THE DISPUTED PRESIDENTIAL ELECTION OF 2000

A History and Reference Guide

E. D. DOVER

GREENWOOD PRESS
Westport, Connecticut • London

Library of Congress Cataloging-in-Publication Data

Dover, E.D. (Edwin D.), 1946–
The disputed presidential election of 2000 : a history and reference guide / by Edwin D. Dover.
p. cm.
Includes bibliographical references and index.
ISBN 0-313-32319-4 (alk. paper)
1. Presidents—United States—Election—2000. 2. Bush, George W. (George Walker), 1946– 3. Gore, Albert, 1948– 4. Electoral college—United States. 5. Contested elections—United States. 6. Contested elections—Florida. 7. United States—Politics and government—1993–2001. 8. Florida—Politics and government—1951– I. Title: Disputed presidential election of two thousand. II. Title.

JK526 2003
324.973′0929—dc21 2002032072

British Library Cataloguing in Publication Data is available.

Library of Congress Catalog Card Number: 2002032072
ISBN: 0-313-32319-4

First published in 2003

Greenwood Press, 88 Post Road West, Westport, CT 06881
An imprint of Greenwood Publishing Group, Inc.
www.greenwood.com

Printed in the United States of America

The paper used in this book complies with the Permanent Paper Standard issued by the National Information Standards Organization (Z39.48–1984).

10 9 8 7 6 5 4 3 2 1

THE DISPUTED PRESIDENTIAL ELECTION OF 2000

To Molly

CONTENTS

PREFACE

The Disputed Presidential Election of 2000 explores the most important features of the disputed presidential election of 2000. Its primary goal is to provide solid background information about the personalities, politics, laws, events, and meaning of the disputed presidential election of 2000. The book contains six chapters that individually focus attention on some of the more unique events that marked the campaign and its aftermath. The first and longest chapter provides a general overview of the election from the earliest days of 1999 when the candidates first emerged to December 12, 2000, when the U.S. Supreme Court decided the final outcome. The second chapter looks at the creation, development, and relevance of the electoral college, an institutional device that is essential for understanding the relationship among the numerous events that occurred in Florida. The two chapters that follow review the major features of the Florida vote controversy. Chapter 3 describes the actual events during the thirty-six-day battle, while chapter 4 explores the cases that made their way through the courts both before and after the election. Chapter 5 explores the inherent financial problems that continue to operate in American federalism where poorly funded counties are given the responsibility for conducting national elections. Finally, Chapter 6 offers a forecast of some long-term consequences of the variety of events that occurred in the 2000 election.

This book also contains three sections that provide valuable information about the election for use by students and researchers. Included here are short biographical accounts of the twenty leading political personalities from the election. The personalities are candidates, leaders of political parties, and the various judges and officials who were involved in the Florida vote controversy. Each of the accounts describes the person's election role and contains features about their educational and professional careers. The primary documents section contains some of the most important court rulings, laws, and voting results of the 2000 election. Among the included material is a complete copy of the ruling of the U.S. Supreme Court in the case of *Bush v.*

Gore and the stinging dissent of Justice John Paul Stevens. Major features of the ruling by the Florida Supreme Court and the decision of the trial court that led to the *Bush v. Gore* case are also included, as are relevant components of the U.S. Constitution, federal election law, and Florida law. Finally, a complete summary of voting results, both by states and by Florida counties, is included. The last major section of the book is an annotated bibliography of major books written in the past few years that discuss various features of the 2000 election. The list of books includes works about the electoral college, the rules by which elections are conducted, the campaign itself, voting results by state and social class, and descriptions of the Florida vote controversy.

INTRODUCTION

The presidential election of 2000 is one of the most unusual political battles in American history. The nation was beginning a new century with the realization that it would also be getting a new president. The incumbent, Bill Clinton, was finishing his second term and was constitutionally ineligible for another. A presidential term of office lasts for four years, but the Constitution's Twenty-Second amendment limits the president to only two terms. Clinton's legacy was unusual; the nation was at peace and its economy was strong, yet many voters were apprehensive about Clinton and happy that his tenure was coming to an end. People believed that the policies of the Clinton administration had been good for the nation and were thankful to Clinton for them, but they did not like Clinton personally. The reason for this dislike was the series of personal scandals that had marked the Clinton presidency, including highly publicized sexual liaisons with White House intern Monica Lewinsky. How these mixed views would translate into votes was often uncertain. This uncertainty would cloud the efforts of Vice President Al Gore to succeed Clinton. Gore wanted to embrace Clinton's policies but not Clinton himself. This was not an easy task, and Gore never did it very well. With Clinton, who had led the Democratic Party for eight years, retiring, the opposition Republicans believed they had an excellent chance to return to the White House they had last occupied when George Bush was president. Their hope rested with Bush's son, George W. Bush, who was governor of Texas. Gore and Bush both had to fight for months to win the nominations of their respective political parties, but they both prevailed and both entered the general election with promising chances. The nation underwent an intense campaign that did not produce a clear leader even as Election Day approached.

Americans divided their votes about equally between the nominees of the two major political parties, casting about 48 percent of their votes apiece for both Bush and Gore. They also cast about 4 percent for the nominees of several minor political parties of which the recently formed Greens were the strongest. They did this after a campaign that lasted for nearly two years and ended with a controversial decision by the Supreme Court. The campaign began on January 3, 1999, when the first of the numerous candidates who would seek the nominations of one of the major parties, in this case Elizabeth Dole, announced her plans. It ended on December 18, 2000, when 538 persons operating through a structure that many Americans thought was no longer relevant, the electoral college, cast 271 votes for Bush and 266 for Gore, with one abstention. Bush won and thus became president, but he had actually lost the popular vote by about one-half million votes. Moreover, Bush's victory had not been certain until six days earlier, when the Supreme Court ruled that certain procedures being used in Florida to recount ballots on old and unreliable machines violated the equal protection clause of the Constitution. The nation had just finished a lengthy election whose outcome was extremely confusing to nearly all observers. Many people wondered about how a nation where millions of people used electronic cards with personal identification numbers to acquire money from ATMs could conduct elections where ballot counters needed to look at the "dangling chads" on punch cards while trying to figure out "the intent of the voter?" This book will help students, researchers, and interested readers make sense of the 2000 election.

KEY PLAYERS IN THE DISPUTED PRESIDENTIAL ELECTION OF 2000

Lamar Alexander, former governor of Tennessee, secretary of education, Republican presidential candidate in 2000.

James Baker, U.S. secretary of state from 1989 to 1993, director of Bush efforts in the Florida vote controversy.

Bill Bradley, former U.S. senator from New Jersey, Democratic presidential candidate in 2000.

Patrick Buchanan, 2000 presidential nominee of the Reform Party, former Republican candidate.

George Bush, president from 1989 to 1993, vice president from 1981 to 1989, father of George W. Bush and Jeb Bush.

George W. Bush, governor of Texas from 1995 to 2001, Republican nominee for president in 2000 and winner of the election.

Jeb Bush, younger brother of George W. Bush, Governor of Florida (1999–), and codirector of Bush campaign in Florida.

Richard Cheney, former congressman from Wyoming, secretary of defense, and Republican vice presidential nominee in 2000.

Bill Clinton, president from 1993 to 2001, first Democrat since Franklin D. Roosevelt to win two presidential terms.

William Daley, U.S. secretary of commerce under Clinton, directed Gore efforts in the Florida vote controversy.

Elizabeth Dole, secretary of transportation under George Bush, Republican presidential candidate in 2000.

Robert Dole, former U.S. senator from Kansas and Senate majority leader, Republican presidential nominee in 1996.

Steve Forbes, owner of *Forbes Magazine*, self-financed Republican presidential candidate in 1996 and 2000.

Albert Gore, Jr., vice president from 1993 to 2001, former Tennessee senator, Democratic presidential nominee in 2000.

Katherine Harris, Florida secretary of state from 1999 to 2002 and codirector of Bush presidential campaign in Florida in 2000.

Joseph Lieberman, U.S. senator from Connecticut since 1988, Democratic vice presidential nominee in 2000.

John McCain, U.S. senator from Arizona since 1986, major rival of George W. Bush for Republican nomination in 2000.

Ralph Nader, consumer advocate and political reformer, Green Party presidential nominee in 1996 and 2000.

William Rehnquist, chief justice of U.S. Supreme Court, leader of the Court's more conservative members.

John Paul Stevens, associate justice of U.S. Supreme Court, leader of the Court's more liberal members.

CHRONOLOGY OF EVENTS

1998

May 11 The first Gallup-CNN-USA Today Poll of the campaign shows 30 percent of Republicans supporting George W. Bush for the presidential nomination. Elizabeth Dole, Dan Quayle, and Steve Forbes follow with the support of 14, 9, and 7 percent, respectively, of Republicans.

October 27 The Gallup-CNN-USA Today Poll now shows Bush with 39 percent support while Dole, Quayle, and Forbes are at 17, 12 and 7 percent, respectively.

1999

January 4 Elizabeth Dole becomes the first candidate to officially enter the race for the Republican nomination.

January 21 Dan Quayle announces his candidacy for the Republican nomination. John Kasich (February 15), Pat Buchanan (March 2), Lamar Alexander (March 9), and Steve Forbes (March 16) announce their campaigns for the Republican nomination.

March 3 Governor George W. Bush of Texas announces his candidacy for the Republican nomination and attains far greater media attention than any of his rivals. Reporters begin describing Bush as the front-runner for the nomination.

May 16 Democratic Vice President Al Gore delivers his first major address as a candidate while speaking about education in Des Moines, Iowa. National media use this as an opportunity to analyze the condition of the Gore campaign.

June 12	Bush makes his first campaign trips to Iowa (June 12 and 13) and New Hampshire (June 14) and once again receives extensive media attention.
June 16	Gore announces his candidacy for the Democratic nomination in his boyhood home town of Carthage, Tennessee.
June 30	Campaign financial reports must be filed with the Federal Election Commission by this day. George W. Bush has raised $36.2 million; Al Gore, $18.5; Bill Bradley, $11.5; John McCain, $6.1; Elizabeth Dole, $3.4; and Dan Quayle $3.1.
August 13	The Iowa Republican Straw Poll takes place. Amid enormous media coverage, Bush wins with 31 percent of the vote. Forbes and Dole follow with 21 and 14 percent, respectively. Alexander withdraws from the race.
September 8	Bradley announces his candidacy for the Democratic nomination in his boyhood home town of Crystal City, Missouri.
September 11–October 20	Several Republican candidates, including Buchanan, Quayle, and Dole, withdraw.
September 25	Gore and Bradley have their first joint appearance of the campaign, speaking individually at a meeting of the Democratic National Convention in Washington, D.C.
September 27	Senator John McCain of Arizona officially announces his candidacy for the Republican nomination while campaigning in Nashua, New Hampshire.
September 29	Gore moves his campaign headquarters from Washington, D.C., to Nashville, Tennessee.
October 9	Gore and Bradley speak individually before the Iowa Democratic State Committee in Des Moines.
October 11	The AFL-CIO endorses Gore, thus providing him with extensive support and resources from organized labor.
October 27	Gore and Bradley hold the first Democratic debate of the New Hampshire campaign at Dartmouth College.
October 28	All Republican candidates, except Bush, debate one another at Dartmouth College in New Hampshire.
December 2	All Republican candidates, including Bush, debate one another in Manchester, New Hampshire.
December 16	Bradley and McCain hold a joint press conference in Clairemont, New Hampshire, to emphasize the need for campaign finance reform.

2000

January 4–February 1	This period covered the most intense part of the campaign leading to the Iowa caucuses and the New Hampshire primary. National television networks begin daily campaign coverage on January 4.
January 4	Elizabeth Dole endorses Bush.
January 7	Forbes begins his attack advertising against Bush in Iowa and New Hampshire.
January 17	Martin Luther King's birthday is marked by demonstrations and remarks by the candidates about the flying of the confederate flag above the South Carolina state capitol.
January 23	A *Des Moines Register* newspaper poll shows Bush and Gore leading in Iowa.
January 24	In the Iowa caucuses, Gore defeats Bradley by 63 to 35 percent while Bush beats Forbes by 41 to 30 percent.
January 27	President Bill Clinton delivers his annual State of the Union Address and uses this opportunity to praise Gore.
February 1	In the New Hampshire primary, McCain defeats Bush by 49 to 31 percent while Gore edges Bradley 52 to 48 percent.
February 2	Bush delivers a controversial speech at Bob Jones University, a conservative South Carolina religious school.
February 2–19	This period was dominated by the campaign between Bush and McCain in the Republican primary in South Carolina.
February 8	Bush wins the Delaware primary with McCain finishing second and Forbes third. Forbes withdraws from the race.
February 12	Deep divisions surface within the Reform Party at its national committee meeting in Nashville, Tennessee. Minnesota Governor Jesse Ventura quits the party.
February 19	Bush wins the South Carolina primary over McCain by 53 to 42 percent.
February 21	Gore and Bradley debate at the Apollo Theatre in Harlem.
February 22	McCain defeats Bush in Michigan by 51 to 43 percent. McCain also wins his home state of Arizona.
February 28	McCain makes a public attack against Religious Right leaders Jerry Falwell and Pat Robertson.

February 29	Bush wins the Virginia primary by 53 to 44 percent. Gore defeats Bradley in Washington State by 60 to 40 percent.
March 1–7	This final week of intense campaigning for the party nominations concludes with eleven primaries on March 7.
March 7	Bush wins seven of the eleven Republican primaries on this "Super Tuesday," including those in New York, Ohio, and California. Gore defeats Bradley in all eleven Democratic primaries.
March 9	McCain and Bradley withdraw, thus ending the campaigns for the party nominations.
March 10–August 17	This period marks the interim between the conclusion of the nomination battles and the beginning of the general election campaign.
March 11	New national polls show the race between Gore and Bush to be very close.
March 27	Gore proposes changes in campaign finance laws and faces greater scrutiny for his role in the 1996 Clinton campaign funding problems.
May 1	Bush proposes partial privatization of Social Security.
July 24	Media begin extensive speculation about Bush's choice of a running mate.
July 25	Bush announces his choice of Dick Cheney as running mate. Democrats begin a series of attacks on Cheney's voting record as a congressman from Wyoming.
July 28	Bush leaves Austin, Texas, for a five-state campaign trip en route to the Republican National Convention in Philadelphia.
July 31–August 3	Republican National Convention meets.
August 3	Bush addresses the nation with his acceptance speech at the Republican National Convention.
August 6–7	Intense media interest and speculation occurs over Gore's possible choice of a running mate.
August 8	Gore announces his choice of Connecticut Senator Joseph Lieberman at a rally in Nashville.
August 10–12	The Reform Party holds an extremely divisive national convention in Long Beach, California. Pat Buchanan wins the nomination but a large faction of the party refuses to support him and nominates John Hagelin of the Natural Law Party as its candidate.
August 12	Gore begins his campaign trip to the Democratic National Convention by addressing environmental issues at Rachel Carson's home in Pennsylvania.

August 13 Bill and Hillary Clinton raise several million dollars in Los Angeles for his presidential library and her Senate candidacy.

August 14–17 The Democratic National Convention meets in Los Angeles.

August 14 Bill Clinton addresses the Democratic National Convention.

August 15 Clinton and Gore appear at a joint rally in Monroe, Michigan, where Clinton introduces Gore as the new leader of the Democratic Party.

August 17 Gore delivers his acceptance speech before the Democratic convention and a national television audience. He prefaces his speech with a lengthy kiss with his wife, Tipper.

August 18–20 Gore begins a series of speeches that emphasize populist economic themes.

August 21 New national polls show Gore taking the lead from Bush.

August 25 Bush delivers a major foreign policy speech in Miami, Florida.

August 28 Gore speaks to seniors in Tallahassee, Florida, about the need to improve prescription drug benefits.

August 30 Gore and Bush advance their education plans.

August 31–September 1 Clinton makes several announcements related to campaign issues. He vetoes a Republican-passed tax change and announces a delay in implementing a missile defense system.

September 3 Bush and Gore announce plans for nationally televised debates.

September 4 Bush accidentally makes a vulgar remark about a *New York Times* reporter while talking in front of an open microphone.

September 5 Bush announces his prescription drug program.

September 6 Gore announces his 191-page tax and economic program.

September 11 The Federal Trade Commission releases a report about how the movie industry deliberately markets violent movies. This report generates numerous remarks by the candidates.

September 12 A new controversy arises about a subliminal message in a Bush television advertisement where the letters "rats" are said to refer to bureaucrats.

September 19 Bush appears on the *Oprah Winfrey Show.*

September 21	Gore calls on Clinton to tap the nation's strategic oil reserve to combat high energy prices. Clinton does so the next day.
September 29	Gore attacks Bush over his environmental proposals, including the proposal for new oil drilling in the Arctic Wildlife Refuge.
September 30–October 2	The candidates prepare for the first debate.
October 3	The first debate between Bush and Gore occurs in Boston. Gore is initially seen as the winner, but criticism of his aggressive behavior eventually hurts him.
October 5	The vice presidential candidates hold their only debate in Danville, Kentucky. The public response to their performance is positive.
October 7	Bush and Gore both campaign in Florida. The competitive nature of this state's vote is becoming apparent to both candidates and news media.
October 10	A new set of national polls show the outcome of the race is too close to call.
October 11	The second presidential debate occurs in Winston-Salem, North Carolina. The major emphasis is on foreign policy, with the candidates agreeing with one another sixteen times.
October 12	The terrorist attack on the U.S.S. *Cole* in Yemen reduces media coverage of the campaign for several days.
October 16	Ralph Nader addresses 15,000 supporters at a rally in Madison Square Garden. This is the first important national television coverage of Nader's campaign.
October 17	The final presidential debate takes place in St. Louis, Missouri. Polls show Gore as the winner, but the television audience is the lowest for any of the debates.
October 19	Bush and Gore emphasize taxes and the economy.
October 22	New media polls show Bush leading by margins of two and four percentage points, all of which are within the polls' margins of error.
October 23	Gore and his surrogates begin a series of attacks against Nader. They tell liberal voters that a vote for Nader will help elect Bush.
October 25	Gore campaigns in Nashville, Tennessee, after appearing to be in trouble in his home state. Bush spends this day in Florida.
October 28	Bush and Gore both campaign in the Midwest.
November 1	Gore campaigns in central Florida along the Interstate Highway 4 corridor between Tampa and Orlando.

November 3 News story breaks about Bush's 1976 arrest in Maine for driving while under the influence of alcoholic beverages (DUI).

November 5 Bush campaigns in Florida.

November 5–6 Final television network polls show the race is extremely close with no clear leader.

November 7 Election Day. Gore receives 48.26 percent of the popular vote, Bush receives 47.81, Nader receives 2.92, and Buchanan receives 0.43. Bush leads the electoral vote with 271 to 267 for Gore, but the twenty-five votes in Florida, where Bush leads, are subject to an automatic recount because of the closeness of the state result.

November 8 Problems about vote recounts in Florida emerge, which lead to legal action by both campaigns. Bush leads by 1,784 votes before the recounts begin. A controversy erupts over the use of a possibly illegal "butterfly ballot" in Palm Beach County.

November 9 Gore demands a manual recount of disputed votes in four Democratic majority counties in Florida—Palm Beach, Volusia, Broward, and Miami-Dade—that had used punch card ballots. Frequently, machines cannot count some of these because the so-called chad remains attached in some way to the ballot.

November 11 The Bush legal team files a lawsuit in federal district court for an injunction to stop the manual recounts because they violate the equal protection and due process clauses of the Fourteenth Amendment to the U.S. Constitution.

November 12 The Palm Beach County Canvassing Board votes to authorize a manual recount of all ballots cast in the county.

November 13 A federal district court rejects a lawsuit from the Bush campaign challenging the manual recounts on equal protection and due process grounds.

November 13 Katherine Harris, Florida secretary of state and a Bush campaign official, rules that all recounts must be completed by November 14 and that she will certify the results that day as official.

November 14 Florida judge Terry Lewis rules that counties must abide by the seven-day deadline for submitting recounts as ordered by the secretary of state but adds that the secretary of state must use reasonable discretion when deciding to reject recounts submitted past the deadline.

November 14	The initial deadline for recounts occurs. Bush's lead has diminished to only 300 votes. Florida Secretary of State Katherine Harris certifies these results as official with the final certification to add only overseas absentee ballots to this total.
November 14	The Miami-Dade County Canvassing Board orders a manual recount of all ballots.
November 15	Broward, Miami-Dade, and Palm Beach Counties provide explanations to the Florida secretary of state to justify extending their deadlines for completing recounts.
November 16	The Florida Supreme Court sets aside the Florida secretary of state's November 14 certification of the election results.
November 17	The federal Eleventh Circuit Court of Appeals rejects the Bush appeal from a federal district court for an injunction to stop the recounts.
November 17	The Miami-Dade County Canvassing Board changes its mind and decides against conducting the manual recounts.
November 18	The inclusion of overseas absentee ballots increases Bush's lead to 930 votes. The Republicans begin a series of attacks against the Democrats for trying to disqualify the votes of overseas servicepeople.
November 18	Democrats file suit in Seminole County, charging the county clerk with illegally permitting workers from the Republican Party to correct mistakes on absentee ballot applications.
November 20	Florida judge Jorge Labarga rules that he cannot overturn the results of Palm Beach County because of the use of the butterfly ballot.
November 21	The Florida Supreme Court rules that the secretary of state abused her discretion by not accepting recounts submitted after November 14. The court extends the deadline for submission of recounts to November 26.
November 22	The Miami-Dade County Canvassing Board says it cannot complete recounts by November 26 and thus suspends them.
November 23	The Florida Supreme Court refuses to order the Miami-Dade County Canvassing Board to continue with the manual recounts.
November 26	The uncompleted recounts are ended, and the vote is certified as final and official by Secretary of State Harris with Bush's lead at 537 votes. Broward County completed its recount, with Gore gaining 567 votes;

Palm Beach County had Gore gaining 215 votes but submitted them ninety minutes too late, and Harris did not accept them.

November 27 Gore files suit in the Florida court of Judge N. Sander Sauls contesting the official certification of a Bush victory by Secretary of State Katherine Harris.

December 1 The Florida Supreme Court upholds the lower court ruling dismissing the challenge to the Palm Beach County butterfly ballot.

December 4 Florida circuit judge Sander Sauls dismisses Gore's challenge to the vote certification.

December 4 The U.S. Supreme Court reverses the earlier decision of the Florida Supreme Court on extending the deadline for recounts. The U.S. court wants the Florida court to clarify the basis of its decision and to show whether it was based exclusively on state statutes, the state constitution, or the court's powers.

December 8 Two separate Florida courts dismiss suits aimed at disqualifying absentee ballots with applications that had been altered by Republican workers.

December 8 The Florida Supreme Court overturns Judge Sauls ruling by a four to three vote and orders a statewide recount of all disputed undervotes, that is, votes that did not record a presidential vote when counted by machine. The court also adjusts the current vote by granting Gore 383 votes from Palm Beach and Miami-Dade Counties. Bush's lead is reduced to only 154 votes.

December 9 The U.S. Supreme Court issues an injunction stopping the newly ordered manual recounts and grants certiorari to review the previous day's decision of the Florida Supreme Court.

December 12 The U.S. Supreme Court overturns the decision of the Florida Supreme Court by a five to four vote, thus ending the legal appeals and the election. Florida's twenty-five electoral votes belong to Bush. The court based its decision on the equal protection clause of the Fourteenth Amendment, charging that the Florida standard of attempting to determine the "intent of the voter" led to inconsistent methods of counting ballots throughout the state.

December 13 Gore concedes the election, and Bush responds by accepting victory. Bush speaks before a joint session of the Texas legislature in Austin.

1

OVERVIEW OF THE 2000 ELECTION

The disputed election of 2000 appears at first glance to be a unique event in American history, but this may not be as true as it seems. In some ways, the election was unique, but in other ways, it was very ordinary when compared to the outcomes of other recent contests. Two types of features defined the 2000 presidential election. One was the combination of unique events that is unlikely to ever be repeated in the same manner in future elections. These events included the battle for executive succession between the governor of Texas and the vice president of the United States in the aftermath of a presidential sex scandal and controversial impeachment trial, and the extraordinary legal and constitutional disputes relating to the counting of flawed ballots in Florida that eventually decided the final outcome of this exceptionally close race.

The second type of feature was the reoccurrence of a variety of electoral patterns that have characterized presidential elections of the recent past. Important here was the nomination of the vice president by the incumbent party when the president retired, something that has now occurred four times since 1960. Also important was the inflated significance of a small number of primary elections in key states in determining the eventual nominees of both major political parties, a pattern that is now about fifty years old. The extensive reliance of most people on various forms of mass media, particularly television, for much of their political information is another election feature that has been of major importance for several decades now. Finally, there was the continuing, although diminished, importance of partisanship at influencing the electoral choices of individual voters.

Political scientists define the unique features as short-term and the recurring ones as long-term and seek to explain the outcomes of all elections by the variety of ways in which the two types combine. The 2000 election involved the occurrence of some unique events within the context of some stable and often unchanging political institutions, beliefs, and practices.

One such example was the nomination of George W. Bush and Albert Gore by the two major political parties. While it is customary to think of these parties as the Republican and Democratic, it is also possible to think of them by the various electoral roles they play in any given election. One party is always the incumbent, while the other is always the opposition. The incumbent party, which was the Democratic in 2000, always has the goal of retaining the presidency, while the opposition party seeks to deny the incumbent another term and win the office instead. In every election since 1956, the incumbent party has nominated the president for another term if he sought it or selected the vice president as a successor if the incumbent did not run. With this in mind, the nomination of Gore should have come as no surprise, because the incumbent, Bill Clinton, was barred by the Constitution from seeking a third term. Gore became the fourth vice president since 1960 to be nominated for president in a year when the incumbent retired. The others were Richard Nixon (1960), Hubert Humphrey (1968), and George Bush (1988).

In those years when the incumbent party nominates the vice president, the opposition tends to select a relatively inexperienced new player on the national political scene. This new leader unites his party around the vague but often inspiring theme that he can lead them to the victory that has been denied them in recent elections. For example, in 1960 John F. Kennedy, at the time a minor leader in the Senate, inspired and then united Democrats with his call to "get this country moving again." His party had suffered overwhelming defeats in both 1952 and 1956. More often than not, this new leader is a governor. Whereas Gore had held elective office for twenty-four years prior to 2000, including eight as vice president, Bush had been governor of Texas for only six years.

THE PARTY NOMINATIONS

A modern nomination campaign begins about one year before the election. Political observers refer to the events of the preelection year as the "invisible primary." This is when candidates raise money, gain endorsements from key party leaders, and generate visible support in public opinion surveys. An unusually large field of twelve Republicans sought the presidency in 2000, but they were opposed by only two Democrats. Bush and Gore succeeded in accomplishing the various political tasks of the invisible primary and by the end of 1999 appeared as almost certain winners of their respective nominations. Each had attained the personal endorsement of nearly every important elected official within his party, had raised far more money than any rival, and had massive leads in the polls.

Bush and Gore were officially nominated at national conventions of their parties during the summer of 2000. Nominating conventions have been integral components of presidential elections since the 1830s. About one year before an election, the national leadership of each party selects a time and date for its convention and then adopts a formula to allocate votes to each state, basing votes on such features as population and past support for the party. Each state then selects delegates to attend the convention. States employ various methods and dates in selecting their delegates during the first months of an election year.

For many years, Iowa and New Hampshire have been the first states to choose delegates, and both states are strongly committed to remaining in the leadoff positions. Iowa uses caucuses, while New Hampshire has a primary election. In a caucus, party members attend meetings at which they choose delegates to attend higher-level meetings where national convention delegates are selected. In a primary, voters cast ballots for president and delegates are later selected to reflect the outcome of the vote. By agreement with the two parties, Iowa holds its caucuses eight days before New Hampshire conducts its primary. No other state can vote until these two states are finished. Iowa had its caucuses on January 24, and the New Hampshire primary occurred on February 1.

These two states exert a disproportionate influence on nominations because most candidates devote a considerable amount of time and money to contesting them and news media tend to report extensively on them. After extensive campaigning, Bush and Gore both won convincing victories in Iowa and headed for the New Hampshire primary widely acknowledged as the front-runners within their respective parties. Gore also won in New Hampshire over his only rival, former New Jersey Senator Bill Bradley, but Bush suffered a serious political setback. Senator John McCain (Arizona) had spent seventy-seven days campaigning in New Hampshire, and, as a result, defeated Bush by the stunning margin of 49 to 31 percent. The Republicans now had a serious battle for the nomination.

The most important day for delegate selection was March 7, when eleven states, including such major ones as California, New York, and Ohio, held primaries. Gore and Bradley campaigned extensively in these eleven states, while Bush and McCain divided their time between these states and several others that had Republican primaries in February. Political observers called March 7 "Super Tuesday." Many people, including the candidates, believed the results of Super Tuesday would determine the nomination. Gore won all eleven states, mostly by wide margins. He attained 84 percent of the vote in California. These defeats led to Bradley's withdrawal from the campaign two days later and clinched the Democratic nomination for Gore.

The February Republican primaries had an unusual rule; they were open to all voters, including Democrats. The first was in South Carolina (February 19) and was followed three days later by primaries in Arizona and Michigan. Balloting occurred in Virginia one week later. Bush and McCain campaigned extensively in South Carolina, starting shortly after the New Hampshire primary. Bush spoke about his conservative views and long-time history in the Republican Party while trying to win the support of his own partisans. McCain drew attention to his Vietnam War record (he had spent seven years as a prisoner of war) and emphasized campaign finance reform. Bush was particularly vulnerable concerning these issues. He had not served in the military and was

With his wife Cindy at his side, Arizona Republican Senator John McCain speaks to supporters at a rally in Nashua, New Hampshire, on February 1, 2000. *Shaun Best/©Reuters NewMedia Inc./Corbis.*

financing his campaign with millions of dollars in private contributions raised from persons associated with major industries. McCain also talked about his military record because South Carolina had the highest percentage of veterans of any state. With regard to campaign finance, he wanted to replace much of the private system of funding with federal assistance for candidates. He also tried to convince Democrats and nonpartisans to cast ballots. He fell short of this goal, however, as Bush won the primary by a margin of 53 to 42 percent.

Important differences occurred in the division of votes in South Carolina. Republicans clearly favored Bush; 69 percent of them voted for him. McCain, however, acquired the votes of 70 percent of the Democrats and 60 percent of the nonpartisans who cast ballots. Bush won the primary because a majority of voters were Republicans.

Two primaries that followed had similar divisions: McCain defeated Bush in Michigan by 51 to 43 percent, while Bush won the Virginia primary by 53 to 44 percent. Bush did not contest McCain's home state of Arizona. Bush won the support of a majority of Republicans in both states, while McCain once again had the solid backing of Democrats and nonpartisans. Republicans cast a majority of the votes in Virginia but only 48 percent of the votes in Michigan, thus explaining Bush's victory in the former state and his defeat in the latter.

Unfortunately for McCain, every Super Tuesday primary was restricted to Republicans, and most of them were not supporting him. McCain had not garnered the backing of a majority of Republicans in any of the contested primaries that had already been held, even New Hampshire. He could not win the nomination without defeating Bush among Republicans in several of the major states, particularly California. Both Bush and McCain proclaimed to California Republicans that he was the proper heir to the political legacy of Ronald Reagan. Republican voters opted for Bush, backing him by 60 to 35 percent. Bush also won six other primaries this day, including the ones in New York and Ohio. McCain quickly ended his campaign, and, as Bradley did among Democrats, officially withdrew from the race two days after Super Tuesday, on March 9.

The battles for the party nominations were intense, but they were also extremely short, with most people having little or no voice in the final outcomes. Several states had voted between January 24 and March 7 and had influenced the ultimate choices, but over thirty states had yet to hold their caucuses or primaries by the end of Super Tuesday. Bush and Gore were the only candidates left on March 10. Florida, which was to have such a major impact on the final resolution of the general election, had no voice in selecting the nominees of the two major parties. The Florida primary was scheduled for March 14, five days after the effective conclusion of the nomination battles within each party.

While the above descriptions indicate that little or no suspense ever existed over the identities of the eventual winners, the nominations of Gore and Bush were not unusual events. Instead, they were consistent with important long-term patterns of recent presidential elections. Gore's nomination was related to the extensive growth in the importance of the vice presidency over the past half century, which, in turn, was related to the growth of the presidency. The vice presidency was of limited political importance during the nineteenth century and the first half of the twentieth and was an unusual place from which to successfully seek a presidential nomination. Prior to 1960, Martin Van Buren was the only vice president to win the nomination of his party when the president retired, having done so in 1836.

When Franklin D. Roosevelt first became president in 1933, he had a personal staff of less than forty persons. Since that time, we have seen the creation of the Executive Office of the President (EOP) and its expansion into a powerful bureaucratic entity with a staff that now exceeds 2,000 persons and that provides the president with important institutional support in a vast array of policymaking areas previously not available to him. The EOP presently contains the White House Office, the Office of Management and Budget, the staffs of the Council of Economic Advisors and National Security Council, and seven more offices that specialize in policies ranging from intelligence to trade. These enable the president to dominate policymaking and planning in such areas as government spending, economics, and national security and to provide full-time employment for much of his campaign staff. The vice presidency is an integral part of this presidential bureaucracy, even having an office in the West Wing of the White House. Prior to Roosevelt, the vice president was not looked upon as a member of the executive branch of government and instead had an office in the U.S. Capitol Building.

One of the most important tasks of the contemporary vice president is to rally his own partisans behind the president. During his eight years in office, Gore spent countless hours speaking at Democratic Party fundraising events; helping members of his party campaign for offices in Congress, statehouses, and city halls; and representing the president as a surrogate at numerous highly publicized political events. Many of the most influential members of his own party had already endorsed Gore and contributed to his campaign long before the first primaries and caucuses occurred. Other Democrats who might have wanted to run for president discovered that Gore had effectively used the advantages of the modern vice presidential office to create a virtually unbeatable effort for the nomination and therefore chose not to oppose him. The events of the past four decades relating to the successes that vice presidents have achieved when seeking their party's nomination indicate the nation will see many more vice presidents win presidential nominations in future years when the incumbent retires.

The nomination of Bush was also consistent with long-term patterns of other recent elections. Like Gore, Bush also began the campaign with some important institutional advantages over his rivals and then exploited them in a highly effective manner that led to an early victory for the nomination. Perhaps his strongest advantage was the strategic position he held as the governor of Texas. A governorship is a particularly useful office from which to seek the nomination of the opposition party today because it provides financial resources that most other political offices usually lack. A candidate for governor in even the smallest states needs to raise several million dollars to compete effectively. If elected, a governor appoints numerous persons to governmental positions, thus acquiring not only their gratitude but also their contributions in his future quests for office. Bush won a narrow victory for governor of Texas in 1994 and then followed with a sweeping reelection triumph in 1998. Texas is one of the nation's largest and wealthiest states. Bush's successes here allowed him to develop a vast list of contributors that he could use in his presidential campaign. Jimmy Carter, Ronald Reagan, and Bill Clinton were governors or former governors when they won their initial presidential terms, and each of them garnered considerable funding from within their own states. In addition to his Texas support, Bush also attained the backing of twenty-seven other Republican governors. These important party leaders provided Bush with access to even more potential contributors. Finally, Bush was also helped by the fact that he had been an active leader in his father's campaigns for president and vice president in several elections in the 1980s and 1990s. These experiences helped acquaint Bush with many

Democratic presidential nominee Al Gore speaks to a crowd at Muscatine, Iowa, on August 20, 2000. *Jim Bourg/©Reuters NewMedia Inc./Corbis.*

important state and local Republican leaders. Bush's successes in Texas convinced many Republicans that he could unite them and win the election. They responded to his vague, but what they also saw as inspiring, calls for party unity and nominated him.

Strong connections to financial contributors are far more important today than in previous elections because of the impact of the Federal Election Campaign Act. This law, enacted in 1972, limits individual contributions to only $1,000. To conduct a successful campaign today, a presidential candidate needs to raise millions of dollars from thousands of individual contributors. Bush

On his way to his party's convention, Republican presidential candidate George W. Bush speaks to a rally at Owensboro-Daviess Airport in Kentucky on July 29, 2000. *Timothy A. Clary/©AFP/Corbis.*

announced his intentions to pursue the Republican nomination in early March 1999. He acquired over $30 million in contributions by July 1 of that year and then increased that to over $70 million by the important primaries of early 2000. He raised this money from over 175,000 contributors. This was the greatest amount of money raised from the largest number of contributors by a presidential candidate in American history. It is unlikely that Bush could have raised this much money without the advantage of being the governor of Texas.

With the conclusion of the primaries, Bush and Gore spent several weeks planning their general election efforts and in choosing vice presidential running mates. Each of them announced his choice about one week before his respective party convention. Bush picked Richard Cheney, who had served as the White House chief of staff under Gerald Ford, as a congressman from Wyoming for ten years, as secretary of defense under Bush's father, and as president of a Texas-based oil company. Gore chose Senator Joseph Lieberman of Connecticut. Lieberman had been a senator for the past twelve years. Prior to that, he had been a member of the Connecticut legislature for ten years and the state's attorney general for five years. The practice of a presi-

Vice President Al Gore, the 2000 Democratic nominee for president, kisses his wife Tipper as he arrives on stage to give his acceptance speech at the Democratic National Convention in Los Angeles on August 17, 2000. *Sam Mircovich/©Reuters NewMedia Inc./Corbis.*

dential candidate selecting his own running mate is a modern development. Prior to 1940, the conventions picked the vice presidential candidates. Frequently, they chose someone the presidential candidate did not want. After the election, the new president usually responded by ignoring the vice president, thus helping make the office even less important.

The party conventions, which occurred in August, were of only limited importance because of the influence of the primary elections. The leading events were the acceptance speeches of Bush and Gore, who outlined their goals before thousands of delegates and millions of television viewers. These were the most widely watched speeches that Bush and Gore delivered during the entire campaign.

THE GENERAL ELECTION

The general election campaign began in mid-August with the conclusion of the national conventions. While Bush and Gore had been campaigning extensively since clinching their nominations in March, their efforts soon took a different turn. Each now had a running mate. In addition, reporters and voters were expressing a greater interest in political events. Finally, both candidates received a significant infusion of federal funding. The Federal Election Campaign Act, discussed earlier, also grants the nominees of the two major parties $20 million (based on the 1974 value of money) to conduct their general election campaigns. The $20 million figure is linked to the Consumer Price Index, a federal statistic used to measure the rate of inflation, and it increases in tandem with the Index. This means that both Bush and Gore received $67.5 million for their efforts in 2000 since inflationary changes now required $67.5 million to buy what $20 million had bought in 1974. The minor political parties received federal funding based on the percentage of the vote they had attained in the previous election, provided it had been at least 5 percent of the total vote cast. Since Reform Party nominee Ross Perot had garnered 7.8 percent of the vote in 1996, this party's 2000 candidate, Pat Buchanan, received $12.4 million. Ralph Nader received no federal funding but made it clear that his major goal in this election was to attain 5 percent of the vote so his Green Party would qualify for federal funding in 2004. Buchanan's appeal was limited because of deep divisions within his party, but Nader posed a serious threat to Gore because of his strong appeal to liberal reformers and environmentalists. Many political observers believed Gore and Nader were competing for the support of the same voters.

American presidential elections are unusual in that they are conducted indirectly through the electoral college rather than directly through popular vote. Each state has the same number of electoral votes as it has seats in both houses of Congress. Several states had as few as three electoral votes in 2000, while California led the nation with fifty-four. The awarding of Florida's twenty-five electoral votes was the prize that both presidential campaigns fought over in the postelection vote-counting controversy. A candidate must win a majority of the nation's 538 electoral votes, that is, 270, to become president. If no one wins that many votes, the Twelfth Amendment of the Constitution provides that the House of Representatives will choose the president from among the top three vote recipients in the electoral college and the Senate will select the vice president from among the two highest choices. The fact that there is an electoral college forces candidates to structure their campaign efforts in ways that provide them with realistic opportunities of winning a combination of states that will yield the requisite majority of electoral votes needed to attain the presidency.

Bush and Gore both counted on winning approximately 200 electoral votes apiece from states where their parties were particularly strong, but this number was far short of the majority requirement. In response, both focused their efforts on states that appeared competitive in the sense that no winner

Green Party presidential candidate Ralph Nader speaks at an election night rally in Washington, D.C., on November 7, 2000. *Brendan McDermid/©Reuters NewMedia Inc./Corbis.*

appeared obvious. Several of these states were from the nation's industrial region: Pennsylvania, Ohio, Illinois, Michigan, and Wisconsin. Others were from the Border region: West Virginia, Kentucky, Tennessee, Missouri, and Arkansas, while two were from the Pacific Northwest: Washington and Oregon. Finally, one state was the most difficult of all—Florida. By the latter part of August, public opinion polls showed the national division of support was evenly divided between the two candidates, with the final outcome unclear. This trend remained unchanged throughout the entire campaign. By November, every major poll indicated that Bush and Gore were locked in a race that was too close to call. Gore was ahead in some of the final polls, Bush in others, but neither led by more than two percentage points. The margin of error for these polls was 4 percent.

The candidates divided their campaign efforts into three distinct periods and pursued different strategies in each of them. The first period ranged from the conclusion of the Democratic convention to the onset of the first televised debate, from August 18 to September 29. Bush and Gore directed their appeals to undecided voters in the most competitive states. They emphasized the issues that polls had indicated such voters considered important, including education, environmental protection, health care and prescription drug coverage for seniors, and the long-term financing of Social Security. The second period covered the four nationally televised debates and concluded after the final debate on October 17. Three of the debates were between the two presidential candidates, while the other matched Cheney and Lieberman against one another. Gore and Bush devoted the days preceding the initial October 3 debate to preparations and avoided public appearances. The debate followed the format that has been used in presidential debates since 1960; a moderator would ask questions of the candidates who would then answer. The candidates could not question one another but they could comment on the answers made by their rival. The moderator alternated questions between the two candidates and then allowed each to make a final statement. The debates lasted ninety minutes.

Bush and Gore appeared to be evenly matched in the first debate, with Gore perhaps a little stronger. Network polls taken immediately afterward indicated that viewers had seen Gore as a slight winner, although some criticized the vice president for his aggressive behavior toward Bush. Gore frequently interrupted Bush, used a number of facial expressions to indicate his disgust for his rival's comments, and attempted on several occasions to extend his speaking time beyond the allotted amount. In addition, news reporters and members of the Bush campaign pointed out that some of Gore's statements had been inaccurate. Public opinion changed by the time of the second presidential debate on October 11; by now, more people thought that Bush had done better.

The vice presidential candidates used a fundamentally different approach in their debate on October 5. Instead of standing at podiums, they were seated at the same table. They were also very polite to one another and spent much of their time explaining the views of their respective running mates. The debate seemed more like a conversation than a confrontation and ended with voters indicating their strong approval of both men. Voters seemed impressed; they had a more favorable opinion of this debate than they had of the one between the presidential candidates.

The second presidential debate used this seated format and focused primarily on foreign affairs. In retrospect, it appears to have been a lost opportunity for Gore. The two candidates agreed with one another eighteen times on foreign affairs issues, thus convincing many voters that few differences existed between them on this crucial area of presidential leadership. There was one important difference that Gore could have emphasized, however, his own personal experience. Through his institutional role as vice president and his political role of personal surrogate for the president, Gore had acquired a considerable amount of experience in developing American defense strategies

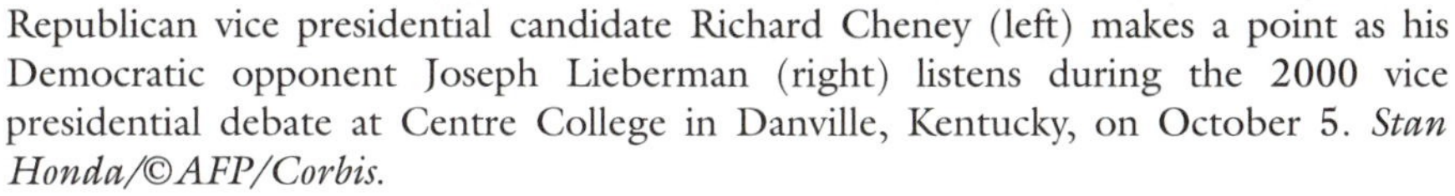

Republican vice presidential candidate Richard Cheney (left) makes a point as his Democratic opponent Joseph Lieberman (right) listens during the 2000 vice presidential debate at Centre College in Danville, Kentucky, on October 5. *Stan Honda/©AFP/Corbis.*

and in meeting and conducting diplomacy with foreign leaders. In contrast, Bush's background as a governor had provided him with few opportunities for working on the international scenes. He had even been embarrassed earlier in the year when he could not name the leaders of several nations. The mass media polls taken after the debate indicated that more viewers thought Bush had performed better and that both candidates were about equally qualified in foreign affairs. International events that followed this debate indicated just how much Gore had lost by not effectively using this debate to demonstrate how his experiences would have been in the nation's and voters' interest. One day after the debate, terrorists bombed a U.S. Navy ship in Yemen, the USS *Cole;* the attack caused millions of dollars in damage and killed seventeen American sailors. News media concentrated their attention on the bombing for several days afterward and ignored the presidential campaign. If Gore had convinced voters of his superior foreign policy credentials during the second debate, the events related to the *Cole* bombing might have provided him with an insurmountable lead among the American electorate.

Debate viewers saw Gore as the winner of the final debate, but this appeared to be a hollow victory. Fewer people had watched it than any of the previous ones, and neither candidate showed any change in his standing in the national polls.

The final period of the campaign encompassed the three weeks between the debates and Election Day, November 7. Bush and Gore directed their efforts toward mobilizing their strongest partisan supporters and encouraging them to vote. This is a necessary task for candidates in all elections because voting in the United States is voluntary. The outcome of an American election often rests on the question of who votes and who does not. Political parties devote millions of dollars to identifying their supporters and in then encouraging them to actually cast ballots. Gore spent much of his time during these three weeks speaking to African-Americans, unionized blue-collar workers, and environmentalists. He talked about the Democratic Party's long-standing record on civil rights while encouraging African-Americans to vote, and while speaking to unionized workers, he talked about how the Clinton administration was responsible for the current prosperity. On several occasions Gore spoke at rallies in his home state of Tennessee, where polls showed he was trailing Bush. Gore also spent some valuable time trying to undermine the growing support for Nader, who was showing surprising strength in several Democratic states; it was possible that Nader could siphon off enough votes from Gore to cost the vice president the election. Gore tried to counter the threat from Nader by speaking about environmental issues in Maine, Michigan, Wisconsin, Minnesota, Oregon, and Washington. He would eventually win all of these states.

Bush concentrated his efforts on mobilizing cultural conservatives who disliked governmental policy on abortion, religion, and gun control, and economic conservatives who wanted less government control of business, education, and retirement programs such as Social Security. He also spoke about morality in government in reference to the personal scandals of Bill Clinton. Like Gore, Bush also made many of his late appeals while campaigning in Florida.

The election was unusually close in both popular and electoral votes. Gore won the popular vote by a narrow margin of 48.4 to 47.9 percent for Bush, thus making this the fourth closest presidential election in American history. Gore received 50,992,335 votes, while Bush garnered 50,455,156. Nader finished in third place with 2,882,738 votes (2.7 percent), while Buchanan trailed with 449,077 votes (0.4 percent). The electoral vote was even closer and unusual in that the second place finisher in the popular vote ran strongest. Bush finished first with 271 votes (including 25 from Florida), while Gore came in second with 267 (Scammon, McGillivrey, and Cook 2001). The last time the winner of the electoral vote lost the popular vote was in 1888.

There were strong differences between the geographic and social group bases of support for each candidate. With respect to geography, Gore won the electoral votes of most states in the Northeast, Midwest, and West Coast regions, while Bush carried nearly every Border, Southeastern, Great Plains, and Mountain state. Gore carried Maine, Vermont, Massachusetts, Rhode Island, Connecticut, New York, New Jersey, Pennsylvania, Delaware, Maryland, and the District of Columbia in the Northeast while losing New Hamp-

On September 28, 2000, Republican presidential nominee George W. Bush greets supporters at the airport in Green Bay, Wisconsin. *Tannen Maury/©AFP/Corbis.*

shire and West Virginia to Bush. He won Iowa, Minnesota, Wisconsin, Illinois, and Michigan in the Midwest and captured Hawaii, California, Oregon, Washington, and New Mexico in the West. Bush carried Alaska, Idaho, Montana, Wyoming, Colorado, Utah, Nevada, and Arizona in the West and North Dakota, South Dakota, Nebraska, Kansas, and Oklahoma in the Great Plains. He added Ohio and Indiana from the Midwest, and perhaps most importantly, won every state in the Southeast. Here, Bush defeated Gore in Virginia, North Carolina, South Carolina, Georgia, Alabama, Mississippi, Tennessee, Kentucky, Missouri, Arkansas, Louisiana, Oklahoma, Texas, and, after five weeks of legal struggles, Florida.

Geographic results sometimes conceal the existence of important socioeconomic and cultural differences among the American electorate. States vary in their preferences because different types of people reside in them. Exit polls, that is, interviews with voters who have just cast ballots, provided a good idea of how these differences influenced the outcome of Election 2000. For example, 57 percent of voters with annual incomes below $15,000 supported Gore, while 59 percent of those with incomes above $100,000 backed Bush. In addition, 71 percent of voters who resided in cities with populations above 500,000 voted for Gore, while 59 percent of those in rural areas supported Bush. Religion also influenced choices; 79 percent of Jewish people backed Gore, while 63 percent of Protestants were for Bush. Gore won the votes of 90 percent of Blacks, while Bush garnered the votes of 54 percent of Whites. Gender and marital status were important; 58 percent of married men voted for Bush while 63 percent of unmarried women voted for Gore. In contrast, married women and unmarried men were both about evenly divided in their support for the two candidates. There were also important distinctions in voting preferences over such public policy questions as gun control, abortion, and attitudes toward Bill Clinton as a person (Pomper 2001, 138). Florida provides a good example of how socioeconomic and cultural differences intersect with geography and influence the distributions of electoral votes.

Florida is the nation's fourth most populous state. It differs from other major states in that it is not dominated by a single metropolitan area such as Chicago in Illinois or New York City in New York. Instead, its people are distributed among several regional centers that differ from one another with respect to both the composition and voting preferences of their populations. Florida had twenty-three seats in the U.S. House of Representatives during 2000. Bush carried thirteen of the districts from which these congressmen were elected by a combined margin of more than one-half million votes. In contrast, Gore carried the remaining ten districts by nearly the same margin. Gore found his greatest support in those regions of Florida that were heavily populated with African-American, Jewish, or blue-collar White voters, while Bush dominated the rural areas and those places with military installations or large numbers of Cuban-Americans or White Protestant retirees. In particular, Gore won in all parts of Miami except in those neighborhoods where many Cuban-Americans reside; in Palm Beach and Broward Counties, which have large Jewish populations; and in the more industrial, governmental, or university cities of Tampa, St. Petersburg, Tallahassee, and Gainesville. Bush ran best in places such as Pensacola and Jacksonville, which have large military installations; the agricultural areas around Ocala and Lakeland; the affluent retirement communities of Sarasota and Fort Myers; and the Cuban-American parts of Miami. Those regions of Florida without large percentages of the particular social groups that preferred Gore and Bush, such as Orlando and Daytona Beach, divided their support about evenly between the two candidates.

OVERVIEW OF THE FLORIDA CONTROVERSY

While many election features were little more than replications of long-term patterns that have governed American elections for many years, one clearly unique feature distinguished this election from all others. This, of course, was the postelection controversy relating to the Florida vote count. This controversy is an extensive topic and is therefore discussed in far greater depth in several other chapters of this book. This chapter provides a short summary of the leading events and shows how they fit into the larger pattern of events that defined the election campaign.

It is difficult to pinpoint the exact time when the possible outcome of the election in Florida first reached the public consciousness. Perhaps it was during the final weeks of the campaign when both major candidates realized how closely divided the state's voters appeared to be in their preferences. Bush and Gore responded by committing significant time and money to Florida after polls indicated that neither of them was ahead in this important state. With Gore holding huge leads in California and New York and Bush being an obvious winner in Texas, Florida was the largest state where the final outcome was unclear. The national news media took these commitments by the major candidates seriously and focused their coverage on the competitiveness of the battle. The final polls relating to Florida were so close that few political observers dared forecast the final outcome. What did seem clear to both Bush and Gore was that the outcome would hinge on voter turnout, that is, which party could do the better job of identifying its supporters and making sure they voted correctly. Both parties prepared for this task by devoting significant time and money to voter registration, delivery of absentee ballots, and Election Day get-out-the-vote drives, and by placing their supporters in the appropriate governmental offices that counted votes.

Florida was one of the first states that concluded its voting on Election Day because it closed most of its polling places at 7:00 P.M. The television networks began reporting the national vote count shortly after 6:00, when balloting stopped in most parts of Indiana and Kentucky. Much to the surprise of many knowledgeable observers, every one of the networks quickly projected that Gore would win Florida's twenty-five electoral votes. Prior to Election Day, the networks had promised they would not project a winner in any state until the polls had closed in that state and would not proclaim a national winner until someone had actually attained the requisite 270 electoral votes. Nonetheless, with Florida in his win column, Gore appeared as the certain winner of the national election. The networks had projected the Gore triumph in Florida on the results of exit polls tabulated by the Voter News Service. This organization is a creation of the networks; it conducts exit polls and makes its findings available to all networks.

There was a problem with the projection, however. Bush was leading in the early Florida vote counts. The Voter News Service projections indicated that Gore would take the lead in the state when the returns from the more populous Democratic counties were tabulated. After it had become apparent that Gore was not gaining ground fast enough to overtake Bush, the networks changed their projections. They removed Florida from the Gore win column and placed it in the undecided group. Several hours later, they declared that Bush would win the state. This victory placed Bush at 271 electoral votes, so every television network proclaimed him the next president. The election seemed over.

Unfortunately for the network analysts, Gore began to gain ground in Florida at a quicker pace than before and soon reduced the Bush lead to less than 2,000 votes. There were also reports of voting irregularities that would lead to a mandatory recount of the entire statewide vote. The networks removed Florida from the Bush victory column, thus reducing the Texas governor's electoral count to only 246. Gore, meanwhile, stood at 267. Neither candidate actually had enough votes to win, although either would win with a victory in Florida.

The recount battle was unusual and bitter, moving through several phases and lasting until the U.S. Supreme Court stopped the recounts on December 12 and effectively ended any chance that Gore had of overtaking Bush. Gore soon conceded defeat, and Bush accepted victory. The first days of the battle involved automatic recounts. Florida law provided for an automatic recount of all ballots if the election was decided by less than one-half of 1 percent of the vote. Bush led after the initial count by 1,764 votes out of a total of more than six million ballots cast. The problem as the Democrats saw it was that the automatic recount would lead to similar results and would produce a Bush victory. They wanted a manual recount of the ballots in four major counties that usually voted Democratic in contested elections. Elections in Florida were conducted by the county clerk in each county with the overall process supervised by the secretary of state. Each county had some discretion in the manner in which it conducted elections, including a choice in the type of ballot it used. Some counties used a punch card ballot, where voters were given a paper ballot and a pointed object, called a stylus, which they could use to punch out a small, numbered perforation that was located next to the name of the candidate of their choice. For example, in Palm Beach County, Bush was listed as candidate number three and Gore was designated as candidate number five. To cast a ballot for Gore, a voter would punch perforation number five and, after casting votes for other offices, turn in the ballot to an election clerk. A counting machine would then tabulate the results. The punch card ballots had a major problem, however. Sometimes the perforations, called "chads" by election personnel, might remain attached to the ballot and not be counted by the machine. There were several reasons for this phenomenon—a voter might not have punched the ballot hard enough to remove the chad, or the voting machine might have been so filled with discarded chads that a voter would encounter difficulty in forcing the chad off a ballot. This counting problem was complicated by the fact that thousands of punch card ballots had not recorded a vote for president. The Gore campaign believed that many uncounted ballots, if inspected manually, would reveal votes for Gore, and they demanded these recounts. The Bush campaign said that such ballots did not record votes because people had chosen not to cast ballots for president. The Bush attorneys spent much of their time during the weeks following the election trying to prevent manual recounts. The Gore campaign asked for manual recounts in only four heavily Democratic counties, however, because of certain peculiar features of Florida election law. A candidate seeking a recount had to request them from individual counties rather than from the entire state.

Manual recounts of thousands of ballots would take a considerable amount of time, and county clerks' offices were not prepared to accomplish this in the time allotted. Florida law required the secretary of state to certify the results as final seven days after an election. Only one of the four Democratic counties completed the manual recounts by that deadline, with the other three counties submitting incomplete results. Bush's lead had declined to only 300 votes with the inclusion of these amended results, but that was still enough for him to win the state.

There were several contradictions in Florida law, however, and they provided Gore with some new opportunities and some threatening pitfalls. Absentee ballots sent from military installations located outside the nation had to be counted if they arrived within ten days of the election, according to federal law. The addition of these ballots expanded Bush's lead to 930 votes. Another problem related to language in the state election law. In one place, the law said that returns submitted after the seven-day deadline "shall be ignored" (Florida Statutes, Title IX, Chapter 102, Section 111), while in another place, the law said they "may be ignored" (Florida Statutes, Title IX, Chapter 102, Section 112). Republican Secretary of State Katherine Harris, who was also a high-ranking official of the Bush campaign, relied on the first of these interpretations in what Democrats said was a partisan attempt to advance Bush's interest. Gore sued and won a ruling by the Florida Supreme Court that overturned this interpretation and adopted the more lenient second one. This court extended the deadline for completing the manual recounts to November 26. When this new deadline occurred, one of the three remaining counties submitted its finished recount; one had abandoned its recount and simply submitted the vote count as of Election Day; and the third county still had a recount in progress. Harris certified the results as official and proclaimed Bush the winner of Florida's twenty-five electoral votes. He was ahead by 537 votes.

There were other problems with the election, including the use of an illegal ballot in Palm Beach County, the so-called butterfly ballot that confused many elderly voters and that probably cost Gore several thousand votes; and the actions by Republican county clerks in Seminole and Martin Counties in correcting mistakes on absentee ballot applications that had been sent out by the local Republican Party. While these problems received some news attention and eventually led to important court cases, they were not a part of the Gore legal strategy. Instead, Gore filed a lawsuit contesting the election shortly after Harris had issued her certification. A trial court refused to help him, but the Florida Supreme Court did. It set aside the certification and ordered a statewide manual recount of all disputed ballots that had not already been counted. The Florida Supreme Court also altered the existing statewide vote totals to reflect manually counted ballots that had not been included in the certification. Bush's lead was reduced to only 154 votes.

The U.S. Supreme Court overturned the Florida Supreme Court on December 12 and ordered an end to the recounts. It also reinstated the results of the earlier certification as the final and official vote in Florida, thus giving Bush a victory by 537 votes in Florida and a national total of 271 electoral votes.

The federal Supreme Court said the recounts violated the Equal Protection Clause of the Fourteenth Amendment where "no state may deprive persons under its jurisdiction of the equal protection of the laws." According to the Court, Florida had violated the amendment by not having a uniform standard for counting disputed ballots and for not counting all of them. Florida law said ballots should be counted if the intention of the voter was clear. While this language seemed reasonable enough, the greater problem was the difficulty of determining voter intent on ballots where chads were only partially removed. Chads might be hanging on to the ballot by one, two, or even four corners. A "hanging" chad was attached to the ballot by two or fewer corners, and a "pregnant" or "dimpled" chad was attached by all four corners but had indications that it had been punched in some way with a stylus. The various counties counted the disputed ballots differently, Palm Beach County recording only hanging chads while Broward County counted both hanging and dimpled ones. The inconsistency in the application of these standards led the federal court, in a controversial and highly criticized five to four decision, to rule that the manual recounts violated equal protection of the laws.

The critics who attacked the Supreme Court for its ruling based their complaints on two factors. First, they believed the five majority justices were motivated by partisan considerations and were more intent on helping to elect Bush than defend constitutional principles. The critics pointed out how inconsistent the content of this ruling was with other equal protection decisions about voting rights. They also complained that the Supreme Court should not have become involved because the Constitution places the primary responsibility for conducting elections with the states. The courts of Florida should have decided the final outcome of that state's election.

Nonetheless, the decision of the Supreme Court was final, and it brought the election controversy to an abrupt end. The electoral votes were cast on December 18, as required by law, and revealed yet another problem. One Democratic elector from the District of Columbia, who was expected to vote for Gore, instead abstained in protest of the lack of congressional representation for the district. The final electoral vote was Bush, 271 and Gore, 266, with one abstention.

REFERENCES

Barone, Michael, Richard E. Cohen, and Grant Ujifusa. *The Almanac of American Politics 2002.* Washington, D.C.: The National Journal, 2001.

Ceaser, James W., and Andrew E. Busch. *The Perfect Tie: The True Story of the 2000 Presidential Election*. Lanham, Md.: Rowman and Littlefield, 2001.

Cook, Rhodes. *Race for the Presidency: Winning the 2000 Nomination*. Washington, D.C.: Congressional Quarterly Press, 2000.

Crotty, William, ed. *America's Choice 2000*. Boulder, Colo.: Westview Press, 2001.

Dover, E. D. *Missed Opportunity: Gore, Incumbency, and Television in Election 2000*. Westport, Conn.: Praeger, 2002.

Goldstein, Michael L. *Guide to the 2000 Presidential Election*. Washington, D.C.: Congressional Quarterly Press, 2000.

Jacobson, Gary C. *The 2000 Elections and Beyond*. Washington, D.C.: Congressional Quarterly Press, 2001.

Jamieson, Kathleen Hall, and Paul Waldman. *Electing the President 2000: The Insiders' View*. Philadelphia: University of Pennsylvania Press, 2001.

Jones, Randall J., Jr. *Who Will Be in the White House? Predicting Presidential Elections*. New York: Longman, 2002.

Lewis, Charles. *The Buying of the President 2000: The Authoritative Guide to the Big-Money Interests behind This Year's Presidential Candidates*. New York: Avon Books, 2000.

Mayer, William G., ed. *In Pursuit of the White House: How We Choose Our Presidential Nominees*. New York: Chatham House Publishers, 2000.

Nelson, Michael, ed. *The Elections of 2000*. Washington, D.C.: Congressional Quarterly Press, 2001.

Polsby, Nelson, W., and Aaron Wildavsky. *Presidential Elections: Strategies and Structures of American Politics*. 10th ed. New York: Chatham House Publishers, 2000.

Pomper, Gerald M., ed. *The Election of 2000*. New York: Chatham House Publishers, 2001.

Rakove, Jack N., ed. *The Unfinished Election of 2000*. New York: Basic Books, 2001.

Sabato, Larry J. *Overtime: The Election 2000 Thriller*. New York: Longman, 2002.

Scammon, Richard M., Alice V. McGillivrey, and Rhodes Cook. *America Votes 24: A Handbook of Contemporary American Election Statistics 2000*. Washington, D.C.: Congressional Quarterly Press, 2001.

Stevens, Stuart. *The Big Enchilada: Campaign Adventures with the Cockeyed Optimists from Texas Who Won the Biggest Prize in Politics*. New York: The Free Press, 2001.

Vanderbilt Television News Archive. *Evening News Abstracts*. Nashville: Vanderbilt University Publications, 2002.

Wayne, Stephen J. *The Road to the White House: The Politics of Presidential Elections*. Boston: Bedford/St. Martin's Press, 2000.

2

THE ELECTORAL COLLEGE: CREATION, DEVELOPMENT, AND RELEVANCE

One of the most significant, and certainly unique, features of the American approach to presidential elections is the electoral college. Indeed, without the electoral college, the Florida vote controversy would not have taken place; none of the candidates would have had any need for recounting or preventing recounts of thousands of disputed ballots. The candidates fought over recounts precisely because the outcome of that battle would result in one of them eventually receiving the twenty-five electoral votes allotted to Florida. Those twenty-five votes were essential for victory for either of the two major candidates. To win the presidency, a candidate must receive a majority of the votes in the electoral college. In 2000, that majority was 270. Without Florida, Bush would have attained only 246 electoral college votes, while Gore would have acquired 267. If the electoral college did not exist and Americans had instead chosen their president exclusively by popular vote, Gore would have won the election by nearly one-half million ballots. Moreover, he would have triumphed without recounts. It is because of this essential fact that this essay on the creation, development, and relevance of the electoral college appears so early in the book. One must fully understand the importance of the electoral college in American political life to appreciate the context of the Florida recount controversy and the rationale behind the vast number of legalistic moves and court cases that followed. The reader is encouraged to read the relevant portions from the United States Constitution and the United States Code relating to the electoral college that appear in the Primary Documents section of this book.

CREATION OF THE ELECTORAL COLLEGE

The electoral college was created in 1787 as part of the original writing of the national constitution. In many ways, its creation was an afterthought. The most important mission of the convention was the creation of a legislative body, Congress, which would share legislative power with the states. The convention needed more than two months to complete this task. Afterward, the convention turned to a secondary problem, the creation of an executive. One part of this problem was the method by which a president would be chosen. There were numerous opinions, but none of them enjoyed widespread support. Some convention delegates wanted the president chosen by a direct popular vote of the people, while others preferred a more indirect method, choice by Congress. The electoral college was a compromise between these two positions.

The opponents of a direct popular vote believed that most citizens would be unaware of the qualifications of the nation's leaders and could therefore not make an informed choice for president. In addition, Southern states feared a loss of influence because slaves, counted individually as three-fifths of a person in the census, were not allowed to vote. Many of the smaller states also believed they would have little influence over the choice of a president because of their limited population numbers. Finally, many of the convention delegates thought that a popularly elected president might develop a personal relationship with the people that would be so powerful it could threaten the role of Congress as a representative institution (Longley and Peirce 1999). With respect to the opposite point of view, perhaps the strongest argument against the leading alternative to popular vote, election by Congress, was that Congress would use its electoral role to control the presidency and make that office ineffective (Kuroda 1994). The electoral college appeared to be a good compromise between these two positions; it would provide an indirect method of presidential choice by a political body having the same number of votes as there were seats in Congress, but it was not Congress itself and therefore could not exert any power over the presidency. The Constitution's Article II provided that each state's electoral vote would be equal to its combined number of seats in Congress. The House of Representatives was based on the representation principle of equality of people, while the Senate's formula was based on the idea of equality of states. The allocation of House seats is determined by the results of a census taken every ten years, while each state always has two senators. The constitution left the choice of electors to the states by providing that electors would be chosen by whichever method a state determined and that votes had to be cast by the electors meeting in the capitals of their respective states. The electoral college was not to meet as a single body at any time and place to prevent any conspiracies or deal making. As part of this goal, the actual counting of electoral votes and the determination of the winner was deemed a responsibility of Congress. While defending the structure and operations of the electoral college, Robert M. Hardaway, author of a major book about the electoral college and the Constitution writes as follows:

> The Electoral College system was overwhelmingly approved, not so much as a compromise but as the result of a realization on the part of the delegates that it offered the best of both legislative and direct election proposals. (Hardaway 1994, 14)

There is some debate about whether the authors of the Constitution intended for the electoral college to actually elect the president. While the constitutional language provides for an election procedure, it also suggests that the authors may have instead wanted the electoral college to serve instead as a nominating body. Article II provided for the House of Representatives to choose the president if the electoral college failed in its designated task. The article required for each elector to cast two votes for president with the stipulation that at least one of those votes had to be for a person who was not a resident of the elector's own state. Many of the Constitution's authors believed that electors would be pressured to vote for a person from their own state or that those electors would not be familiar with prominent leaders of other states (Best 1996). The two-vote requirement meant that every member of the electoral college would cast at least one vote for a person of national importance. To win the election, a candidate needed the support of a majority of electors and had to acquire more votes than any other candidate. There were two possible scenarios where no person might fulfill these requirements; two candidates would tie for first place, or no candidate would receive the support of a majority of electors. In either instance, Article II provided that the House of Representatives would then choose the president. The House would make its selection from among the top two candidates in the event of a tie for first place, or, if no candidate had a majority, from among the top five vote getters. Each state would have one vote in this House election. While most of the Constitution's authors expected George Washington to win the first election with little or no opposition, they were not so sure about the likelihood of majority winners emerging in subsequent years. Many of them assumed the House would choose most of the nation's presidents with the electoral college serving primarily as a nominating body (Longley and Peirce 1999).

One unusual feature of the electoral college was the method designated for choosing the vice president. This office was created during the convention's latter stages as a solution to the two unrelated problems of a presiding officer in the Senate and succession to the presidency in the event of a vacancy in that office. The vice president would be the second highest vote getter in the electoral college and would have the responsibility of presiding over the Senate. This created some ambiguity over whether the vice president was a member of the executive or legislative branches. Since he had no executive responsibilities, he was usually treated as a legislative branch member until the middle part of the twentieth century (Kuroda 1994, Dover 2002).

EARLY HISTORY OF THE ELECTORAL COLLEGE

Initially, the electoral college worked much like the authors of the Constitution intended. The nation's first presidential election took place during the early months of 1789. The Continental Congress, the governing body between the end of the Revolutionary War and the new government provided for in the Constitution, enacted laws that required the states to write laws relating to the choice of electors. The states were to complete the actual selection of those electors by the first Wednesday in January 1789. The electors would cast their votes on the first Wednesday in February, and the new congress would meet on the first Wednesday in March to count the votes and announce the winners. While there were some problems, the election was successful. Eleven states participated; Rhode Island and North Carolina were excluded because they had yet to ratify the Constitution. There was no uniform method among the states for choosing electors. Six states opted for legislative choice of electors, while five enacted popular choice methods. New York, a legislative-choice state, demonstrated the pitfalls of this approach when the two houses of its legislature deadlocked over its choice and failed to reach a compromise. New York did not vote for president in this first election. Ten states, with a total of sixty-nine electoral votes, chose the first president. All sixty-nine electors voted for George Washington. Approximately half of the electors, thirty-four, also voted for John Adams, while the remaining thirty-five divided their votes among a wide variety of other persons, with John Jay finishing in third place with nine votes. Washington and Adams were thereby elected as president and vice president.

One important feature of this election was the fact that most, and probably all, of the electors believed they were voting for Washington for president and for someone else, Adams and Jay, for example, for vice president. They did not see themselves as casting their constitutionally mandated two votes for two presidential candidates as was intended for by the authors of Article II (Kuroda 1994). This belief would continue through subsequent elections and would eventually have a profound effect on the electoral college.

Additional events also contributed to the development of the electoral college in directions not intended by the constitutional authors. In discussing the creation and subsequent history of the electoral college, Lawrence D. Longley and Neal R. Peirce attribute its changes to five factors, with the rise of political parties being of the foremost importance. The Constitution makes no mention of political parties, but these nongovernmental organizations have become major components of contemporary American politics. Many informed observers believe that American government simply cannot function unless political parties fulfill the role of aggregating varieties of interests into governing coalitions. The constitutional doctrines of federalism, separation of powers, checks and balances, and respect for individual rights also lead to the dispersion of governmental power among a vast number of competing institutions. Policymaking all too frequently becomes extraordinarily difficult in these circumstances. Parties have risen to fill the leadership void created by the Constitution, and they help institutions work by providing a common set of political goals for officeholders.

The rise of parties affected presidential elections by eliminating the idea of electors making free choices from among a variety of presidential candidates. Instead, most potential electors identified with individual parties and announced in advance how they intended to cast their votes. Moreover, parties also began nominating candidates for president and vice president and in so doing eliminated the nominating function of the electoral college. Parties started by using congressional caucuses, meetings where all congressional members of the party would convene, to designate their nominees. By the 1830s parties were relying on national conventions where hundreds of delegates from state party affiliates would convene to nominate the candidates.

Longley and Peirce also attribute changes in state laws to the transformation of the electoral college. While about half of the states employed legislative choice of electors in 1789, that method eventually became unpopular and was discarded in favor of popular vote approaches. By 1832, twenty-three of the nation's twenty-four states had enacted laws that placed the choice of electors with the voters rather than with the legislature. In addition, those states had also adopted the general ticket method of electoral vote allocation. In this system, candidates for the electoral college are listed on the ballot as members of a party slate rather than as individuals as in 1789. Citizens cast their ballots for one party slate, and victory was then awarded to the slate with the largest number of votes. With this change, electoral college members have been reduced in status to little more than party officials casting their votes for the nominees of the party that nominated them. The U.S. Supreme Court upheld a state law requiring potential electors to sign pledges promising to support the candidates of their party if they wish to be placed on a ballot as a party candidate for the electoral college [*Ray v. Blair*, 343 U.S. 214 (1952)]. The practice of direct choice of electors by the voters of a particular state is not mandated by the Constitution, and this fact may have led to some confusion in the Florida legislature in 2000. The Constitution says that electors must be chosen by whatever method the legislature of a state directs. The states now use the general ticket method, but they do have the constitutional right to use a different method. There is a provision in the U.S. Code, section 6 of Title 3, which is reprinted in the Primary Documents Section of this book, that requires states to decide on which method they will use for choosing electors before an election takes place. The Florida legislature did not appear to understand this provision of federal law when they threatened to choose a separate slate of electors favoring Bush if Gore won with the manual recounts. In addition, when state legislatures delegate the choice of electors to voters, they are bound by the provisions of the Fourteenth Amendment. This amendment, adopted in 1868, prevents states from denying persons the equal protection of the laws. This was the constitutional provision used by the U.S. Supreme Court in stopping the manual recounts of disputed ballots and that eventually led to the triumph of George W. Bush.

Finally, Longley and Peirce write about the influence of the Twelfth Amendment, a significant reform that was added to the Constitution in 1804. This amendment altered the language from Article II and acknowledged the impact of the changes mentioned above. The amendment could not have been adopted without the troubling experiences of the two preceding elections, however. George Washington sought reelection in the nation's second presidential election in 1792, which was the last one conducted under the initial rules without major difficulties. Congress had changed some of the dates; electors were chosen in early November, cast their votes in December, and Congress counted ballots in January. These dates have remained unchanged since that time. Each of the 135 electors from fifteen states voted for Washington, while a majority also voted for Adams, thinking of the two as candidates for president and vice president. The remaining electors voted for Washington and New York Governor George Clinton, seeing Clinton as a candidate for vice president.

Washington retired after two terms, and the battle for succession was both intense and surprising. The nation now had two active parties, the Federalists and the Democratic-Republicans. The Federalists advanced Adams for president and Thomas Pinckney for vice president in the election of 1796. Thomas Jefferson and Aaron Burr were nominated as the presidential and vice presidential candidates of the Democratic-Republicans. The election was close: Adams received seventy-one electoral votes while carrying nine states, and Jefferson won sixty-eight votes and carried seven states. Adams was the obvious winner. There was a major problem with the vice presidency, however. Many of the electors did not vote for the vice presidential candidates advanced by the two parties. As a consequence, Pinckney finished in third place with fifty-nine electoral votes. Jefferson, the major rival of Adams and the leader of the opposition party, was the nation's new vice president by virtue of attaining the second largest number of electoral votes. Because of the partisan rivalry between the two, Adams could not assign any important executive responsibilities to Jefferson.

The problems inherent in the electoral college became even worse in 1800. Both Adams and Jefferson ran again, with Jefferson winning this election by a similarly close margin of seventy-three to sixty-five electoral votes. There was more party unity this time, perhaps too much, because Burr also received seventy-three votes. The House of Representatives had to choose between Jefferson and Burr. The problem to many people was that most electors had intended for Jefferson to be president and Burr to have the second office, but there had been no way for them to make their preferences known. Burr responded to this dilemma by running for president in the House election, and he received the support of many of its Federalist members. Jefferson eventually won, but only after the House had conducted thirty-six ballots. This battle, coupled with the outcome of the 1796 election, led to the adoption of the Twelfth Amendment. Electors would now cast separate ballots for president and vice president. If no candidate receives a majority of the electoral vote, the House chooses the winner, but their choice is now restricted to only the top three vote getters rather than the top five as initially provided in Article II. The Senate chooses the vice president from among the top two vote getters in the event that no one attains a majority of the electoral vote for that office.

THE ELECTORAL COLLEGE AFTER THE TWELFTH AMENDMENT

The adoption of the Twelfth Amendment had two effects. First, it eliminated the problems that had developed from the initial language of the Constitution by repealing the provision that electors must cast two undesignated votes for president. Second, it informally recognized political parties as the nominating institutions in presidential elections by providing separate ballots for president and vice president. Nonetheless, additional problems surfaced in subsequent years, particularly in 2000, which was nearly two centuries after the adoption of the amendment.

The first trouble occurred in the election of 1824. It developed primarily because the political parties failed to deliver on the change they had created from the initial language in the Constitution. The parties failed to make nominations in 1824, and in response, the nation temporarily returned that role to the electoral college. With the electoral college serving as the nominating devise, the choice of president was placed squarely in the House of Representatives, much as the authors of the Constitution had intended. The final outcome was highly divisive, however, and served to bring forth the same arguments that had been employed at the constitutional convention against congressional choice of the president.

With respect to the political context of the election of 1824, the Federalist Party had ceased to exist by this time, and its demise left only one party in existence, the Democratic-Republicans. The Federalist Party declined significantly after John Adams lost the election of 1800. It competed in national elections for nearly two decades after that but never won, nor did it appear likely to do so. It ceased its efforts entirely after 1816. There was no immediate problem; James Monroe was unopposed for a second term in 1820, but the lack of a rival damaged the ruling Democratic-Republicans in the battle for a successor to Monroe in 1824. This party eventually became so diverse in its appeals that it appeared to stand for little. It had so many factions it disintegrated in 1824 when some of its leading factions advanced their own presidential candidates in that year's election. There were four candidates in 1824—all claimed membership in the Democratic-Republican Party—but none could unite their partisans into a common cause and win access to the ballot in every state. As a result, no candidate won either a majority of the electoral or popular vote. The two strongest were Andrew

Jackson, who attained 41.3 percent of the popular vote and ninety-nine electoral votes while carrying eleven states, and John Quincy Adams, who garnered eighty-four electoral votes, 30.9 percent of the popular vote, and seven states. The others, William Crawford and Henry Clay, each won three states. Crawford finished third in electoral votes, with forty-one votes, but fourth in the popular vote, with 11.2 percent, while Clay finished third in the popular vote with 13 percent but fourth in electoral votes with only thirty-seven votes.

Since no candidate had a majority of the electoral vote, the House of Representatives decided the election. A significant factor was that Clay, out of consideration for his fourth place electoral vote finish, was Speaker of the House. He actively supported Adams, and his backing proved crucial. Adams was elected because thirteen state delegations voted for him on the one and only ballot. Jackson won the support of seven states, and Crawford of four. Since the parties had failed to control nominations, the electoral college reduced the number of eligible candidates to three, and the House chose the president from that list.

There was a problem, however, as Adams soon named Clay as his secretary of state. While there is no evidence that Adams and Clay had made any deal relating to support and appointment, their opponents, particularly Jackson, made such accusations. The House election of Adams and his subsequent appointment of Clay convinced many people of the undesirability of allowing the House of Representatives to choose the president. A redefined party system was in existence by 1828. Jackson's supporters had created the Democratic Party, while Adams and Clay were responsible for starting the National Republican Party. This latter entity did not last long and was succeeded by the Whig Party in 1834. The Whigs were, in turn, replaced by the current Republican Party in the election of 1856. Since that time, the two major parties have performed the role of nominating the two final candidates for president, with the electoral college serving as the electing institution.

Two elections in the post-Civil War period were also defined by electoral college difficulties. In 1876, voters appeared to have chosen the Democratic nominee Samuel Tilden for president over the Republican Rutherford Hayes by a margin of over 250,000 popular votes and an electoral vote count of 203 to 166. Tilden amassed 51 percent of the popular vote compared to Hayes's total of 48 percent. Unfortunately for Tilden, there were serious discrepancies in the vote count in three former confederate states: South Carolina, Louisiana, and Florida. In each of these three states, competing governmental institutions submitted final vote tallies that showed the party of the leaders of those institutions winning the state. Initially, Tilden had been leading in all three. In addition, each state submitted two lists of electors, one of which supported each of the major political parties. Congress was required to select the proper slate of electors from each state. It responded by appointing a commission comprised of five House members, five senators, and five justices from the Supreme Court to investigate the claims and decide which slates to accept. The commission's findings had to be approved by both houses of Congress to take effect. The Democrats controlled the House and responded by naming three members of their own party and two Republicans to the commission, while the Republicans, in control of the Senate, named three of their members and two Democrats. The Supreme Court named its five seniormost associate justices: two Republicans, two Democrats, and one nonpartisan. The nonpartisan soon resigned from the court to become a Democratic senator from Illinois, so the next judge in seniority, a Republican, replaced him. The commission voted eight to seven, strictly on party lines, to seat the Republican electors. The Senate accepted this decision, but the House indicated it would disapprove. In a move of historic significance, a number of Southern congressmen agreed to vote for the Republican slates in exchange for an end to Reconstruction and the appointment of several Southerners as executives in the new Republican administration. This deal made, the disputed electors went to Hayes, who won the presidency through an electoral vote count of 185 to 184 despite the fact that he had lost the popular vote. Without the existence of the electoral college, Tilden would have become president. The Congress responded to this controversy by enacting a law, which is still in effect today, that says Congress must accept the slate of electors that is certified as official by a state's governor unless it can be proven that such a slate was chosen in a fraudulent manner.

The second difficult election occurred twelve years later in 1888. The Democrats nominated Grover Cleveland for a second term as president, while the Republicans choss Benjamin Harrison. The election was close, as were most of the elections, during this time, with Cleveland garnering 48.6 percent of the popular vote compared to Harrison's 47.8 percent. While this margin may not seem large, only 0.8 of 1 percent, it was large when compared to its two predecessors. The popular vote difference in the election of 1880 was only 0.02 percent, and Cleveland had won the popular vote when seeking his first term in 1884 by only 0.25 percent. There was an important difference between the elections of 1884 and 1888, however. Cleveland had won the electoral votes of twenty of the nation's thirty-eight states in 1884, but in 1888 he carried only eighteen. Two of the states he had carried in 1884, New York and Indiana, went for Harrison in this more recent election. As a result, Harrison won the electoral vote by an overwhelming margin of 233 to 168. Cleveland won the popular vote by scoring massive victories in the former confederate states, where nearly all voters supported the Democrats. Harrison won most of the other states by far closer margins. Cleveland had more votes, but Harrison had a broader and more national base of support. The election of 1888 was the last time when the winner of the popular vote did not also win the electoral vote, until the election of 2000.

RELEVANCE OF THE ELECTORAL COLLEGE

There have been fifty-four presidential elections in American history and in only four of those did the winner fail to finish first in the popular vote. On the basis of this fact one might be encouraged to believe that the electoral college is getting far too much attention and assume that it amounts to little more than a ceremonial event with little political significance. It would be wrong to make such an assumption. There has been a lively debate for many decades now about the relevance and usefulness of the electoral college. In this section, I review the arguments in support of and in opposition to the usefulness of this constitutional device.

The existence of the electoral college places certain political requirements on presidential candidates that might well not happen otherwise. One of these is that a candidate, to be successful in a presidential quest, must develop support throughout the nation rather than restrict it to one of two regions. The size of a victory in any one state is not of particular importance to the final outcome of a presidential election. What is important is the fact that such a state level pattern of support occurred. A presidential candidate receives the entire electoral vote of a particular state simply by receiving more popular votes in that state than any other aspirant for the office. Bush defeated Gore by less than 600 votes in Florida and received the entire bloc of that state's electoral vote; Gore defeated Bush by more than 1.7 million votes in New York and received the entire bloc of that state's electoral vote. Gore would still have won the New York electoral vote if his victory margin had been only 0.7 million votes, or only 600 votes. The key requirement for a candidate to win the presidency is to attain a majority of the entire national electoral vote, which is presently 270. This requires conducting a campaign aimed at winning just enough popular support in a particular combination of states to result in the acquisition of the requisite number of 270 electoral votes. Candidates must conduct nationally focused campaigns if they wish to accomplish this goal. Judith A. Best, author of a number of works about the electoral college and who has testified before Congress on the desirability of retaining it, says that this political need for a national campaign forces a candidate to develop a consensus in support of his election. She adds that such a political need is also in the nation's best interest (Best 1996).

One of the more significant features of the operation of the electoral college is the existence of what Best and other writers call the "magnifier effect." Here, a popular vote victory in a particular state, regardless of how small it might be, magnifies the size of the actual victory. If the occurrence of this phenomenon is observed on a national scale, a small popular vote victory may appear as a large electoral vote triumph. For example, in the election of 1960, John F. Kennedy received 49.72 percent of the popular vote, while Richard Nixon attained a nearly equal percentage of 49.55. Kennedy carried several states by popular vote margins comparable to his national total. The electoral vote tally told a different story, however. It created an impression that

Kennedy had won the election by a solid and significant margin. Kennedy won 303 votes compared to Nixon's 219. The magnifier effect made Kennedy's victory look larger than it actually was. Best says this effect helps create a popular mandate behind the winner but does not exaggerate it.

The magnifier effect can also prove helpful for the nation in that it can produce a clear winner in situations when the voters may not have chosen one. Three elections from different time periods illustrate this fact. In the elections of 1860, 1912, and 1992, Abraham Lincoln, Woodrow Wilson, and Bill Clinton, respectively, finished first in the popular vote in campaigns in which there were more than two major candidates. Lincoln attained 39.8 percent of the popular vote, Wilson 41.8, and Clinton 43.4. None of these are convincing victories. The distributions of electoral votes in these elections provided more convincing evidence for claims of victory, however. Lincoln attained 180 votes of the 303 that were cast in 1860; Wilson garnered 435 out of 531, while Clinton won 370 votes from the grand total of 538 that comprised the electoral college of 1992. The size of these electoral vote triumphs allowed these presidents to claim popular mandates even though their actual votes may have suggested otherwise. All three were able to govern effectively afterward.

There are many critics of the electoral college who see little merit deriving from the institution. Instead, they view it as an outdated and undemocratic entity that poses the threat of occasionally obstructing the choices of the people from winning the presidency. Two such critics are David Abbott and James Levine, who find the general ticket method of vote allocation where the winner in a given state receives all of that states' electoral vote as favoring certain groups and regions within American society while punishing others. The groups that are helped tend to be concentrated in particular states, and their overwhelming support for one candidate in a close election frequently proves decisive in the outcomes of those states. Some groups whose members are concentrated in a few competitive states include Jews, Italian-Americans, suburbanites, and groups with narrowly defined interests such as Cuban-Americans in Florida. Other groups that are more dispersed throughout the nation and that have less ability to concentrate their votes behind one candidate in a key state are African-Americans and Hispanics. While these groups are some of the most numerous of all of the nation's minorities, they are also found in all states (Abbott and Levine 1991).

In addition to their focus on voter groups, certain states, as argued by Abbott and Levine, may enjoy unusual advantages or disadvantages because of their size and their levels of political competitiveness. The mathematics of electoral vote distribution tends to favor small states in the sense that each state, regardless of size, receives two votes for its representation in the Senate. Despite this fact, more populous states may actually benefit far more from the distribution of electoral votes simply because of their political competitiveness. Candidates tend to devote far more time and resources to a few large states because the outcomes in those states are frequently in doubt and the relative size of those states can unduly affect the final outcome of the national results. This pattern of campaigning often gives the larger states more influence over the issues that dominate a campaign. Moreover, Abbott and Levine also find representation problems in the sense that rapidly growing states may be penalized in their vote allocations because the federal census is compiled only once every ten years. Such states may have allocations of electoral votes that are based on outdated population totals. For example, in the election of 2000, New York had thirty-three electoral votes, and Texas had thirty-two. These allocations were based on the census of 1990. The census of 2000 led to a change in the distribution of votes between these two states, with New York now being entitled to only thirty-one and Texas to thirty-four. While these altered numbers were based on the population as it actually existed during the 2000 election, they will not take effect until the next election in 2004. Related to this phenomenon of inaccurate vote allocations is the fact that states with relatively high participation rates may also be penalized because such rates are relevant only within the context of the vote in that particular state and have little or no bearing on the nationwide electoral vote totals.

Abbott and Levine are also critical of the electoral college for contributing to distorted interpretations of election outcomes. Unlike Best, discussed above, they believe the magnifier effect is detrimental to governing in the sense that it creates illusions of landslide victories by winners of close elections. For example, in 1980, Ronald Reagan attained 50.7 percent of the popular vote compared to 41 percent for the defeated incumbent president, Jimmy Carter, and 6.6 percent for the third party challenger, John Anderson. Stated differently, Reagan won the support of approximately half of the nation's voters, while the other half wanted other candidates. However, the results of the electoral college told another story. Reagan won forty-four states and 489 electoral votes, while Carter garnered six states and the District of Columbia for a total of forty-nine electoral votes. Anderson, who failed to carry any state, received no electoral votes. The outcome of the electoral college suggests that Reagan had acquired a strong mandate to govern, but did he? Was his electoral total merely an illusion created by an undemocratic and artificial entity that lost its original purpose over two hundred years ago?

The electoral college is a controversial, but also defining, feature of American presidential elections. It has lost much of its intended purposes: to provide a means of nomination in a dispersed nation without political parties or good communication; to prevent a president from building a personal following from among the populace that might make the executive office unduly powerful; to give the states control of elections in a nation that lacked a strong central government; and to permit the House of Representatives to actually choose the president in most elections. Its only remaining purposes seem questionable. Is it an institutional device that forces candidates to build national rather than regional followings, as some of its defenders argue, or has that consensus building role been destroyed by nationwide television, which is now the major media by which presidential candidates reach much of the American public? Does it create an electoral mandate for the winner through the magnifier effect that permits the victorious candidate to claim popular leadership, or does it instead create an illusion of widespread support for the first-place finisher in a close election? Does it create winners out of losers when the second-place finisher in the popular vote wins a majority of the electoral vote and the presidency, or does it reward the candidates whose support is most dispersed throughout the nation? Are the values that allegedly derive from the existence of the electoral college worth the trouble that existed in Florida when the popular vote indicated that a clear winner had emerged in Gore, or was the outcome of Election 2000 such an anomaly that we should look on it as little more than an oddity and continue conducting our elections as we have for more than two hundred years? Should we keep or abolish the electoral college?

One of the authors who was quoted in this essay, Robert Hardaway, writes that the major reason why efforts aimed at changing the manners in which we conduct our elections, including even the retention or abolishment of the electoral college, always fail is because Americans lack a national consensus on what kind of change we want. At this writing, there seems to be little that will be done in either the nation or in Florida to alter the ways in which elections are run except to eliminate the outdated punch card ballot that caused so much trouble and replace it with more accurate types of ballot methods of more recent origin. This is a limited change and does not question the basic assumptions and values underpinning the current system that we now use. This pattern of advancing only limited change in the wake of major troubles, such as adopting the Twelfth Amendment after the original electoral system failed, has been a major feature of American elections for more than two centuries now and is unlikely to change anytime soon. With this, one should conclude that the electoral college, viewed either as a viable national consensus builder or as an outdated and undemocratic anachronism, depending upon one's point of view, will very likely be with us for many decades to come simply because we do not or cannot agree on its usefulness or on its possible replacement.

REFERENCES

Abbott, David W., and James P. Levine. *Wrong Winner: The Coming Debacle in the Electoral College*. Westport, Conn.: Praeger, 1991.

Best, Judith A. *The Choice of the People? Debating the Electoral College*. Lanham, Md.: Rowman and Littlefield, 1996.

Dover, E.D. *Missed Opportunity: Gore, Incumbency, and Television in Election 2000*. Westport, Conn.: Praeger, 2002.

Glennon, Michael J. *When No Majority Rules: The Electoral College and Presidential Succession*. Washington, D.C.: Congressional Quarterly Press, 1992.

Hardaway, Robert. *The Electoral College and the Constitution: The Case for Preserving Federalism*. Westport, Conn.: Praeger, 1994.

Kura, Alexandra. *Electoral College and Presidential Elections*. Huntington, N.Y.: Nova Science Publishers, 2001.

Kuroda, Tadahisa. *The Origins of the Twelfth Amendment: The Electoral College in the Early Republic, 1787–1804*. Westport, Conn.: Greenwood Press, 1994.

Longley, Lawrence D., and Neal R. Peirce. *The Electoral College Primer 2000*. New Haven, Conn.: Yale University Press, 1999.

3

THE FLORIDA VOTE CONTROVERSY: MAJOR POLITICAL AND LEGAL ISSUES

Almost certainly, the defining characteristic of the 2000 presidential election was the Florida vote controversy and the vast array of court cases, including a landmark one by the U.S. Supreme Court, that developed from it. This chapter and the next focus on the major developments of this controversy. This chapter provides a narrative of the leading events of the continuing battle over vote counts and of the responses by the Bush and Gore campaigns to a series of developments over which they had limited control. The following chapter focuses specifically on the legal rulings that came from these court cases and from a variety of other recent cases relating to the constitutional theme of equal protection of the laws that was used by the Supreme Court to stop manual recounts of Florida ballots. Both chapters are written from the perspective that the states hold the primary responsibility within the American constitutional tradition for conducting elections and that the federal role is limited.

This chapter begins with the circumstances and events of November 8, the day immediately after the election. As mentioned previously in chapter 1 of this book, television viewers had already encountered a few problems relating to Florida during election night when the various television networks relied on exit polls and proclaimed Gore as the winner of the state's twenty-five electoral votes, retracted their forecast, awarded the state to Bush, and then retracted that award several hours later. With the conclusion of the initial vote count in the state, Bush led Gore by a scant 1,784 votes out of more than six million that had been cast. The Texas governor could not yet claim the state's electoral votes and the presidency, however, because Florida law required an automatic recount in any election when the margin of votes separating a winner from the next highest finisher was less than one-half of 1 percent. The mandatory recount would not be completed for several days, so the outcome in both Florida and the nation remained uncertain.

THE PALM BEACH COUNTY BUTTERFLY BALLOT

While several days would pass before the official state recount was completed, another controversy erupted that would dominate the Florida election for several days: the presence and possible detrimental effect of the so-called butterfly ballot in Palm Beach County. At the center of this problem, and of the others that were to arise during the coming days, was the use of the punch card ballot. As mentioned in chapter 1, this balloting method requires the voter to use a stylus and punch a perforated opening on a paper card ballot to record a vote. With such a method, each candidate's name is listed on the ballot in some predetermined order with a number placed next to a specific perforated opening where one can record a vote for that candidate. For example, if a voter wishes to cast a ballot for the candidate designated as number 18, he or she inserts the stylus into the perforation marked 18 and punches it from the card.

Florida law required that the names of all candidates for any partisan office to be chosen in a given election had to be listed on the ballot in the order in which each political party's candidate for governor had finished in the most recent election for that office. Since the last election for governor of Florida had been in 1998 and the winner had been Republican Jeb Bush, a brother of Governor Bush, the Republican nominees for all offices to be voted on in Florida in 2000, including president, had to be listed first. The remaining candidates were to be listed in the same order in which their nominees had finished in the last governor's race. These names were to be followed in the ballot listing by the names of candidates from political parties that had not competed in the election for governor in 1998. This law meant that the Democratic nominee for every office decided in 2000 had to be placed second on every ballot. The usual practice in both Florida and other states using punch card ballots is to list the names of all candidates in a column on the left side of the ballot with the perforations placed in a column on the right side.

In all, there were ten presidential candidates on the Florida ballot, including the two major party nominees of Bush and Gore, their leading minor party rivals Ralph Nader and Patrick Buchanan, and six nominees of smaller minor parties. The Palm Beach county clerk, Teresa LaPore, a Democrat, had initially created a ballot that listed all ten candidates on one sheet of paper in the proper order as required by state law. Unfortunately, she had to employ an unusually small print size to accomplish this. LaPore was concerned that many elderly voters—Palm Beach County has a disproportionately high number of retirees—would have difficulty reading the ballot's small print. To create a ballot with larger print and still keep the ballot on one page, she placed the candidates' names in two columns, one on the left side of the page and one on the right, while having the perforations in the middle. The left column included the first six party names in the precise order as required by law, while the right contained the last four names. The related perforation numbers were identified by arrows, but the order in which they were placed on the ballot did not correspond to this legally required rank order, however. The names on the left side of the ballot were denoted by odd-numbered perforations, while the ones on the right were identified with even numbers that were interspaced between the odd numbers. For example, the order of parties, candidates, and perforation numbers on the left were as follows: Republican, George W. Bush (3); Democratic, Al Gore (5); Libertarian, Harry Browne (7); Green, Ralph Nader (9); Socialist Workers, James Harris (11); and Natural Law, John Hagelin (13). Those on the right were as follows: Reform, Patrick Buchanan (4); Socialist, David McReynolds (6); Constitution, Howard Phillips (8); and Workers World, Monica Moorehead (10). The perforation numbers appeared in numerical order on the ballot, but the candidates' names alternated from one side of the page to the other. The first number, 3, corresponded to Bush from the left side; the next, 4, corresponded to Buchanan from the right; the next, 5, corresponded to Gore on the left; and the following one, 6, corresponded to McReynolds from the right. The term "butterfly" derived from the ballot design because the perforations in the middle were surrounded on both sides by two lists of candidates that superficially looked like wings.

While the intentions behind this ballot design were probably benevolent, with the primary goal being to increase the voters' convenience, the eventual result was quite the opposite. Thousands of elderly voters were confused by the unusual ballot design and all too frequently cast mistaken ballots for

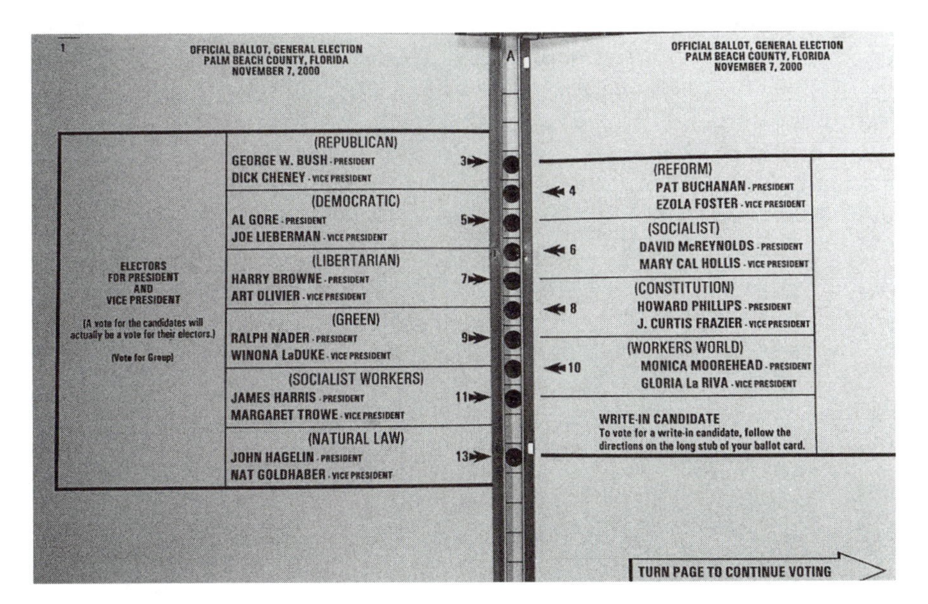

The infamous butterfly ballot used in Palm Beach County, Florida. Confusion arose among some voters over whether to punch 4 or 5 to vote for Al Gore. *Marc Serota/ ©Reuters NewMedia Inc./Corbis.*

candidates other than the one they wished to support. Some people who wanted to support Gore punched the perforation for Buchanan instead or punched the one immediately below Gore for Socialist David McReynolds. Some of these voters, discovering their errors, compounded them by then punching the Gore number, thus disqualifying their ballots because they had now cast two votes for president. One of the great unanswered mysteries that developed from this controversy, and one that was all too frequently raised by Republican defenders of Bush's resistance to Gore's challenges, was why had these people, upon discovering their errors, not simply turned in their spoiled ballots and asked for replacements. Moreover, why had the Democratic Party, which controlled the Palm Beach county clerk's office and thereby possessed the legal responsibilities for conducting elections, not been more vigilant in pretesting this new ballot design in ways that might have exposed the confusion long before election day? These questions were never answered.

The butterfly ballot posed two problems for Gore. One was that some of his supporters simply punched the wrong perforation, usually the number 4 space that was identified for Buchanan. The second problem related to the overvotes that occurred when voters actually cast two ballots, one for Gore and one for some other candidate, with the vote for Gore likely having been cast after a person had discovered his or her mistake. The combined effects of these two problems were significant and may have been the major reasons why Gore lost Florida. If problems relating to the butterfly ballot had not existed, the early evening network forecasts that awarded Florida's electoral votes to Gore might have been accurate after all. Buchanan received 3,704 votes in Palm Beach County compared to only 561 in Miami-Dade and 789 in Broward Counties, both of which are more populous than Palm Beach. In fact, Buchanan did not receive 1,000 votes in any Florida county other than Palm Beach. In addition, the *Miami Herald* newspaper, which sponsored and conducted a complete recount of all disputed ballots during the months following the conclusion of the vote controversy, reported that more than 20,000 overvotes had been cast in Palm Beach County with 5,264 recording votes for Gore and Buchanan, 2,862 supporting Gore and David McReynolds from the Socialist Party, and 1,319 backing Gore and Libertarian candidate Harry Browne (Merzer and the staff of the *Miami Herald* 2001, 189). The combined effects of these two problems may have cost Gore as many as 10,000 votes.

The immediate problem for the Gore campaign relating to the butterfly ballot, which seemed to be the victim of this flawed design, was to decide upon a course of action. There appeared to be three options, none of which was very promising. The campaign could ask a judge to reapportion the overvotes according to the same distributions of votes that had been recorded in other Florida counties; it could instead ask that a judge hear testimony from individual voters who believed they had incorrectly punched the wrong perforations and then readjust their votes upon request, or it could ask for a new election in Palm Beach County to be conducted with a properly designed ballot (Toobin 2001, 35).

The first two options seemed improbable; few observers expected judges to take the radical step of reapportioning votes from spoiled ballots or correcting personal mistakes. A new election would be problematic because federal law required uniform dates for presidential elections and voters in a second election would have knowledge of the national outcome and might very well readjust their votes in ways that might produce a different result. Nader, for example, had attained nearly 100,000 votes in Florida. Eventually, the Gore campaign attempted nothing in relation to the butterfly ballot design simply because none of the options seemed to offer any realistic promise of overturning the apparent Bush victory. The overvotes remained uncounted and unavailable in the final tally as the Democrats instead directed their attention to other ballot-related issues.

MANUAL RECOUNTS AND HANGING CHADS

The Gore campaign chose to direct its attention to the problem of undervotes in the hopes that this avenue might provide a greater opportunity for victory. An undervote is a ballot that does not record a vote when tabulated by a counting machine. There were over 60,000 presidential undervotes throughout Florida in 2000. Of course, many of the undervotes contained no presidential preferences simply because some people had chosen to abstain in that contest. The punch card ballots caused another problem, however, that was unique to them and that may have inadvertently expanded the number of undervotes. The paper covering the perforations, generally referred to as chads, sometimes remained attached to the ballots after being poked by a stylus and because of this were not always tabulated by the automatic counting machines.

The undervote problem the Gore campaign concentrated its attention on stemmed from the peculiar nature of punch card ballots and the fact that some chads remained attached to ballots. Terms that were new to much of the American electorate were soon introduced into everyday vocabulary. A hanging or dangling chad was attached to the ballot by at least two corners. A pregnant chad was attached at four corners but had obviously been punched because it bowed forward allowing light to show. A dimpled chad was still attached to the ballot but contained a pinprick indicating that a voter had attempted to punch the perforation but had not done so hard enough to dislodge or bend the chad. The question that had to be determined by an elections official was whether to include any or all of these types of ballots in the final count. A machine count that had failed to tally them initially on election night would probably miss them once again during the mandatory recount for exactly the same reasons as before. The only way to count ballots with hanging, pregnant, or dimpled chads was by manual inspection.

One might well place the blame for these incomplete ballots on voters who improperly used a stylus, but there were other problems that often accounted for the problems. The book *The Miami Herald Report: Democracy Held Hostage* discussed how voting machines often become so jammed with discarded chads that voters sometimes encountered difficulties in forcing the perforations open and completely removing the chads from their ballots. The above mentioned difficulties could result from old or badly maintained voting machines (Merzer and the staff of the *Miami Herald* 2001).

While the Florida state government of Florida had the primary responsibility for conducting elections, it had delegated much of it to county governments. Counties had to decide on which type of ballots they would use and then had to purchase and maintain the requisite equipment. The most widely used alternative ballot to the punch card is the optical scan. Here, a voter darkens a small circle or square on a ballot with a pencil mark that designates his or her choice. The counting machines then read the marks and record the votes. In comparison of the two approaches, 2.6 percent of Florida punch card ballots used in the 1996 election did not record a vote for president while only 0.2 percent of optical scans recorded no such vote (Merzer and the staff of the *Miami Herald* 2001, 62).

The Gore campaign decided to concentrate its challenge on the undervotes in three Democratic counties that used punch card ballots, Broward, Miami-Dade, and Palm Beach, and on Volusia County, another with punch cards, which had sent forth some inaccurate vote totals on election night that were later rescinded. The Gore totals had once been overstated by more than 16,000 votes in Volusia County. The Gore campaign wanted to supplement the mandatory machine recounts with manual recounts of the undervotes in these counties to acquire some additional votes that the machines could not count. Why these particular counties and no others? Florida law provided that candidates seeking challenges of election outcomes had to focus on counties where there may have been errors rather than on statewide results. In addition, some of the more Republican oriented counties had used optical scans that had few errors while the more Democratic counties had used the less reliable punch cards. The Bush campaign responded by opposing the Gore efforts at securing manual recounts.

Robert Zelnick has discussed the strategies that were employed by the Gore and Bush campaigns with respect to the manual recounts and he compares them on several key matters of contention. Zelnick said the Gore campaign wanted to claim a moral basis for an election victory by emphasizing that the Democratic ticket had won the national popular vote. The Bush campaign sought to counter this claim by saying the election was over, that Bush had won in Florida and therefore in the nation and that the public interest demanded that recounts stop. Zelnick adds that Gore wanted to strengthen his demands for manual recounts by advancing the argument that far too many Florida voters had been disenfranchised by faulty voting equipment, that all votes should be counted, and that the most flexible standards relating to chads should be used. Florida law was silent on how to count ballots with attached chads; the standard it used for counting disputed ballots was the "intent of the voter." The Bush campaign wanted to stop the recounts entirely, or if that was not possible, to limit either the jurisdiction or discretion of county canvassing boards in finding new votes from the machine rejected undervotes. Zelnick concluded his strategic discussions by saying the Gore campaign wanted to rely on the rulings of the liberal and Democratic Florida Supreme Court as the final arbiter of the controversy while the Bush campaign preferred to place its faith in the more conservative and Republican oriented U.S. Supreme Court (Zelnick 2001, 4–7).

There was an interesting contradiction in Florida law that set the stage for some of the major legal action that was to follow. Florida law required that the secretary of state certify the results of the election as official seven days after the vote had been conducted. In this instance the certification would have had to take place on November 14. The contradiction related to

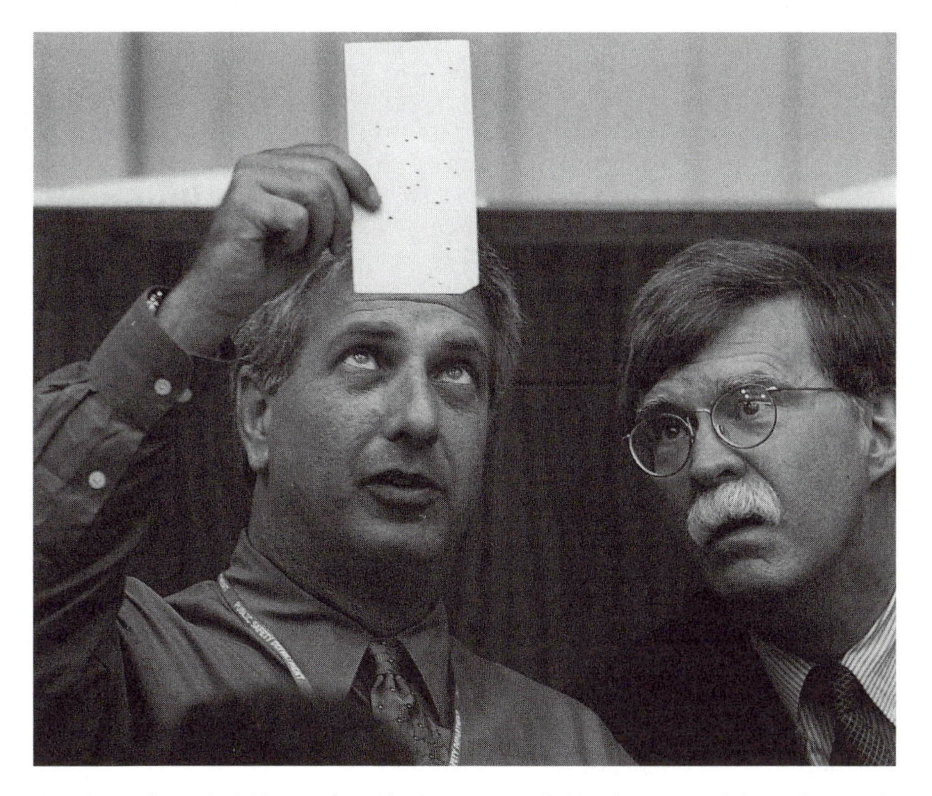

On November 20, 2000, Judge Charles Burton (left), chairman of the Palm Beach County Canvassing Board, and Republican attorney John Bolton (right) review ballots during the Florida presidential ballot recount. *Rhona Wise/©AFP/Corbis.*

statutory language about the amount of discretion the secretary of state could use in accepting election returns that arrived after the seven-day limit. The timeline was particularly important this year because of the large number of undervotes that were being recounted manually. One phrase in state law said late returns "shall be ignored," while another suggested the secretary of state could use some discretion in refusing them. When referring to late returns, it said "such returns may be ignored."

The seven-day deadline was important to Bush because many of the large Democratic counties that were conducting manual recounts could not complete them within the allotted time period. The Bush campaign had just recently suffered an important setback when a federal district court rejected its petition to halt the manual recounts. It now sought to force the recount teams to rely upon the most restrictive standard of accepting undervotes, the existence of hanging chads. It also wanted to have the recounts completed within the seven-day requirement. It appeared that the Bush campaign had a strategically placed and valuable ally in Secretary of State Katherine Harris for enforcing the seven-day limit. Harris, elected to office in 1998, was an active leader of the Florida Republican Party and one of the directors of the Bush presidential effort in the state during 2000. Democratic critics often accused her of making partisan rulings on discretionary matters to enhance Bush's prospects.

Bush quickly suffered several more legal setbacks. On November 14, a Florida state judge delivered what appeared to be a Bush victory when he upheld the authority of the secretary of state to refuse returns submitted after the seven-day period, but he added language that soon proved detrimental to the Bush strategy. The judge, Terry Lewis, ruled that the secretary of state could not merely ignore late returns; she was required to use reasonable discretion when doing so. Lewis had interpreted the contradictory phrases in a way that made "may be ignored" into the proper legal standard. Harris implemented the seven-day rule, included only the new vote totals that were submitted, and informed counties with incomplete submissions to justify their requests for additional time. By this time, only one of the four counties, Volusia, where Gore had requested manual recounts, had completed them. In a somewhat surprise move, the canvassing board in Miami-Dade County voted to suspend the manual recounts after concluding that enough time was not available to complete them. There were about 10,000 overvotes that had not been inspected. The two remaining counties, Palm Beach and Broward, requested more time to complete their recounts, but Harris refused. In all, this combination of events produced two new lawsuits from the Gore campaign. One sought to compel Miami-Dade County to complete its manual recount, while the other asked the Florida Supreme Court to set aside the certification that Harris had just made. With certification, Bush was ahead, but his margin had declined to only 300 votes.

Gore's legal actions met with mixed results. He lost in the effort to have Miami-Dade County continue with the recounts, but he was successful in the attempt to overturn Harris. The Florida Supreme Court overturned her decision on November 16 and ordered the recounts to continue in those two counties. The reason for the different rulings, one not ordering a resumption of recounts while the other required them, was that the court was supporting the choices of the respective county canvassing boards. Miami-Dade did not want to continue, but the other two counties did, so the court supported each of them in their preferences. Five days later this same court ruled that Harris had abused her discretion in refusing to accept recounts after November 14 and extended the deadline for completing them another five days, until November 26. This extension allowed Broward County enough time to complete its recounts, but Palm Beach County submitted its results ninety minutes after the 5:00 P.M. deadline the Supreme Court had set. With one set of new results recorded and one refused, Harris certified the election as official. Prior to the certification, Bush had led by 930 votes; with it, his lead was diminished to only 537 votes.

As mentioned above, Bush's lead was only 300 votes after the initial certification on November 14 and 537 votes after the final one on November 26. During the twelve days between those times, he had expanded his lead over Gore to 930 votes with the counting of some absentee ballots that had been sent from overseas locations, most of which were military. These ballots constituted yet another part of the continuing vote controversy. A federal law, designed to promote voting participation by armed forces personnel, required states to accept absentee ballots sent from overseas locations provided those ballots had been correctly signed and mailed by Election Day and had arrived within ten days after the election. Several years earlier the state of Florida had signed a consent decree with the federal government because its law allowed only seven days. Most of these ballots favored Bush; hence his gain to a margin of 930 votes, but a substantial number lacked such required features as postmarks or signatures. Usually, absentee ballots lacking the required information are not counted. Anticipating a problem, the Bush campaign accused the Gore campaign of trying to prevent servicemen from voting. Since the Gore campaign had based its argument for manual recounts on the proposition that all votes should be counted, it could do little to resist the Republican claim without appearing hypocritical and self-serving.

Other legal issues that were related to features of the vote controversy surfaced in various Florida courts during this time. One involved the standards counties could use when counting the disputed undervotes. Palm Beach County had adopted the most restrictive standard of counting only those disputed ballots with hanging chads, that is, the chad had to be detached at two corners for the ballot to be tallied as containing a legal vote. Florida law was quite confusing on this point. It provided that the standard to be used in counting ballots was "the intent of the voter." The Palm Beach County canvassing board had reasoned that the presence of a hanging chad indicated the voter had intended to cast a ballot. It rejected the more lenient standards of pregnant or dimpled chads, completely attached perforations that had indentations or pinpricks. These would be counted only if a ballot contained several similar markings for other contested offices. Ironically, Broward County had completed its recounts while employing the more lenient standards, while Palm Beach County had failed to complete its work. Gore challenged the Palm Beach County interpretation in court and lost.

Yet another problem existed in Seminole and Martin Counties, and it raised a threat that could have cost Bush the election. In each county, the local Republican Party had printed and mailed applications for absentee ballots to party members. Those persons wanting such ballots merely had to fill out the request form and mail it to the clerk in their respective county. There was an important omission on the forms; however, there was no printed space for the required voter identification number. As with the overseas ballots, the usual practice would be to disregard these applications because of their defective nature. The county clerks, who were Republicans, allowed party workers opportunities and office space to correct these omissions by writing the identification numbers on the applications. Several thousand Bush ballots resulted from these corrected forms. Democrats sought to have the ballots disqualified because of the actions of the Republican officials, but their lawsuits eventually failed. Separate rulings in two trial courts on December 8 dismissed these cases. The Gore campaign did not participate directly because of its stand that all votes should be counted.

The official certification by Harris on November 26 contributed to even more litigation as the Gore campaign sought to have it overturned. Its legal team filed a petition to contest the election in a Florida district court in the capital city of Tallahassee. While the Gore campaign was pursuing its goals through the Florida courts, the Bush campaign was looking to the federal judiciary for relief, but its efforts continued to bear little fruit. An appeals court upheld the ruling of a federal district court that had rejected Bush's efforts to stop the recounts.

Gore's initial step in contesting the election took place in the district court of Judge N. Sander Sauls on December 2. The trial lasted for only two days, with Sauls ruling against Gore on December 4. Gore appealed to the Florida Supreme Court immediately. This court overruled Sauls four days later and then added 383 votes to Gore's total from the completed recounts in Miami-Dade and Palm Beach Counties that Harris had rejected. It then ordered a complete manual recount in all Florida counties that had not already conducted them. With this, the Bush lead declined to only 154 votes. The Bush campaign appealed this ruling to the U.S. Supreme Court in what soon became the case of *Bush v. Gore*. The full text of the rulings of Judge Sauls and the Florida Supreme Court are reprinted in the Primary Documents section of this book.

Florida Secretary of State Katherine Harris speaks at the Florida state capital on November 26, 2000, after signing documents certifying the state's twenty-five electoral votes for George W. Bush. *Peter Muhly/©Reuters New-Media Inc./Corbis.*

THE U.S. SUPREME COURT RULES

An additional, and, as matters eventually turned out, final phase of the legal battle was developing before the U.S. Supreme Court. The first case to reach the high court was *Bush v. Palm Beach County Canvassing Board*. This was an appeal of the Florida Supreme Court ruling that extended the certification deadline to November 26. The federal court overruled the Florida court on December 4 and set aside the decision extending the deadline. It returned the case to the Florida Supreme Court with instructions for that court to clarify the reasons for its decision. The Florida court had to determine whether it had based its decision exclusively on Florida statutes, which is what the federal Supreme Court said mattered, or whether it had relied on other factors such as the Florida constitution or the rules it had created. These latter options were not to be permitted. The federal court based its ruling on the fact that the U.S. constitution places the responsibility for determining the manners in which members of the electoral college shall be chosen exclusively with the legislatures of the various states. Federal laws require that electors must be chosen according to state laws that were already in effect at the time of an election. The U.S. Supreme court was concerned that the Florida Supreme Court may have been adding conditions to the certification law that had not been in existence at the time of the November 7 election.

The next matter before the U.S. Supreme Court was a request by the Bush campaign to stop the statewide recounts that had been ordered by the Florida Supreme Court in its ruling of December 8. The federal court, just one day later on December 9, ordered these recounts to stop and then scheduled a hearing on the Bush appeal of the Florida Supreme Court's ruling. This case became known as *Bush v. Gore*.

The final judicial decision in this lengthy battle came on December 12 when the U.S. Supreme Court found that the Florida Supreme Court had violated the equal protection clause of the Fourteenth Amendment by ordering statewide recounts without the existence of a uniform standard for determining the intent of the voter. This was an extremely controversial ruling in which the five most conservative members of the court constituted a majority of one in a five to four vote. The decision was soon praised by Republicans, condemned by most Democrats, and attacked by a wide variety of legal scholars as being both inconsistent with previous court rulings on equal protection and voting rights and motivated by partisan considerations where the main intent was to secure the election of Republican Bush. The complete text of the decision is reprinted in the Primary Documents section of this book, but it is also summarized in the following passage in which the court discusses the type of standards that had been employed in counting the punch card ballots.

Much of the controversy seems to revolve around ballot cards designed to be perforated by a stylus but which, either through error or deliberate omission, have not been perforated with sufficient precision for a machine to count them...the Florida Supreme Court has ordered that the intent of the voter be discerned from such ballots. For purposes of resolving the equal protection challenge, it is not necessary to decide whether the Florida Supreme Court had the authority under the legislative scheme for resolving election disputes to define what a legal vote is and to mandate a manual recount implementing that definition. The recount mechanisms implemented in response to the decisions of the Florida Supreme Court do not satisfy the minimum requirement for non-arbitrary treatment of voters necessary to secure the fundamental right. Florida's basic command for the count of legally cast votes is to consider the "intent of the vote." This is unobjectionable as an abstract proposition and a starting principle. The problem inheres in the absence of specific standards to ensure its equal application. The formulation of uniform rules to determine intent based on these recurring circumstances if practicable and, we conclude, necessary...The want of those rules here has led to unequal evaluation of ballots in various respects...the standards for accepting or rejecting contested ballots might vary not only from county to county but indeed within a single county from one recount team to another...The State Supreme Court ratified this unequal treatment...Upon due consideration of the difficulties identified to this point, it is obvious that the recount cannot be conducted in compliance with the requirements of equal protection and due process without substantial additional work...Because it is evident that any recount seeking to meet the December 12 date will be unconstitutional for the reasons we have discussed, we reverse the judgment of the Supreme Court of Florida ordering a recount to proceed.

The decision also produced four dissenting opinions, one from each of the justices who comprised the minority. These dissents focused on such issues as the inconsistency with which the court had acted in overruling a state court on state election matters and on how the U.S. Supreme Court may have inflicted permanent damage on itself in the eyes of many American voters by making a decision that seemed aimed more at electing Bush rather than protecting constitutional rights. One of the strongest remarks in this regard came from Justice John Paul Stevens, who ended his dissent with the following stinging comment. Justice Stevens' dissent is also reprinted in the Primary Documents section.

What must underlie petitioners' entire federal assault on the Florida election procedures is an unstated lack of confidence in the impartiality and capacity of the state judges who would make the critical decisions if the vote count were to proceed. Otherwise, their position is wholly without merit. The endorsement of that position by the majority of this Court can only lead credence to the most cynical appraisal of the work of judges throughout the land. It is confidence in the men and women who administer the judicial system that is the true backbone of the rule of law. Time will one day heal the wound to that confidence that will be inflicted by today's decision. One thing, however, is certain. Although we may never know with complete certainty the identity of the winner of this year's Presidential election, the identity of the loser is perfectly clear. It is the Nation's confidence in the judge as an impartial guardian of the rule of law.

The court decision on December 12 led to the immediate conclusion of the election disputes and of the election itself. With no remaining options still available, Gore conceded defeat to Bush, who responded several hours later by delivering his acceptance speech before a joint session of the Texas legislature. With this, the disputed election of 2000 was finally over.

The legal and unprecedented drama over the counting of disputed ballots in Florida lasted for thirty-six days and gave a distinct and unusual meaning to the year's choice of a president. It raised some significant questions about the continued validity of the electoral college as the devise that actually chooses the president. It thrust state and federal courts into controversial roles for which they had only limited experiences and may have helped undermine the faith that people have in the neutrality of the judiciary. Finally, and perhaps most importantly, it exposed before the nation and world some very unfortunate and dysfunctional features of the manners in which America runs its elections, with the extreme partisanship of the officials who have the responsibility for conducting elections being perhaps the most glaring.

THE *MIAMI HERALD* REPORT

Throughout the controversy, the Gore campaign sought to have the most lenient standards used for counting the punch card ballots while the Bush campaign fought against any recounts. The Bush victory before the U.S. Supreme Court meant that thousands of questionable ballots would not be officially counted and included in the final tally. Nonetheless, ballots are public property and cannot be hidden from scrutiny. Shortly after the conclusion of the various legal battles, a consortium of newspapers, led by the *Miami Herald*, sponsored a count of the 64,248 punch card ballots that did not record a presidential vote to determine which candidate would have won if the ruling of the Florida Supreme Court had stood. The outcome was surprising: Bush would have won and would have done even better than without the recounts. This research project used a variety of standards to count the disputed ballots and therefore projected several possible outcomes.

If all ballots had been counted using the most lenient standard, every pinprick or hanging chad counted, Bush would have won in Florida by a margin of 1,665 votes, more than three times the 537-vote difference that was recorded in the final legal count. Bush would also have won if a more exacting standard where pinpricks were counted only if they had appeared on other parts of a ballot was employed, although his margin of victory would have been smaller. He would have won in this manner by 884 votes. The outcome would have been closer if the Palm Beach County standard that Gore objected to had been used, where at least two corners of the chad had to be detached for a ballot to count. Bush would have won in this manner by only 363 votes. Finally, an irony of the *Miami Herald* count was that Gore would have won the election by a narrow margin of three votes if the most demanding standard had been employed, the one preferred by the Republican Party and the Bush campaign, where only ballots with completely detached chads had been counted (Merzer and the staff of the *Miami Herald* 2001, 168).

While the battle over the punch card ballots had been the most intensely fought legal struggle of the election controversy, the intervention by the U.S. Supreme Court on the side of Bush may have had far less effect on the final outcome than what many observers expected at the time. *The Miami Herald Report* (Merzer and the staff of the *Miami Herald* 2001) indicates that Bush still would have won if Gore had gained his wish that every vote should be counted. Another possible outcome was that the election would not have been decided by the electoral college since neither candidate would have attained a majority and would instead have been decided by the House of Representatives in conformity with the Twelfth Amendment. With each state having one vote and with the Republicans having a majority in the House,

Bush would still have won the election. Gore lost the election in two ways: (1) his failure to capture some key states such as the usually Democratic state of West Virginia or his home state of Tennessee, and (2) with respect to Florida, Gore may very well have suffered the greatest setback to his chances with the Palm Beach County butterfly ballot whose confusing design might well have cost him several thousand votes.

REFERENCES

Dershowitz, Alan M. *Supreme Injustice: How the High Court Hijacked Election 2000.* New York: Oxford University Press, 2001.

Dionne, E.J., Jr., and William Kristol. *Bush v. Gore: The Court Cases and the Commentary.* Washington, D.C.: The Brookings Institution, 2001.

Gillman, Howard. *The Votes That Counted: How the Court Decided the 2000 Presidential Election.* Chicago: The University of Chicago Press, 2001.

Greene, Abner. *Understanding the 2000 Election: A Guide to the Legal Battles That Decided the Presidency.* New York: New York University Press, 2001.

Greenfield, Jeff. "*Oh Waiter! One Order of Crow!*" New York: G.P. Putnam's Sons, 2001.

Issacharoff, Samuel, Pamela S. Karlan, and Richard H. Pildes. *When Elections Go Bad: The Law of Democracy and the Presidential Election of 2000.* Rev. ed. New York: New York Foundation Press, 2001.

Jarvis, Robert M., Phyllis Coleman, and Johnny C. Burris. *Bush v. Gore: The Fight for Florida's Vote.* New York: Kluwer Law International, 2001.

Kaplan, David A. *The Accidental President.* New York: HarperCollins, 2001.

Kellner, Douglas. *Grand Theft 2000: Media Spectacle and a Stolen Election.* Lanham, Md.: Rowman and Littlefield Publishers, 2001.

Merzer, Martin, and the staff of the *Miami Herald. The Miami Herald Report: Democracy Held Hostage.* New York: St. Martin's Press, 2001.

New York Times. 36 Days: The Complete Chronicle of the 2000 Presidential Election Crisis. New York: Time Books, Henry Holt and Company, 2001.

Posner, Richard A. *Breaking the Deadlock: The 2000 Election, the Constitution, and the Courts.* Princeton, N.J.: Princeton University Press, 2001.

Rakove, Jack N., ed. *The Unfinished Election of 2000.* New York: Basic Books, 2001.

Sabato, Larry J. *Overtime: The Election 2000 Thriller.* New York: Longman, 2002.

Sammon, Bill. *At Any Cost: How Al Gore Tried to Steal the Election.* Washington, D.C.: Regnery Publishing, 2001.

Simon, Roger. *Divided We Stand: How Al Gore Beat George Bush and Lost the Presidency.* New York: Crown Publishers, 2001.

Tapper, Jack. *Down and Dirty: The Plot to Steal the Presidency.* New York: Little, Brown, and Company, 2001.

Toobin, Jeffrey. *Too Close to Call: The Thirty-Six-Day Battle to Decide the 2000 Election.* New York: Random House, 2001.

Washington Post. Deadlock: The Inside Story of America's Closest Election. New York: Public Affairs Press, 2001.

Zelnick, Robert. *Winning Florida: How the Bush Team Fought the Battle.* Stanford, Calif.: Hoover Institute Press, 2001.

4

THE FLORIDA VOTE CONTROVERSY: MAJOR COURT CASES

This chapter, like chapter 3, deals directly with the events and legal rulings of the Florida vote controversy. It focuses attention on the most important of the court cases that developed during this time and explores the legal basis for those decisions. The chapter is subdivided into two parts. The first part deals with the rulings of the various Florida courts relating to specific aspects of the controversy and the decision of the U.S. Supreme Court in the most important of all cases, *Bush v. Gore*. The second part looks at the general direction of legal rulings that the U.S. Supreme Court has developed over the past several decades concerning equal protection of the laws as they relate to voting rights. This section is designed to give the reader a strong understanding of the historical foundation, or perhaps the lack of it, as some critics argue, that the Supreme Court used to justify its ruling.

CASES OF THE FLORIDA CONTROVERSY

The legal actions that comprised the Florida vote controversy developed in several directions simultaneously. Some cases eventually formed the foundation of the *Bush v. Gore* decision, while others seemed to have little bearing on this final Supreme Court decision and are today important mainly because they were related in some way to election troubles. The discussion below looks at this variety of cases in a way that categorizes them according to the various legal issues raised. The cases described here are drawn from a list of leading Florida cases prepared by Howard Gillman (2001) and published in his book, *The Votes That Counted: How the Court Decided the 2000 Election*.

The Gore campaign did not challenge several election-related matters in court because either the legal options appeared unpromising or the possible political damage to its cause seemed too great. Nonetheless, these matters did not stay out of the legal system as other persons brought suit. There were three major issues in this category: the legality of the "butterfly ballot" from Palm Beach County, the practice of Republican county clerks in Seminole and Martin Counties allowing officials from their own political party to correct mistakes on absentee ballot applications that the party had prepared, and the extra time (ten days) allowed for absentee ballots originating from overseas locales to be counted as official. The cases were decided in a relatively short period of time, only twenty-two days. The first ruling from a trial court came on November 20, while the final decision from the relevant appeals court was read on December 12. In each instance, state and federal trial courts appeared very reluctant to intervene in an election dispute and instead deferred to the prior judgment of the executive branch of Florida government. The appeals courts upheld the trial courts decisions.

With respect to the first issue mentioned above, the validity of the butterfly ballot and a demand that a new election be ordered in the county, the trial judge in the case of *Fladell v. Palm Beach County Canvassing Board,* Jorge Labarga, ruled that he lacked the authority to order a revote in a presidential election (Gillman 2001, 217). Two state trial judges ruled in separate opinions on December 8 that the actions of the Republican county clerks were not sufficient to reject the absentee ballots in Seminole and Martin Counties. Finally, a federal district court judge ruled that the consent decree between Florida and the U.S. government allowing ten days for absentee ballots to arrive from overseas locations was acceptable even though Florida law specified that absentee ballots had to be received within seven days of an election. All four trial courts were unwilling to overturn the discretionary decisions made previously by elections officials.

There is an interesting legal principle underlying all of these cases: a lack of effort by trial courts to reject routine election practices because those practices might have contributed to minor violations of equal protection of the laws. The disputes that eventually brought about these lawsuits also created or enhanced conditions of unequal and nonuniform practices in the conduct of elections. The existence of a confusing butterfly ballot in one Florida county and not in any of the remaining 64 of the state's counties certainly created some conditions where voting was more difficult and more prone to error in one place than in others. The trial court did not see this as a violation of equal protection. This same interpretation also applied in the two cases relating to the relabeling of absentee ballot applications by Republican Party officials. Many Florida voters in other counties had their applications rejected because they had committed some errors, yet this was still not significant enough to warrant action under the doctrine of equal protection. Finally, ten days were allowed for absentee ballots to arrive from overseas locations. Why were the same ten days not allowed for absentee ballots to arrive from any other locations, even from places within the United States? One could certainly use this argument to challenge the practice on equal protection grounds, but the federal trial court did not do so. I do know from personal experience—I worked as an Army postal clerk in the late 1960s at a military post office in Seoul, South Korea—that mail delivery from overseas military bases to places within the United States is frequently quicker than from places actually located within the nation itself. All the actions mentioned above resulted in the existence of some unequal circumstances in the casting of votes, yet all were considered by the relevant trial courts to be within the boundaries of acceptable behavior. Courts do not view inconsistencies such as these to be violations of equal protection of the law.

A second set of legal actions, which were brought by the Gore campaign, challenged the discretionary decisions of county elections officials and were frequently more successful than the above mentioned cases. The court decisions here were not based on equal protection of the laws but rather on abuse of discretion. One dealt with the standards a county canvassing board could employ when it conducted manual recounts. The canvassing board in Palm Beach County had adopted one of the stricter standards for discerning the intent of the voter, which was a general standard established by Florida law as to the counting of ballots. The Palm Beach recount standard required that chads had to be detached from at least two corners of a ballot for that ballot to be counted as a vote. The legal challenge sought to have a more lenient standard employed that would require counting of the so-called dimpled chads. These were ballots containing indentations on a chad but where all corners of the chads were still attached to the ballot. The case, *Florida Democratic Party v. Palm Beach Canvassing Board,* ended with the trial judge ruling that the board had to consider the intent of the voter when inspecting ballots characterized with dimpled chads. The same trial judge, in a subsequent ruling, said that courts could not require a county canvassing board to accept a dimpled chad ballot if the board had not discerned the intent of the voter from it.

As discussed in the previous chapter, Gore did not fare particularly well in gaining votes through the manual recounts with the adoption of the two-corner standard in Palm Beach County, but he had better success in several of the other urban Democratic counties since they adopted more lenient standards. Unfortunately for Gore, Miami-Dade County stopped their recounts well before finishing them while charging that enough time was not available to finish the task. Gore sued, but the Florida courts were unwilling to overrule the discretionary decisions of a county board and refused to order the officials to resume the recount. Once again, judges were showing a reluctance to intervene with the choices of elections officials, even if this meant that certain ballots would be subject to manual recounts while others would not.

Gore was more successful in the lawsuits he advanced against Secretary of State Katherine Harris over the misuse of her discretion. His first challenge against the actions of the state's highest election official, which occurred in *McDermott v. Harris,* was over Harris's announcement that she would reject all recounts that were not completed within seven days of the election. Gore failed in his attempt to have this ruling overturned as the trial judge ruled that the secretary of state did have the power to reject late returns. This same judge did add that Harris could not arbitrarily deny the late recounts; she would need a valid reason for rejecting specific ones. Of course, Harris, as an official of the Bush campaign in Florida, did reject all of the late returns, including some that arrived about one hour after the deadline from Palm Beach County. Gore was far more successful in defeating Harris when his challenges were reviewed by the Florida Supreme Court. In a unanimous decision in *Palm Beach County Canvassing Board v. Harris,* the Florida Supreme Court ruled that Harris could not ignore the late returns from Palm Beach County because the recounts had been legally authorized by the processes available under Florida law. The Florida Supreme Court then extended the date for county canvassing boards to finish recounts by five days to allow time for Palm Beach County to complete their work. Unfortunately for Gore, the county did not finish its recounts within this new timeline either.

While the Gore campaign and its allies sought legal relief through the Florida courts, the Bush campaign went directly to the federal courts instead. Initially, Bush failed to attain what he wanted, but this pattern would soon change. In what became a precursor of the eventual U.S. Supreme Court decision in *Bush v. Gore,* the Bush campaign charged in a federal district court that the practice of courts ordering manual recounts only in the counties that Gore wanted and to conduct them without uniform standards was a violation of due process of law and equal protection of the law. The federal trial court rejected this claim and the Eleventh Circuit Court of Appeals upheld the court ruling by a vote of eight to four.

Bush attained a significant victory in the case of *Bush v. Palm Beach County Canvassing Board* on December 4 when the U.S. Supreme Court overturned the decision of the Florida Supreme Court in the above mentioned case of *Palm Beach County Canvassing Board v. Harris.* The federal court returned the case to Florida while instructing the Florida court to clarify the reasons for its decision. The Florida Supreme Court had to determine whether it had arrived at its decision on the basis of state law or on the basis of other factors such as the state constitution or the court's equity powers. This was an important distinction because the U.S. Constitution says that members of the electoral college must be chosen by a method that is determined by the legislatures of each state. Federal law requires that these relevant state laws must be in effect at the time of the election. The U.S. Supreme Court appeared to be saying that if the Florida Supreme Court had based its decision on factors other than state law, then it might have violated federal law. While states are responsible for conducting elections and for writing necessary laws relating to them, federal law is superior to state constitutions and state court rulings in this instance.

The final exchange of legal battles between the two political campaigns and the two supreme courts occurred over the efforts by Gore to contest the decisions of the secretary of state related to the uncompleted recounts. In *Gore v. Harris* the vice president wanted the courts to order that all uncounted undervotes in both Miami-Dade and Palm Beach Counties be inspected manually to determine the intent of the voter. He charged that "a receipt of a number of illegal votes or rejection of a number of legal votes sufficient to change or place in doubt the result of the election" had occurred. This was the standard required in Florida law to contest an election outcome. The trial court judge, N. Sanders Sauls, ruled against Gore on December 4, but the Florida Supreme Court applied this same legal standard and ruled in Gore's favor four days later. The Florida Supreme Court went further then previously expected, however, and ordered a statewide recount of all undervotes previously uninspected. This ruling remained in effect for one day as the U.S. Supreme Court quickly set it aside and then scheduled an immediate appeal of the Florida Supreme Court's decision.

The final and certainly most important of all court decisions in this controversy was the U.S. Supreme Court's ruling in *Bush v. Gore* on December 12 that effectively ended the recounts and decided the presidential election in favor of Bush. The constitutional issue the federal court used was equal protection of the laws. If Florida were to conduct manual recounts of disputed ballots as ordered by the state's highest court, it would deny equal protection of the laws to some of its citizens because the lack of uniform standards meant that identical ballots would be counted differently in different counties. With this, the legal disputes and the election itself rapidly ended.

ELECTIONS AND EQUAL PROTECTION OF THE LAW

In relying upon the equal protection clause of the Fourteenth Amendment in *Bush v. Gore,* the U.S. Supreme Court appeared to depart significantly from their actions in previous cases relating to voting rights. In general, the court has overturned a number of state election laws on equal protection grounds, but it has tended to rule in ways that extended the franchise to a greater number of persons while doing so. Most Supreme Court decisions relating to the voting rights–equal protection theme have been advanced in cases dealing with racial discrimination or legislative apportionment. They do not result from alleged lacks of equal protection that might arise from the discretionary choices of state and county election officials over ballot style and counting methods.

The Fourteenth Amendment was ratified in 1868, shortly after the conclusion of the Civil War. Its major purposes were to secure citizenship rights for the former slaves who had been granted their freedom through such devices as the Emancipation Proclamation and the Thirteenth Amendment. The Fourteenth Amendment begins by saying that "All persons born or naturalized in the United States and subject to the jurisdiction thereof are citizens of the United States and the State wherein they reside." In addition to granting citizenship to former slaves, this clause was also intended to overrule a Supreme Court decision of 1857, *Dred Scott v. Sandford,* which ruled that slaves could not be citizens. The Fourteenth Amendment also placed important restrictions on states to prevent them from discriminating against their Black citizens. Two of these provisions are the due process and equal protection clauses that read, "nor shall any state deprive any person of life, liberty, or property, without due process of law; nor deny to any person within its jurisdiction the equal protection of the laws."

In the decades following adoption of the Fourteenth Amendment, the Supreme Court overturned a number of state laws it believed had been designed primarily to restrict the voting rights of Blacks. Two of the more significant rulings came in challenges to the devices of "grandfather clauses" and "white primaries." The grandfather clause was struck down in 1915 in the case of *Guinn v. United States* (238 U.S. 347), while the white primary fell in the 1944 case of *Smith v. Allwright* (321 U.S. 649). The grandfather clause exempted all persons and their lineal descendants from state literacy tests for voter registration if they had voted on or before January 1, 1866. It was designed to create a barrier to voter participation by Black persons. The date is significant; the Fourteenth Amendment was not adopted until 1868. Laws creating white primaries were quite frequent in one-party Southeastern states where the Democratic Party tended to dominate elections. The laws specified that political parties were private organizations and could therefore select their own members. The majority Democrats responded by limiting their membership to Whites. Since the winners of primary elections almost always went on to win the general elections, this legal device served the purpose of excluding Black voters from any significant involvement in state elections. The Supreme Court ruled that political parties were quasi-public organizations that performed a significant public role and acted under state authority. Parties could therefore not limit their membership to members of only one race. In more recent years, the court has upheld provisions of the Voting Rights Act, a federal law enacted in 1965 that was designed to overcome a variety of measures that some states employed to prevent Blacks from voting. Among these are the use of racially biased literacy tests, unusual hours for voter registration, creation of electoral districts that dilute the voting power of Black citizens, and a variety of other similar activities.

The Supreme Court has also used the equal protection clause to strike down legislative apportionment practices of state governments. It did so because these practices sometimes have the effect of diluting the importance of individual votes. The Court opened the door to this issue in 1962 when it ruled that "the right to relief under the equal protection clause is not diminished by the fact that the discrimination relates to political rights" (*Baker v. Carr,* 369 U.S. 186). Granting relief of this nature had been a problem before 1962 in that earlier courts had seen apportionment as a political question, a matter that should have been left to the elected institutions of government rather than to the courts for resolution. The Supreme Court ruled that the apportionment plan of the Tennessee legislature violated the equal protection clause because the various districts from which legislators were elected were of vastly different populations. This decision led to an even more extensive ruling two years later in the case of *Reynolds v. Sims* that expanded participation even more. In once again raising questions about the apportionment of state legislatures, the Supreme Court overturned an Alabama statute while then requiring that future apportionments of state legislatures had to be made exclusively on the basis of current populations. The Court summarized its position by saying that the "concept of equal protection has been traditionally viewed as requiring the uniform treatment of persons standing in the same relation to the governmental action questioned or challenged." In a clause that may contradict the rationale from the *Bush v. Gore* (531 U.S. 98) decision, the Court added in this 1964 decision that "the equal protection clause guarantees the opportunity for equal participation by all voters in the election of state legislatures" (377 U.S. 533).

The Supreme Court made every one of the above mentioned rulings in the direction of expanding voter participation. The Court removed barriers that some people had constructed in hopes of preventing other people from enjoying their full rights as American citizens. The Court did not limit its efforts at expanding participation to equal protection arguments, however. It also relied on such constitutional rights as freedom of speech to strike down legislatively imposed limits on campaign spending (*Buckley v. Valeo*, 424 U.S. 1, 1976) and the right of freedom of association to bring a halt to the decades old practices of reliance on political patronage in governmental job hiring (*Rutan v. Republican Party of Illinois*, 497 U.S. 62, 1990). All of these efforts had the political effect of expanding voter participation.

The unusual feature of the *Bush v. Gore* decision as it relates to the equal protection clause and other parts of the constitution is that the Supreme Court did not follow the direction and theme of its past decisions and try to expand the right to vote. Instead, it reduced the ability of persons to vote by rejecting recounts of virtually all ballots that were less than perfect. Several years before the 2000 election the Florida legislature adopted the legal standard that vote tabulations needed to be based on the intent of the voter. This meant that elections officials had to determine from available markings or whatever other factors might exist exactly what the voter had wanted. The legislature had not required that a ballot be without flaws to be counted. The requirement was simply that a ballot counter had to record a vote if he or she could determine what the voter had intended. For example, if a voter had drawn a circle around the name of a candidate rather than punched out the chad on the ballot, that voter's act should have been considered as valid if the elections official could have discerned the identity of candidate for whom the voter had wanted to cast a ballot.

The debate over the counting of undervotes from the defective punch card ballots was essentially a debate over who could vote, and this is what the courts have generally looked at in advancing equal protection arguments. The fact that some voters had to cast ballots through defective punch card devices while others had the opportunity to use the more reliable optical scan equipment is as much an equal protection matter as the lack of uniform standards across counties for determining the intent of voters who submitted ballots with some type of attached chad. A continuation of past court practices of extending the right to vote to an even greater number of people should have resulted in a ruling where the maximum possible number of ballots would have been manually reviewed with the broadest possible standard for determining that intent employed to determine the intent of the voters. This change of direction by the Court from its earlier policies on expanding voting participation may have been as significant a development from the *Bush v. Gore* ruling as was the eventual election of Bush to the nation's highest political office.

REFERENCES

Dershowitz, Alan M. *Supreme Injustice: How the High Court Hijacked Election 2000.* New York: Oxford University Press, 2001.

Dionne, E.J., Jr., and William Kristol. *Bush v. Gore: The Court Cases and the Commentary.* Washington, D.C.: The Brookings Institution, 2001.

Gillman, Howard. *The Votes That Counted: How the Court Decided the 2000 Presidential Election.* Chicago: The University of Chicago Press, 2001.

Greene, Abner. *Understanding the 2000 Election: A Guide to the Legal Battles That Decided the Presidency.* New York: New York University Press, 2001.

Greenfield, Jeff. "*Oh Waiter! One Order of Crow!*" New York: G.P. Putnam's Sons, 2001.

Issacharoff, Samuel, Pamela S. Karlan, and Richard H. Pildes. *When Elections Go Bad: The Law of Democracy and the Presidential Election of 2000.* Rev. ed. New York: New York Foundation Press, 2001.

Jarvis, Robert M., Phyllis Coleman, and Johnny C. Burris. *Bush v. Gore: The Fight for Florida's Vote.* New York: Kluwer Law International, 2001.

Kaplan, David A. *The Accidental President.* New York: HarperCollins, 2001.

Kellner, Douglas. *Grand Theft 2000: Media Spectacle and a Stolen Election.* Lanham, Md.: Rowman and Littlefield Publishers, 2001.

Merzer, Martin, and the staff of the *Miami Herald. The Miami Herald Report: Democracy Held Hostage.* New York: St. Martin's Press, 2001.

New York Times. 36 Days: The Complete Chronicle of the 2000 Presidential Election Crisis. New York: Time Books, Henry Holt and Company, 2001.

Posner, Richard A. *Breaking the Deadlock: The 2000 Election, the Constitution, and the Courts.* Princeton, N.J.: Princeton University Press, 2001.

Rakove, Jack N., ed. *The Unfinished Election of 2000.* New York: Basic Books, 2001.

Sabato, Larry J. *Overtime: The Election 2000 Thriller.* New York: Longman, 2002.

Sammon, Bill. *At Any Cost: How Al Gore Tried to Steal the Election.* Washington, D.C.: Regnery Publishing, 2001.

Simon, Roger. *Divided We Stand: How Al Gore Beat George Bush and Lost the Presidency.* New York: Crown Publishers, 2001.

Tapper, Jack. *Down and Dirty: The Plot to Steal the Presidency.* New York: Little, Brown, and Company, 2001.

Toobin, Jeffrey. *Too Close to Call: The Thirty-Six-Day Battle to Decide the 2000 Election.* New York: Random House, 2001.

Washington Post. Deadlock: The Inside Story of America's Closest Election. New York: Public Affairs Press, 2001.

Zelnick, Robert. *Winning Florida: How the Bush Team Fought the Battle.* Stanford, Calif.: Hoover Institute Press, 2001.

5

FEDERALISM AND THE FLORIDA VOTE CONTROVERSY

Observers of the political events and legal decisions that marked the Florida vote controversy might wonder how such a mess could ever occur in the affluent and democratic United States. How was it possible that the world's most important economic, political, and cultural power, a nation where millions of citizens communicate with one another in cyberspace, could employ such antiquated voting mechanisms that contenders for the presidency were reduced to arguing over the counting of ballots characterized by "dimpled chads?" Few Americans completely understood the complex reasons for the existence of the electoral troubles of 2000. Many were increasingly embarrassed by what appeared to be a mediocre functioning of governmental institutions during the five weeks of the vote-counting controversy. They were also disappointed by the Supreme Court decision that seemed to leave as many questions unanswered as it addressed. The explanation of how such a controversy could ever happen and why it unfolded as it did to some extent rests in the existence and continued operation of American federalism. This chapter focuses on American federalism in an attempt to explain the origins of the electoral problems that defined, but which were not limited to, the counting of votes in Florida.

There is a widespread belief within the academic discipline of political science that federalism is the most significant American contribution to political thought. Federalism is an American invention; we created it when we adopted our national constitution in 1787, and we have used it as the foundation of our governmental order ever since. One can see proof of the importance of federalism as an approach to government in the fact that a significant number of nations have followed our example by creating their own federal systems modeled on ours. Some of them have succeeded, such as Australia, Canada, Germany, India, Mexico, and Switzerland. Others have failed completely, with the nation ceasing to exist, as happened with the Central American Federation in the 1830s and Yugoslavia in the 1990s. The Central American Federation lasted for less than ten years and then dissolved into the nations of Guatemala, Honduras, El Salvador, Nicaragua, and Costa Rica. Most recently, the federal system of Yugoslavia, which was created shortly after the end of World War I, collapsed and now also consists of five separate nations. The American federal system faced a similar threat of dissolution with the Civil War, but the victory of the union side ended that problem. Finally, the fate of some federal systems remains uncertain, with Nigeria a case in point. The Nigerian federal system, established in the early 1960s with the end of British colonial rule, has undergone a number of revisions over the past forty years as leaders attempt to salvage it within a nation bitterly divided by ethnic and religious strife. Despite this checkered pattern of success and failure, American federalism has been an important approach to government throughout the world over the past two centuries.

GENERAL OVERVIEW OF AMERICAN FEDERALISM

Federalism is a political structure where the people, acting through a constitution, divide the authority of government between a nation and several states in such a way that neither level of government serves as an agent of the other and where both levels have independent authority over some areas of public policy. William Riker, one of the foremost authorities on federalism, writes that such systems tend to come into existence in places where the lack of social unity is resolved by creating a governmental structure where local majorities can substitute their own views within their own regions for the views of national majorities on certain policy questions (Riker 1964). The federal structure that presently exists within the United States was created with the drafting of the constitution but has undergone a variety of alterations since that time. Nonetheless, the primary decisions of that convention are still intact and serve to define contemporary American government. At the heart of the structure is the division of legislative authority between the national government and the states.

The first part of the constitution, Article 1, which creates both the federal system and the Congress, begins with a statement that is significant in defining American federalism. It reads, in part, "All legislative powers herein granted shall be vested in a Congress of the United States..." The key federal phrase in this statement is "herein granted." It means that the political entity know as "the people," acting collectively through the device of a constitution, created Congress and gave it some, but not all, legislative power. The "herein granted" phrase means that Congress can enact laws only in those policy areas in which it has a grant of power. Congressional powers can be expressly mentioned in various parts of the constitution, or they can be implied from that express language. These two categories of power are known in constitutional law as "expressed" and "implied," respectively. An example of an expressed power is the taxing and spending clause of Article 1 Section 8 Subsection 1. It reads as follows:

> The Congress shall have Power to lay and collect Taxes, Duties, Imposts and Excises, to pay the Debts and provide for the common Defense and general Welfare of the United States; but all Duties, Imposts, and Excises shall be uniform throughout the United States.

Article 1 Section 8 contains eighteen subsections that grant Congress a variety of powers. These powers include the regulation of commerce among the states and with Indian tribes and foreign nations; the creation and operation of post offices and military and naval forces; the coining of money; the establishment of copyrights and standards for weights and measures; and the important ability of Congress to determine the methods it wishes to employ to implement its powers. This last power is granted in Article 1 Section 8 Subsection 18 and is the source of the implied powers. It grants Congress the power to do the following:

> To make all Laws which shall be necessary and proper for carrying into Execution the foregoing Powers, and all other Powers vested by this Constitution in the Government of the United States, or in any Department or Officer thereof.

The phrase "necessary and proper" has been interpreted by both Congress and the nation's courts to mean that Congress has the ability to employ any method it might choose to implement its powers provided the chosen method is not prohibited by the constitution.

All constitutional language relating to congressional powers was originally found in the eighteen subsections of Article 1 Section 8, but that is no longer true. The power has been increased over the past two centuries through the enactment of several constitutional amendments. One such amendment, which was quite relevant in the Florida vote controversy, is the Fourteenth Amendment, which was added to the constitution in 1868. This is a lengthy amendment that was designed to deal with the constitutional rights of former slaves who had been given their freedom through the Civil War, Abraham Lincoln's Emancipation Proclamation, and the Thirteenth Amendment. One of its provisions is the requirement that prohibits states from denying persons the equal protection of the laws that the Supreme Court relied upon in the case of *Bush v. Gore*. The fifth and final section of the Fourteenth Amendment reads as follows:

> The Congress shall have power to enforce, by appropriate legislation, the provisions of this article.

While the constitution provides a substantial number of powers to the national government and a considerable amount of flexibility in their applications, it actually leaves most governmental powers to the states. This act is accomplished through the very broad language of the Tenth Amendment. This amendment divides governmental powers as they relate to the states into three broad categories: those powers that belong to the national government, those powers that are denied to the states, and those powers that do not belong to either of these first two categories. Powers comprising this latter group are called "reserved." Roger Taney, Chief Justice of the Supreme Court from 1836 to 1864, described the reserved powers as "the power to govern men and things" and said they comprise the policy areas of health, safety, welfare, and morals. The Tenth Amendment reads as follows:

> The powers not delegated to the United States by the constitution, nor prohibited by it to the States, are reserved to the States respectively or to the people.

The constitution does not neatly sort all powers into precise categories with some being exclusively national and others exclusively state. Instead, it provides both levels of government with the authority to participate in the same policy areas in an undefined but shared manner. These powers are called "concurrent" because both governmental levels possess them. The manners in which these powers are to be shared are usually determined by the workings of the national and state political processes. One such shared power is taxation. The national government attains its power over taxation from the taxing and spending clause of Article 1 Section 8, while the states derive their power from the Tenth Amendment. The ability of Congress to tax does not bar the states from also doing so.

An important shared power that was relevant in the Florida vote controversy relates to elections for members of Congress and for the president. There are two constitutional references to this sharing of power: Article 1 Section 4 focuses on congressional elections, while Article 2 Section 1 describes the processes that must be used for choosing members of the electoral college in presidential elections. Both clauses place the primary responsibility for holding elections with the states but also permit Congress to enact uniform requirements in specific circumstances. Article 1 Section 4 reads

> The Times, Places, and Manner of holding Elections for Senators and Representatives, shall be prescribed in each state by the Legislature thereof; but the Congress may at any time by Law make or alter such Regulations, except as to the Places of choosing Senators.

There are two different clauses in Article 2 Section 1 that relate to state and national governmental roles in choosing members of the electoral college. The first of these, which comprises the second paragraph of the section and focuses attention on the power of states to hold congressional elections, grants the primary power to the states. It reads, in part,

> Each State shall appoint, in such Manner as the Legislature thereof may direct, a number of Electors, equal to the whole number of Senators and Representatives to which the State may be entitled in the Congress;...

As with congressional elections, the constitution also gives most power to the states in choosing members of the electoral college, but it also provides some power to the national government. The limited grant of electoral power to the national government appears in the fourth paragraph of this section and reads

> The Congress may determine the Time of choosing the Electors, and the Day on which they shall give their vote; which shall be the same throughout the United States.

THE ROLE OF COUNTIES IN AMERICAN FEDERALISM

The states have the constitutional responsibility for delivering the vast array of governmental programs and services that characterize life in the United States. Most of the everyday features of government that Americans have, such as education; environmental controls; law enforcement; fire protection; health care; social services; regulation of land, property, and motor vehicles; marriage laws; transportation; building codes; and so on fall under the responsibility of the states. Sometimes the states deliver these services directly to citizens by creating agencies for that purpose, while in other circumstances, the states create vast networks of local governments and then delegate the responsibilities to them. There are about 85,000 local governments in the United States. While they often differ in their sizes and roles, they all share one feature in common: they are the creations of their respective states and derive all their legal powers from them. They carry out their assigned tasks with some, although frequently not much, state supervision, and attain most of their sources of funding either directly, as in the case of financial grants, or indirectly, as in the ability to enact taxes of their own, from their states. Sometimes, local governments supplement their finances with federal aid. One of the leading types of local governments in the nation is the county, and one of the usual responsibilities of nearly every county government is the conducting of elections.

Florida performs its electoral role in a manner that is similar to that of other states. As mentioned in previous chapters, Florida assigns the responsibility to an elected official, the secretary of state, while delegating much of the actual work to elected officials in the various counties, the county clerks. Nearly all of these persons attain their positions through partisan elections, that is, to be nominated for office they must win the primary election of one of the political parties, and if successful, must then compete in the general election as the nominee of that party. While many voters may find the offices of secretary of state and county clerk to be of little interest and whose actions seemingly have no effect on their daily lives, these offices attract the interest of the political parties simply because of their importance in conducting elections. Far more voters are concerned with the identity of the person who will become governor than with secretary of state and direct more of their concern in local affairs to competitive campaigns for sheriff, mayor, and positions on county commissions and school boards than they do for county clerk. The responsibilities for conducting elections are not even the most important for the officials entrusted with them; these officials have other tasks that take up much more of their time. Secretaries of state often register corporations, audit state agencies, and keep vast arrays of records. County clerks also have a variety of tasks that usually involves the compiling of many different types of records and issuing permits such as marriage licenses. Elections are only part of a vast set of responsibilities generally assigned to the officials the states designate to conduct them and elections are usually among the least important of those assigned tasks.

There are two problems that I focus on in this chapter that relate to the ways in which states and their counties conduct elections; the general patterns in the financing of state and county government and of how these patterns can influence the conducting of elections, and the temporary nature of the election role as it presently exists within the assigned offices that are entrusted with it.

The first of these patterns, the financing of state and county governments, is a widespread problem throughout the nation. The distribution of power within the American federal system places extensive responsibilities on the governments that are least capable of paying for them. We prefer to have most governmental services provided at the local level, and this is exactly how the governmental system has responded, yet the structure of public finance leaves those local governments with only limited funding to carry out their numerous responsibilities. The federal government dominates the most lucrative types of taxation, while the states rely upon the ones that follow in their ability to produce revenue. Local governments, such as counties, are often left with the least-productive types of taxation to finance their myriad activities.

The most productive type of taxation is on income because it can yield revenue from virtually all economic transactions. In addition, income taxes tend to be progressive in the sense that the marginal rates increase with higher levels of income. For example, a person with a relatively low income might be taxed at a 10 percent rate, while a person with a much higher income might be taxed at a rate of 20 percent. Income taxes are the largest source of revenue for the national government and the second largest for the states. These taxes accounted for about 53 percent of federal revenue in 1995 and about 38.2 percent of state receipts. Local governments acquire only limited funding here; only 4.6 percent of their 1995 revenue came from income taxes (Walker 2000, 214–217).

The second and third strongest types are payroll and consumption taxes, respectively. Payroll taxes are enacted on salaries and wages, while consumption taxes are placed on purchases. The largest payroll taxes in the nation are the federal levies collected through the Social Security and Medicare programs. These taxes generally yield far less revenue than income taxes because they are limited to only the first $85,000 of a person's annual salary and therefore cannot reach all forms of incomes. The tax rates are also lower than those for income taxes as well. The national government dominates payroll taxes, garnering about 39.8 percent of its annual revenue from these sources. State and local governments acquire only a very negligible portion of their revenue from payroll taxes. The most common form of consumption taxes are those that are placed on retail sales. Known as sales taxes, these taxes are even more limited than payroll taxes in their revenue yield because they can reach only those transactions that involve the sale or purchase of goods. Most services are exempt from sales taxes. These taxes are the leading sources of revenue for most states and provide about 49.8 percent of annual state revenue. As with income and payroll taxes, consumption taxes provide only a very limited portion of local governmental revenue; in 1995 they accounted for 14.9 percent of local revenue.

In comparison, the two most lucrative types of taxation, income and payroll, collectively account for more than 90 percent of federal revenue but yield less than 40 percent of state funding and less than 5 percent of local monies. The combination of income, payroll, and consumption taxes account for about 90 percent of state money but provide less than 20 percent of the revenue of local governments. The domination of the most lucrative types of taxation by the higher level governments in the federal system means that local governments must rely on less-effective taxes for their funding. The most common sources of their monies are property taxes. Property taxes are usually limited to land, and real estate as personal property is often taxed under the larger sources discussed above. These taxes yield about 74.8 percent of local revenue (Walker 2000, 217).

Local governments tend to encounter two major problems through their reliance on property taxes. First, there may be legal limits that are unrealistically low. These limits may be set by a state constitution or statute or they may be enacted in voter referendums. It is far easier for voters who are angry at the performance of government to act out their frustrations on local property tax sources than on the federal or state taxes. The so-called tax revolts of recent decades have often resulted in reductions of property taxes, while other taxes have tended to remain untouched. The second problem local governments often encounter is that considerable amounts of property may not be taxable either because it is owned by national, state, or local governments, or because state statutes have provided tax breaks to certain persons or groups. Some of the most common recipients are nonprofit organizations or certain businesses that receive special tax benefits for locating or remaining in a particular locale. The combined effects of the low yielding property tax added to a number of exemptions often leaves local governments with limited revenue.

Local governments are not always left without adequate resources to conduct their affairs; there are significant amounts of national and state financial aid available. The main problem here is that much of that aid is designated for specific activities rather than for general purposes. The largest portion of state financial assistance to local governments, slightly more than 60 percent, must be spent on education. There are also designated funds for public assistance, transportation, law enforcement, and a vast array of other governmental activities. This pattern is important because it means that less than 8 percent of state financial aid to local governments can actually be used for general purposes, such as conducting elections at the county level (Walker 2000, 217).

The second problem arising from the American federal system that relates to the Florida vote controversy is the limited and temporary nature of election activity. We do not have elections every day or even every month in this nation. Instead, we have them only on predesignated dates every few years. There are two dates that are significant with respect to federal elections. In 1845, acting on its constitutional power to set uniform times, places, and manners for elections, Congress designated the first Tuesday after the first Monday in even numbered years as the day in which states had to conduct elections to select members of Congress. The law also provided that all states that allowed voters to select members of the electoral college—and all but one state did so at that time—had to have voters make those selections on this national election day. In response to this law, state governments tended to schedule elections for their own and local officials on these same days. An important effect of this law is that election-related activity tends to be temporary every other year. For example, the Florida secretary of state and the various county clerks were quite busy between September and November 1998 registering voters, conducting elections, and counting ballots for members of Congress, state officials such as governor, and many local positions. Their tasks ended shortly after the election results were certified as final. They had few election-related activities to perform until the next tally occurred in November 2000, when they once again devoted several months to the same activities as in previous earlier elections. It is very easy for a local government that has a responsibility for conducting a task only on discrete occasions to devote little time between those intervals to any problems that might exist. At the conclusion of any given election, a county clerk's office would simply collect its voting machines and store them until the next election two years later while giving little or no thought to any problems that might exist with them. Even though there were troubles with the voting machines, such as many being decades old and poorly maintained, local officials usually had not only limited funding with which to address these problems, but also far more pressing responsibilities. They had to make choices about how to allocate their limited funds. Repairing or replacing antiquated voting equipment that would be used only on limited occasions all too often took a low priority to such matters as purchasing equipment for police, fire, or emergency services or a vast array of other activities that poorly funded county governments were required to perform.

The embarrassing problem of chads dangling from punch card ballots and clogging uncleaned counting machines that had been invented during the 1960s is understandable in light of the nature of the distribution of power and money within the American federal system. Also understandable within this same context is the existence of an unusual and particularly confusing butterfly ballot in Palm Beach County and the fact that a fairly large number of newly registered voters, many of whom were poor and members of racial minority groups, were not listed on voter sheets at the precincts where they were entitled to vote. Equally understandable is the partisan-enhancing behavior of a number of county election officials who may well have abused the discretion that accrued to their offices in a largely unsupervised federal system. As a nation, we have assigned a vast array of responsibilities to our state and local governments but we have provided them with limited resources and even less guidance for carrying them out. A look at many of the problems that arose with the Florida vote controversy shows how the limitations of the American federal system are partly to blame.

One of the first problems to emerge in the controversy was the use of the butterfly ballot in Palm Beach County. The federal system played a significant role here in the sense that Florida had assigned the responsibility for conducting elections to its individual county clerks and had granted those clerks broad discretion in fulfilling that task. This discretion was so broad and unsupervised that the Palm Beach county clerk actually used it to create and implement a new ballot design that eventually proved to be an electoral disaster for her own political party. The U.S. Supreme Court ruled that the methods Florida employed in its manual recounts of ballots were inconsistent enough to warrant a violation of the equal protection of the laws, but this same court did not see an equal protection problem in the fact that states and even counties within the same state could create their own ballot designs and that these might be discriminatory.

There was another feature of the butterfly ballot, as well as all other designs of ballots used in Florida, which derives from features of American federalism. This was the requirement that the names of Republican candidates always had to appear first on every ballot used in Florida during the election of 2000. As mentioned earlier in this book, Florida law required that the names of the candidates of the political party that received the most votes in the last election for governor be placed first on all ballots. This helped Bush because it reduced the chances that a confused voter would punch the wrong numbered perforation and spoil his ballot. Gore lost far more votes through the butterfly ballot than Bush. The law relating to ballot name placement had been written decades earlier by Florida Democrats who hoped to secure an electoral advantage for themselves. Florida has been a traditional Southern state until recently in the sense that it nearly always supported Democratic candidates in most elections. Jeb Bush is only the third Republican governor in Florida since the end of Reconstruction in the 1870s.

One can see another example of the inequities that can come from the local use or abuse of discretion in the controversy related to absentee ballots in Seminole County. Here, the Republican county clerk allowed officials of his own party to correct mistakes on applications for absentee ballots and thereby helped Bush attain several thousand votes that might have been lost otherwise.

The unequal distribution of resources among counties that results from the nature of the American federal system can also be seen in differences that occurred among Florida counties in their choices of voting equipment. Each county in Florida had the responsibility to decide what kinds of voting equipment it would employ and then had to purchase and regularly maintain that equipment. Some counties, many of which were large, urban, and often poorly funded, relied on punch cards because they had been doing so for decades and did not wish to use their limited monies for purchasing newer and more accurate methods such as those relying on optical scans. Variations in local standards for counting attached chads were not the only unequal feature of the Florida election; different uses of voting equipment across various counties were also an important matter. One voter might be required to cast a ballot in her county on a punch card and then face a 2.6 percent chance that her vote would not be counted, while another person in a different county would cast a vote through an optical scan approach and face only a 0.2 percent chance of casting an unreadable ballot. This inequity results from differences in the financial resources of local governments and in the discretion that such governments use when allocating their funds.

One of the more unfortunate problems in Florida was that many African-Americans who had registered to vote for the first time in their lives reported to their polling precinct only to learn that their names had not been included on the precinct voting lists. This omission had occurred because the various county clerks' offices were understaffed and had not anticipated the large number of new voters who would register within the final days before the election. The clerks quite simply had failed to place the names of newly registered voters on the precinct lists. By themselves, these omissions should not have prevented individuals from casting ballots. The precinct election officials had telephones, or sometimes laptop computers, which they could use to contact the county clerks' offices for verifications. Unfortunately, many of the precincts that were located in the poorer areas of Florida did not have the laptops, and the limited staffing of the Clerks offices often created great difficulties in contacting the office by telephone to verify registration. Some potential African-American voters simply left the precincts in frustration after the election officials were unable to verify their registration. The poor distribution of voting resources throughout Florida contributed to a widespread perception that racism was still an operating feature of American government.

The inequities that existed in the voting methods in Florida were not deliberate in the sense that they had been implemented with the intent of aiding the Republican Party at the expense of the opposition. Instead, they resulted primarily from the discrimination that is inherent in the American system of federalism. American federalism is often characterized by inequitable distributions of resources both among and within the states. In addition, it encourages inequities through the arbitrary uses that some local officials frequently make of the discretion that often accompanies grants of power.

The problems of inequity discussed here are not unique to Florida and are not limited to elections. They occur in every state and city and surface in virtually every aspect of public policies. Great inequities exist across the nation and within individual states with respect to the quality of schools, fire and police departments, hospitals, public assistance, and emergency facilities among others. The operations of many of these governmental programs are similar to the election processes where antiquated punch card ballots are filled with dangling chads. The equipment and staffing are inadequate because the American federal system did not provide the local governments charged with their delivery the resources necessary to do the job.

REFERENCES

Anton, Thomas J. *American Federalism and Public Policy: How the System Works*. New York: Random House, 1989.

Beer, Samuel H. *To Make a Nation: The Rediscovery of American Federalism*. Cambridge, Mass.: Belknap Press of Harvard University Press, 1993.

Bender, Lewis G., and James A. Stever. *Administering the New Federalism*. Boulder, Colo.: Westview Press, 1986.

Conlan, Timothy. *New Federalism, Intergovernmental Reform from Nixon to Reagan*. Washington, D.C.: Brookings Institution, 1988.

Derthick, Martha, ed. *Dilemmas of Scale in America's Federal Democracy*. Cambridge: Cambridge University Press, 1999.

Donahue, John D. *Hazardous Crosscurrents: Confronting Inequality in a Time of Devolution*. New York: Century Foundation Press, 1999.

Durland, William. *William Penn, James Madison, and the Historical Crisis in American Federalism*. Lewiston, N.Y.: E. Mellon Press, 2000.

Ferejohn, John A., and Barry R. Weingast. *The New Federalism: Can the States Be Trusted?* Stanford, Calif.: Hoover Institution Press, 1997.

Greve, Michael S. *Real Federalism: Why It Matters, How It Could Happen*. Washington, D.C.: AEI Press, 1999.

Hanson, Russell L., ed. *Governing Partners: State-Local Relations in the United States*. Boulder, Colo.: Westview Press, 1998.

Kee, James Edwin, and John Shannon. *Transforming American Federalism: The Role of Crisis, Consensus, and Competition*. Washington, D.C.: Urban Institute, 1992.

Kincaid, John, ed. *American Federalism: The Third Century*. Newbury Park, Calif.: Sage, 1990.

Maxwell, James A., and J. Richard Aaron. *Financing State and Local Governments.* Washington, D.C.: Brookings Institution, 1977.

Nice, David C. *Federalism: The Politics of Intergovernmental Relations.* New York: St. Martin's Press, 1987.

Ostrom, Vincent. *The Meaning of American Federalism: Constituting a Self-Governing Society.* San Francisco: ICS Press, 1991.

O'Toole, Laurence J., Jr. *American Intergovernmental Relations: Foundations, Perspectives, and Issues.* 3d ed. Washington, D.C.: Congressional Quarterly Press, 2000.

Peterson, Paul E. *The Price of Federalism.* Washington, D.C.: Brookings Institution, 1995.

Peterson, Paul E., Barry G. Rabe, and Kenneth K. Wong. *When Federalism Works.* Washington, D.C.: Brookings Institution, 1986.

Riker, William H. *Federalism: Origin, Operation, Significance.* Boston: Little, Brown, 1964.

———. *The Development of American Federalism.* Boston: Kluwer Academic Publishers, 1987.

Sanford, Terry. *Storm over the States.* New York: McGraw-Hill, 1967.

Smith, James C. *Emerging Conflicts in the Doctrine of Federalism: The Intergovernmental Predicament.* Lanham, Md.: University Press of America, 1984.

Walker, David B. *The Rebirth of Federalism.* 2nd ed. New York: Chatham House Publishers, 2000.

Wildavsky, Aaron. *Federalism and Political Culture.* New Brunswick, N.J.: Transaction Publishers, 1998.

Zimmerman, Joseph F. *Contemporary American Federalism: The Growth of National Power.* New York: Praeger Publishers, 1992.

6

THE LONG-TERM SIGNIFICANCE OF THE DISPUTED ELECTION OF 2000

It is nearly certain that some long-term consequences will result from the unusual events of the 2000 election. Perhaps less obvious, but equally if not more certain, is that some additional consequences will follow from the very ordinary and much less debated events that marked this same election. As mentioned earlier in chapter 1, presidential elections are decided by combinations of several long-term sets of events, or factors, that recur from one election to another with a number of short-term sets of events that are specific to a given campaign. This chapter directs attention to the leading events that characterized the 2000 election and provides some forecasts about the way in which they might influence future elections. The first topic considered is the possible significance of the events that were unique to 2000, including all aspects of the Florida vote controversy. The second topic looks at the potential importance of the recurring events of the 2000 election. Themes reviewed here include presidential incumbency, nomination processes, the role of mass media, and the current structure of partisanship in voter choice.

EVENTS UNIQUE TO 2000

By far, the most unique event of the 2000 election was the Florida vote controversy and all that derived from it, including the unprecedented intervention by the Supreme Court and the ascension to the presidency of a candidate who lost the popular vote. While certainly dramatic and fundamental components of an important time in American history, the Florida vote controversy will probably have only a very limited impact on future elections. It may have a much greater impact on a number of governmental institutions such as the electoral college, the courts, and the American system of federalism, however.

It is virtually certain that all state governments, Florida in particular, will correct the worst features of voting that proved to be such an embarrassment in the 2000 election. By this writing in early 2002, Florida has already outlawed the punch card ballot from all future elections. A person will have to visit a museum rather than a polling precinct to find dangling, pregnant, and dimpled chads in any part of the state of Florida. Other states have followed Florida's lead: the technological quality and counting accuracy of the ballots and voting machines that will be used throughout the nation in the election of 2004 will be vastly superior to those of 2000. Congress has already indicated the extent of its interest in helping by providing financial grants to states and counties for the one-time purchase of state-of-the-art voting machines and ballots. One long-term effect of the vote controversy has been to bring about an immediate and long overdue upgrading of voting equipment and the elimination of antiquated systems that remained in use long after their defects had become known.

A much greater change could result with the electoral college if the confusing pattern of 2000 occurs again. As discussed in chapter 2, the electoral college has undergone some significant changes since its inception, transforming from what may have initially been designed as a nominating body into the actual electoral structure. Despite its constitutional standing, the electoral college has seemed unimportant in nearly all presidential elections and has worked as a mere formality after the voting has occurred, serving to ratify the popular vote choices. It has served one valuable purpose, however. It has magnified the sizes of victory margins and has thereby increased the legitimacy of the election winners. It has also made close elections appear less close and made modest victories seem far more sweeping. There was not one instance during the twentieth century where the candidate who won the popular vote failed to win the election. The outcome of 2000, where the second-place finisher in the popular vote became president, has challenged the legitimacy of the electoral college but has not destroyed it. The electoral college should survive the 2000 election and continue virtually unchanged if future elections conclude as most of the previous ones have, with the popular vote winner also securing a majority of the electoral vote.

However, two different scenarios could undermine the legitimacy of the electoral college. Both scenarios share one feature in common—several elections occurring over a relatively short period of time also conclude with the popular vote winner losing the electoral vote and the election. The first scenario distributes these unusual results about evenly between the two political parties, with each party losing through the electoral college what it believes it had won with the popular vote. Both parties would adopt the view that they had been victims of an antiquated system. They would likely unite in an effort to bring it to an end and would find widespread public support for their endeavor. This situation would result in the adoption of a constitutional amendment that would eliminate the electoral college and provide for a direct popular vote choice for the president. Unlike the unity here, the second scenario could be far more troubling. One of the political parties, say the Republicans, would continue losing the popular vote but would also secure electoral vote majorities by winning the support of most of the low population states in the Great Plains and Rocky Mountain regions. The election of a series of minority presidents from the same political party would most likely destroy the legitimacy of the electoral college and lead to vocal demands for a constitutional amendment allowing for a direct popular vote. Despite the fact that the status quo worked for them, Republicans would probably be unable to resist these demands and would be forced to support a constitutional amendment.

It is likely that neither of these two scenarios will occur. The election of 2000 was unusually close; it had the fifth-closest popular vote and third-closest electoral vote margins in American history. In most elections, the two major candidates are separated by several percentage points in the popular vote, 51 to 47 percent, for example, and perhaps as many as one hundred electoral votes. A popular vote difference of only a few percentage points will produce a convincing majority victory in the electoral college. Unless the nation has several more elections within the immediate future that conform to either of the scenarios mentioned above, and it probably will not, the electoral college should remain in existence and unchanged for many years to come. People are reluctant to make very many sweeping political changes unless a significant crisis forces them to do so.

The Supreme Court may not fare as well. The criticism of the *Bush v. Gore* ruling has been particularly strong from two groups of people who have been among the Court's most important supporters: Democrats and other political liberals on the one hand and lawyers and constitutional law scholars on the other. Both sets of critics allege, and with some justification as pointed out in earlier chapters, that the Supreme Court acted in a direction inconsistent with many of its past rulings relating to both the conduct of elections and equal protection of the laws. These two groups believe that the five-member court majority voted as Republicans rather than as jurists in deciding the issues relating to the election. Some leading critics, including constitutional law scholar Alan Dershowitz, go so far as to say that the majority would have ruled differently if Gore had been leading in the Florida vote and Bush had been the candidate demanding manual recounts.

The long-term problem the Supreme Court faces is that it could lose the public respect that is so vital for its continued functioning as a significant component of the separation of powers system. The Supreme Court lacks any formal methods of enforcing its decisions; it must rely on federal and state executives and legislatures to implement its rulings. There are many examples in American history where these institutions have ignored court rulings that they did not like. One was the negative response by many Southeastern states to the racial desegregation decision of *Brown v. the Board of Education* in 1954. While the Supreme Court had ruled that racially segregated schools violated equal protection and ordered the practice to end with "all deliberate speed," many states refused to comply until they were forced to do so by the federal government, which often threatened to use military force. The Court eventually won the battle over desegregation, but it did so by relying primarily on its one great advantage, the widespread belief by many Americans that courts are esteemed nonpolitical institutions that decide cases and controversies through the application of neutral principles of law. The Supreme Court will not be as effective as it has been if it ever loses this advantage. Justice John Paul Stevens indicated his concern for the potential of this loss when he wrote in his dissenting opinion in *Bush v. Gore* that the judicial system was the greatest loser.

There have been important differences throughout the nation over the past five decades in levels of political support for the Supreme Court. Many liberals have been grateful for the landmark decisions relating to freedom of expression, privacy, due process, and equal protection that the Court has advanced, while numerous conservatives have been equally critical of the Court and its rulings with respect to many of these same topics. With *Bush v. Gore,* the Supreme Court angered some of its most ardent supporters without necessarily gaining the backing of the conservatives, who generally prefer a vastly reduced role for government. A lack of political support from both liberals and conservatives might well undermine the long-term legitimacy and power of the Supreme Court. Judges who are viewed by most people as "politicians in robes" tend to have very limited influence.

The Florida vote controversy could well enhance the implementation of some necessary long-term changes in the operations of the American federal system, but many of these changes are not new and have been underway for some time. As shown in chapter 5, local and county governments have been treated poorly by the federal system, being expected to provide a vast array of public services while having access to only limited amounts of money when doing so. There is a need to either strengthen the financial capacities of these local governments or remove some of their responsibilities and place those with state governments. This latter course of action seems to be more probable. State governments have been expanding their policy roles in recent years by assuming administrative control of programs that had either been federal or local in nature. Public education provides an important example. The two most recent presidents, Bill Clinton and George W. Bush, both made increased state funding and control of public education the centerpieces of their policy agendas when they were governors. Clinton and Bush were also representative of a trend among governors and other state leaders; they wanted their states to assume greater roles in a wide variety of policies traditionally considered as local responsibilities. The centralization of financing and control of elections in state rather than in county officials is very likely to result from this long-term governmental trend as well as from the specific events that marked the 2000 election. The *Bush v. Gore* decision will result in the creation of new state standards for conducting elections and counting ballots.

RECURRING EVENTS OF 2000

Perhaps the greatest legacy of the 2000 election will be a continuation of several long-term factors that have defined presidential elections in recent decades. These include such matters as the dominant effect of incumbency, the proliferation of nominating primaries, and the tendency of many states to schedule them at increasingly earlier dates, the influence of mass media values in campaigns with particular emphasis on the "horse race," and voting results that reflect deep and somewhat permanent divisions between geographic regions, economic interests, and social classes.

Until recently, partisanship was the most significant factor in determining the final outcome of presidential elections. Political scientists had responded to this fact by developing a set of categories to explain outcomes that were based on the particular ways in which partisanship operated in any given election. All elections were either "maintaining," where the majority party won, "deviating," where the minority claimed victory, or "realigning," where the partisan loyalties underwent fundamental changes and resulted in the rise of a new majority party. This has changed in recent years, as the strength of incumbency is now the most important determinant of election outcomes. There are several ways to describe this phenomenon; some writers have seen elections as retrospective evaluations of the national administration (Fiorina 1981), and others have seen elections as resting on the performance of the executive (Wattenberg 1991). I have argued that three categories of elections now occur: those with strong incumbents, where the president wins a second term; those with weak incumbents, where the chief executive fails in his attempt at reelection; and those with surrogate incumbents, where the vice president becomes the standard bearer of the presidential party in those years when the president cannot or does not seek another term. This last type of election took place in 2000 for the fourth time in the past four decades (Dover 1994).

Incumbency has become the dominant factor because of the enormous growth in the size and scope of the presidency over the past few decades. This growth has occurred both institutionally and rhetorically. The institutional growth is seen in the expansion of the presidential office in such policy areas as national security, budgeting and government management, and economic planning. The rhetorical role has developed through the ability of a president to develop a personal following and define the nation's political agenda through the use of television (Dover 1998). The strength of presidential incumbency in explaining the outcomes of national elections has been significant in every campaign since 1956; it reasserted itself in 2000 and will do so once again in 2004 and 2008. The presidential election of 2004 will not be decided on the basis of issues that developed because of the Florida vote controversy of 2000. It will be decided by the strength of George W. Bush in both defining and resolving the nation's problems and in building a personal following that transcends the bounds of party loyalty. Bush will be judged on his responses to the events of September 11, 2001, on his economic policies, and on how effectively he uses television and other channels of mass media to convince people of the superior qualities of his leadership.

A second recurring feature of modern elections has been the growing use of presidential primaries to determine nominations. As discussed earlier in chapter 1, candidates for president must now devote considerable time and effort to raising the millions of dollars required for contesting the extensive number of primary elections. States have now begun the practice of scheduling many of the primaries at relatively early dates during the election year to attract the candidates and news media and generate interest among their own voters. Most primaries in 2000 had been completed before April 1, and the nominees of both parties had become obvious by that time. This pattern will be even more pronounced in 2004. The first votes of that election year will be held in Iowa and New Hampshire during the late weeks of January. Other states can hold their primaries at any time after the first week of February 2004. With so many primaries taking place so early during the year, it is virtually certain that the nation will know the identities of the inevitable nominees of both parties, and incumbent George W. Bush will certainly be one of them, by mid-March 2004. This selection of presidential nominees through a series of early year primaries is one event of 2000 that will continue nearly unchanged into the next few elections.

Another long-term feature of the 2000 election that will return virtually unchanged is the dominance of mass media in providing most of the information that voters have about the campaign and the candidates. For some time now, political reporters have tended to describe campaigns in "horse race" terms, that is, by which candidate is winning and which ones are not, and to treat the candidates who perform best in this context as qualified for office. Reporters tend to direct much of their attention to such factors as the amount of money and number of key endorsements the candidates have raised and of how the candidates are faring in public opinion surveys. They also focus much of their news coverage on the attacks that candidates make upon their rivals as depict these attacks as key components of the personal quests by candidates for acquiring competitive advantages. Despite some very extensive criticism after every election, mass media organizations continue with this pattern of coverage because they believe the candidates are actually behaving in a competitive manner and they view competition as a test of a potential president's leadership skills. With this in mind, one recurring feature of the 2000 election that will be repeated in future years will be the patterns of news coverage where reporters see campaigns as little more than personal quests for power between self-motivated individuals who have only limited ties to major political institutions and social movements.

A final feature of the 2000 election that exhibited long-term trends likely to be repeated in coming years was the discrepancy between the popular and electoral votes. The general distributions of both categories of votes were discussed in some detail in chapter 1. This chapter examines how these distributions are reflective of larger divisions that exist within the American political order. The divisions took place in several dimensions: geographic, socioeconomic, and cultural, but all three of these categories are supportive of one another. Differences among people as reflected geographically can be observed by focusing attention either on entire states or on leading political subdivisions such as congressional districts or counties that exist within states. In addition, people of differing socioeconomic wealth or cultural preferences tend to reside in similar locales. Differences among voters with respect to these two categories can be observed through the use of public opinion surveys that were taken either during the election campaign or at balloting precincts on Election Day. Survey results of this latter type are called exit polls. The major geographic, socioeconomic, and cultural differences among the national electorate were briefly described in chapter 1.

Regardless of whether one relies on geographic or on socioeconomic-cultural indicators to observe the divisions in the 2000 election, it is important to realize that these divisions were not unique to 2000 but were reflective of recurring patterns of other recent elections. Very strong socioeconomic and cultural differences now exist among the nation's various regions. The Northeast, Great Lakes, and Pacific Coast states are very reliable supporters of Democratic candidates, while the Southeast, Border, Great Plains, and Mountain states are equally reliable sources of Republican strength. Ronald Reagan garnered a landslide reelection triumph in 1984 with the electoral votes of 49 states and a voter coalition that cut across all existing political divisions. The four elections since that time have been far more competitive, and when reviewed together, reveal a strong and fairly permanent division of political preference within the nation. This chapter looks at the preferences of the various regions as expressed in the past four elections, from 1988 to 2000. The emphasis will be on the geographic distributions of preferences as shown in statewide voting as reflected in the electoral college and in voting through more localized places as expressed in congressional districts.

The Northeastern states have become strongholds of the Democratic Party in recent elections and are becoming even stronger Democratic supporters through each election cycle. Three states in the region, Massachusetts, Rhode Island, and New York, as well as the District of Columbia, have voted Democratic in the past four elections. Seven other states from the region; Maine, Vermont, Connecticut, New Jersey, Pennsylvania, Maryland, and West Virginia, have voted Democratic on three occasions since Reagan's victory in 1984. The one remaining state, New Hampshire, has split its votes evenly between the two parties during this time, supporting each party two times. In those few instances when some Northeastern states back Republican presidential candidates, their support lags far behind the nationwide showings of the Republican Party. The Northeast is the nation's most urban and socially liberal region and appears to be reacting negatively to the increasingly conservative and fundamentalist Christian trend of the Republican Party that has been occurring since the early 1990s.

In contrast, the Southeastern states have been moving increasingly toward the Republicans during this same time. Seven of the thirteen Southeastern states have cast their lot with the Republicans in all four of the presidential elections since 1984. Moreover, they have done so by one-sided margins. The seven states are Virginia, North Carolina, South Carolina, Alabama, Mississippi, Oklahoma, and Texas. The partisan preferences of these states have been Republican for some time. The last time Virginia and Oklahoma voted Democratic in a presidential election was in 1964, while the remaining states last supported a Democratic candidate in 1976. Several of the remaining Southeastern states have supported Democrats in recent years; Kentucky, Tennessee, Arkansas, and Louisiana voted for Bill Clinton in both 1992 and 1996 and for Jimmy Carter in 1976 but returned to their Republican preferences in 2000 and voted for Bush. These four states have voted Republican in every other presidential election held since 1968. Georgia has also voted Democratic three times since 1968, but differed slightly from these other states. It supported Democratic candidates in 1976, 1980, and 1992.

The Southeastern state that is becoming increasingly unusual in its voting preferences is Florida. Florida is now the nation's most rapidly growing state and appears to have become one of its most competitive. Florida has voted Republican in all but two elections since 1968, going for Carter in 1976 and Clinton in 1996, but the closeness and divisiveness of its vote in 2000 indicates the rapid growth of the state's population has now made this a competitive place. Florida's rapid population growth helped it gain two additional seats in the House of Representative from the 2000 census. This will make Florida even more valuable as a site for campaigning in future elections. The state will have 27 electoral votes in 2004 and 2008 and probably even more after the census of 2010. Other than Florida, the remaining Southeastern states appear unlikely to change much from their current status as Republican strongholds.

The Midwestern states are competitive and will likely be the places where most presidential elections of the near future are decided. Democratic candidates have run particularly well in Minnesota, Iowa, and Wisconsin, having carried each of them in every one of the past four elections, and in Illinois and Michigan, which they have taken three times. Ohio and Missouri are the two most competitive Midwestern states, having divided their votes evenly between Republicans and Democrats. Both voted Republican in 1988 and 2000 and Democratic in 1992 and 1996. The remaining five Midwestern states, Indiana, North Dakota, South Dakota, Nebraska, and Kansas, are strong supporters of the Republican Party and have not voted for a Democratic presidential nominee since 1964. None appears likely to cast its electoral votes for a Democratic contender anytime soon.

Finally, the Western states appear to be dividing into two different political camps. The coastal states of Washington, Oregon, and California are increasingly voting for Democratic nominees and are doing so in ways reflective of the patterns exhibited in the Northeast, by margins that are becoming more extensive over time. California was one of the nation's most competitive states until the 1990s. Today, a recently acquired nonwhite population majority is rapidly transforming California into one of the nation's most Democratic states. Statewide elections in California are rarely close these days. Oregon and Washington are following similar trends, although not as marked as those in California. Hawaii, which has voted Republican in only two presidential elections in the forty years since it became the nation's newest state, continues as the best Democratic state in the Western region. The remaining Western states are exceptionally Republican and are likely to remain so. New Mexico is competitive; it has voted Democratic by close margins in each of the past three elections. In contrast, no other Western state has voted Republican more than twice since 1948. The Republican strongholds are Alaska, Idaho, Montana, Wyoming, Colorado, Arizona, Utah, and Nevada.

The consistency of these statewide voting patterns is supported by the divisions that existed in the balloting for members of the U.S. House of Representatives in 2000. The House is a particularly valuable place to look for such consistencies because the apportionment of seats is based on population. Each state with at least two seats in the House creates districts where each House member is elected individually. The U.S. Supreme Court, in a set of rulings that originated in the *Baker v. Carr* decision discussed in chapter 4, has required that House districts have approximately the same population. While there may have been some differences in the population of the various House districts in 2000 since the census upon which the new apportionments will be based had not yet been completed, the size of these differences was relatively small. This makes it possible to compare the results of presidential with congressional voting to discern the existence of important underlying electoral patterns. Elections for seats in the U.S. Senate or for the governorships of states do not provide these same opportunities since every state has two senators and one governor regardless of population.

A comparison of the results demonstrates that a strong relationship exists between voter choices for these two levels of government. The same political party carried both the presidential and House votes in a majority of the nation's congressional districts. As shown in Table 1, 182 districts voted Republican for both president and congress, while 170 districts voted Democratic for both offices. Only 84 of the nation's 436 districts (the District of Columbia is here considered as one congressional district) split their votes, that is, supported the presidential candidate of one party for president and the candidate of the other party for a seat in the House. As an indication of the closeness of the national divisions, these districts divided their votes about

Table 6.1
Relationship between Presidential and Congressional Voting

	Democratic House Candidate Elected in 2000	Republican House Candidate Elected in 2000	Total
District Carried by Gore	170	40	210
District Carried by Bush	44	182	226
Total	214	222	436

Gamma = .89

equally between the two parties, with forty of them voting Democratic for president and Republican for Congress while the other forty-four voted Republican for president and Democratic for Congress. These divisions, coupled with the fact that the Republican Party now controls the House of Representatives by less than ten votes, indicates that the nearly equal division of support that characterized the election of 2000 is not a unique feature of the presidential vote but is instead a reflection of the nearly even divisions of political opinions and preferences that presently exist throughout the nation.

The closeness of the variety of elections that took place in 2000 indicates that the nation is divided into two relatively equal voting blocs that tend to resurface in a number of different political forums. These blocs did not come into existence with the election of 2000, however. Instead, they have been developing for many years and will continue to function in much the same form during the next few years as they have in the recent past. One of the most important long-term features of the disputed presidential election of 2000 is that the divisions of popular and electoral votes, the divisions of positions in Congress and other governmental offices, will very likely continue to divide in much the same manner for the next few years as they did in this particular year. The nation does not have a majority party. It has two powerful minority parties that compete with one another in the most intense of ways: by spending millions of dollars on campaigns, by fighting one another in every possible forum including courts, and by constantly challenging one another over virtually every public policy question that arises. They do all this in the hopes of acquiring those few extra votes that will make an electoral victory possible.

In summary, several long-term consequences of the election of 2000 are likely, but the most important ones should be those that are reflective of themes that recur over a number of elections. These include the importance of incumbency as a factor in voter choice, the dominance of primary elections as the preferred method for nominating candidates, the reliance on television as the major source of political information, and the existence of a nearly equal division of opinion between two nationwide voting blocs that are based on geographic, socioeconomic, and cultural differences. Less important in the immediate future are the more unique features of election 2000. The nation will probably not make any changes in the operations of the electoral college but will instead continue to watch it functioning much as it has for the past two centuries. There will probably be limited changes in the financing of local governments in the American system of federalism, although there most certainly will be some very significant upgrading in the quality of voting equipment. Finally, there should be some decline, but probably not too much, in the moral authority of the U.S. Supreme Court to convince people that it is actually interpreting the constitution in an unbiased and nonpolitical manner.

REFERENCES

Barone, Michael, Richard E. Cohen, and Grant Ujifusa. *The Almanac of American Politics 2002.* Washington, D.C.: The National Journal, 2001.

Ceaser, James W., and Andrew E. Busch. *The Perfect Tie: The True Story of the 2000 Presidential Election.* Lanham, Md.: Rowman and Littlefield, 2001.

Cook, Rhodes. *Race for the Presidency: Winning the 2000 Nomination.* Washington, D.C.: Congressional Quarterly Press, 2000.

Crotty, William, ed. *America's Choice 2000.* Boulder, Colo.: Westview Press, 2001.

Dover, E.D. *Missed Opportunity: Gore, Incumbency, and Television in Election 2000.* Westport, Conn.: Praeger, 2002.

———. *The Presidential Election of 1996: Clinton's Incumbency and Television.* Westport, Conn.: Praeger, 1998.

———. *Presidential Elections in the Television Age: 1960–1992.* Westport, Conn.: Praeger, 1994.

Fiorina, Morris. *Retrospective Voting in American National Elections.* New Haven, Conn.: Yale University Press, 1981.

Goldstein, Michael L. *Guide to the 2000 Presidential Election.* Washington, D.C.: Congressional Quarterly Press, 2000.

Jacobson, Gary C. *The 2000 Elections and Beyond.* Washington, D.C.: Congressional Quarterly Press, 2001.

Jamieson, Kathleen Hall, and Paul Waldman. *Electing the President 2000: The Insiders' View.* Philadelphia: University of Pennsylvania Press, 2001.

Jones, Randall J., Jr. *Who Will Be in the White House? Predicting Presidential Elections.* New York: Longman, 2002.

Lewis, Charles. *The Buying of the President 2000: The Authoritative Guide to the Big-Money Interests Behind This Year's Presidential Candidates.* New York: Avon Books, 2000.

Mayer, William G., ed. *In Pursuit of the White House: How We Choose Our Presidential Nominees.* New York: Chatham House Publishers, 2000.

Nelson, Michael, ed. *The Elections of 2000.* Washington, D.C.: Congressional Quarterly Press, 2001.

Polsby, Nelson, W., and Aaron Wildavsky. *Presidential Elections: Strategies and Structures of American Politics.* 10th ed. New York: Chatham House Publishers, 2000.

Pomper, Gerald M., ed. *The Election of 2000.* New York: Chatham House Publishers, 2001.

Rakove, Jack N., ed. *The Unfinished Election of 2000.* New York: Basic Books, 2001.

Sabato, Larry, J. *Overtime: The Election 2000 Thriller.* New York: Longman, 2002.

Scammon, Richard M., Alice V. McGillivrey, and Rhodes Cook. *America Votes 24: A Handbook of Contemporary American Election Statistics 2000.* Washington, D.C.: Congressional Quarterly Press, 2001.

Stevens, Stuart. *The Big Enchilada: Campaign Adventures with the Cockeyed Optimists from Texas Who Won the Biggest Prize in Politics.* New York: The Free Press, 2001.

Vanderbilt Television News Archive. *Evening News Abstracts.* Nashville: Vanderbilt University Publications, 2002.

Wattenberg, Martin P. *The Rise of Candidate-Centered Politics: Presidential Elections in the 1980's.* Cambridge, Mass.: Harvard University Press, 1991.

Wayne, Stephen J. *The Road to the White House: The Politics of Presidential Elections.* Boston: Bedford/St. Martin's Press, 2000.

BIOGRAPHIES: THE PERSONALITIES BEHIND THE DISPUTED ELECTION OF 2000

ALEXANDER, LAMAR (1940–)

Lamar Alexander was a leading candidate for the Republican nomination in the elections of 1996 and 2000. He made his greatest impact in 1996 when he emerged as one of the three strongest rivals of Senator Robert Dole, the front-runner for the Republican nomination that year. He competed in the two earliest voter tests of the modern nomination system, the Iowa caucuses and the New Hampshire primary, and finished in third place both times. Dole won in Iowa, while Patrick Buchanan finished second. Dole and Buchanan exchanged places in New Hampshire, with Buchanan having won. After these strong showings, Alexander continued his quest for several more weeks but could not repeat these performances. He discontinued his efforts in mid-March shortly after losing several Southeastern primaries, including the one in his home state of Tennessee.

With Democratic incumbent Bill Clinton winning a second term in 1996, Alexander set out to compete for the Republican nomination in 2000. He was generally looked on by a wide variety of observers and political activists as one of the potentially strongest candidates during the early months of 1999, but he soon encountered some serious difficulties in generating support. Alexander found that time had passed him by. Most Republican officials and financial contributors were now looking for a new leader who could bring about the victory that they believed was within their reach. The candidate who seemed to fill this role was Texas governor George W. Bush. Bush dominated the political news of early 1999 with his great successes in raising money, endorsements, and high poll standings, while Alexander trailed far behind in each of these crucial tests of candidate strength. The Alexander campaign collapsed in August 1999 with the Iowa Republican Straw Poll. This event was part of a party fundraising drive; any person who bought a $25 ticket could attend and cast a vote for a presidential candidate. The votes would not result in any delegates to the national nominating convention but were important nonetheless in illustrating the extent of each candidate's political following. After losing badly to Bush, Alexander quickly ended his campaign. Alexander was noteworthy during the 2000 election mainly because he often accused Bush of attempting to buy the nomination and did so again with his withdrawal announcement. Bush had raised far more money than any other Republican candidate. News media promptly responded to Alexander's attacks and began directing attention to Bush's finances.

Alexander brought a strong record of accomplishments to his presidential quests. He graduated from Vanderbilt University in 1962 and from New York University Law School in 1965. He was elected to the first of his two terms as Governor of Tennessee in 1978 and to his second term four years later. Alexander later served as President of the University of Tennessee and joined the Bush administration as the Secretary of Education in 1991. Alexander returned to public office in January 2003 as a newly elected U.S. senator from Tennessee.

BAKER, JAMES A. III (1931–)

James Baker was a major player in the Florida vote controversy, where he served as director of the Bush legal and political efforts. He brought twelve years of the highest-level governmental experience to this battle from his work in the Republican administrations of Ronald Reagan and George Bush. Baker had been the initial White House Chief of Staff for Reagan, serving in that capacity from 1981 to 1985. Reagan then appointed Baker as the Secretary of the Treasury in 1985, a major position that requires significant political advice for the President relating to matters of governmental finance and economics.

Baker was a Houston, Texas, attorney and long-time personal friend of the vice president George Bush. He had made his initial entry into national politics as a major organizer for Bush in 1980 when Bush ran against Reagan for the Republican presidential nomination. After serving in the Reagan administration, Baker resigned from his treasury post in 1988 to become a major director of Bush's campaign for the presidency. Bush named Baker to the most important cabinet post in the national government, secretary of state, upon winning the election. Baker held this position until 1992 when he returned for a second time as the White House Chief of Staff. The Bush presidency was in trouble in 1992, defeat seemed a strong possibility. Baker took the chief of staff position to help Bush retain the presidency. Bush, of course, lost to Clinton. With this, Baker returned to the practice of law in Houston, Texas.

Baker was not involved in the campaign of George W. Bush in 2000 until the Florida vote controversy. He was brought into the fray because of the need by Bush for a senior and experienced political operative to direct the battle against the recounts. Baker quickly became the public face of the Bush legal efforts, although he was not the attorney who argued any of the actual lawsuits. He was the coordinator of the legal efforts, the main political strategist, and the public spokesman for Bush. Baker tried to create the public view that the election was over and that Bush had won. Any attempts by Gore and the Democrats to challenge the results, either by demanding recounts only in selected places or by contesting decisions of Florida election officials, were described by Baker as nothing more than partisan efforts to steal the election from its proper winner, Bush.

Baker was born in Houston in 1930 and received his baccalaureate degree from Southern Methodist University in 1953. He graduated from that same university's law school five years later. While he was not appointed to any major political position in the second Bush administration, Baker has the necessary political skills for dealing effectively with difficult circumstances. He may be called on in some future controversy.

BILL BRADLEY (1943–)

Bill Bradley was the leading opponent of Al Gore for the Democratic presidential nomination in 2000. Bradley was born in Crystal City, Missouri, in 1943. He graduated from Princeton University with honors in 1965 where he complemented his academic accomplishments with a successful performance as the star of the university's basketball team. He won a gold medal as a member of the U.S. Olympic basketball team in 1964. After his graduation, Bradley was a Rhodes Scholar and received a master of arts degree from Oxford University in 1968. He spent eleven years, from 1967 until 1977, as a professional basketball player with the New York Knicks of the National Basketball Association.

Bradley was elected to the U.S. Senate from New Jersey in 1978 and served three terms, a period of eighteen years, in that chamber. During his Senate tenure, Bradley served as chairman of the Finance, Energy and Natural Resources committee. He was considered as a possible candidate for president by a number of his colleagues and by a vast array of political observers. Bradley retired from the Senate in 1996 and began a quest for the presidency. He announced his candidacy in early 1999 from his boyhood hometown in Missouri.

The Democratic campaign of 2000 attracted only two candidates with Al Gore having a strong advantage because of his position as vice president. Gore was encountering some troubles in generating much enthusiasm, however, and this appeared to open the door to a possible victory by Bradley. The two candidates had raised nearly the same amount of money by the end of 1999, but Gore had garnered a larger number of endorsements from key Democratic Party leaders and higher support from partisan voters as recorded in public opinion surveys. Bradley and Gore had several debates during the latter months of 1999 with Gore often performing better and winning greater audience support.

Bradley gambled that he could upset Gore in either of the two early tests of voter support in 2000, the Iowa caucuses on January 24 and the New Hampshire primary eight days later. He spent several million dollars and valuable campaign time in both states but fell far short in his efforts. Bradley lost the Iowa caucuses to Gore by a margin of 63 to 35 percent, although he ran much better in New Hampshire. He lost this state by only four percentage points, 52 to 48. Nonetheless, these losses hurt Bradley's chances. The next major set of battles for the Democrats was the eleven primary elections of March 7. This day had been designated as "Super Tuesday" because of the large number of major primaries to be decided, including ones in California and New York. While Bradley campaigned extensively in all of these states, the mass media and many voters had given up on his chances. Bradley lost all eleven states to Gore, including a landslide drubbing by 84 to 16 percent in California, and ended his candidacy four days later. Whether he will attempt a second presidential bid at some future date, perhaps in 2004, is uncertain at the time of this writing.

BUCHANAN, PATRICK (1938–)

Patrick Buchanan has been a major player on the political stage for many years and was the nominee of the Reform Party in 2000. He first emerged as a player in national politics as a White House aide for Richard Nixon during the five-and-a-half years of the thirty-seventh president's term of office. One of his major roles for Nixon was speechwriting, particularly for Vice President Spiro Agnew. Buchanan was the author of several of Agnew's most famous speeches and originated a number of the vice president's more memorable lines. Buchanan also worked on the White House staff of Ronald Reagan for two years. Buchanan established much of his public persona through television. He served as a member of several major news and commentary broadcasts, the most important being on the weekly Cable News Network public affairs program *Crossfire*. Buchanan worked as the conservative voice in a program where the guest of the week was questioned by one liberal and one conservative reporter.

Buchanan was increasingly critical of the policies of the Bush administration. In 1992 he announced that he would oppose Bush for the Republican nomination in hopes of emphasizing the conservative values that he thought were being downplayed or ignored by Bush. Buchanan started his efforts in the New Hampshire primary, where his powerful showing indicated the depth of dissatisfaction that many Republicans had for Bush. Buchanan attained 37 percent of the vote, while Bush recorded only 53 percent. Bush's total was considered to be a disappointing performance by an incumbent president within his own political party. With this showing, Buchanan challenged Bush in four additional primaries in Maryland, Georgia, South Dakota, and Colorado. He attained about one-third of the vote in each state and ended his candidacy. Many Republicans said that Buchanan had set the stage for Bush's defeat by Bill Clinton.

Buchanan sought the Republican nomination once again in 1996. He was a more formidable candidate this time, finishing a strong second to Robert Dole in Iowa and then defeating Dole in the New Hampshire primary. Buchanan's win in New Hampshire frightened many Republicans, who soon united in their efforts against him. Buchanan did not win another primary that year and withdrew his candidacy in late March after losing to Dole in California. Once again, many Republicans believed that Buchanan had cost them the general election with his powerful attacks against the candidate who eventually won the nomination.

Buchanan ran for the Republican nomination once again in 2000 but by now had few followers within his own party. He abandoned his quest in September 1999 and joined the Reform Party that had been started a few years earlier by Ross Perot. Buchanan won the Reform nomination, but bitter infighting among party members had the political effect of making the nomination worthless. Buchanan attained only 0.4 percent of the vote in 2000, and the Reform Party lost its designation as a major party and the federal funding that accompanies such status. The party had received $12.4 million in federal funding in 2000 because its candidate in 1996, Ross Perot, had acquired 7.8 percent of the popular vote.

Buchanan was born in 1938 in Washington, D.C., and graduated from Georgetown University in 1961. He received a master of science degree from Columbia University in 1962.

BUSH, GEORGE (1924–)

George Bush has served in a variety of political positions over the past four decades and managed to fill one additional one during the election of 2000. Bush is the father of the Republican nominee George W. Bush and is the only vice president of the twentieth century to have won the presidency upon the retirement of the incumbent. Both of these factors were important in 2000.

Bush was born in Milton, Massachusetts, in 1924. His father, Prescott Bush, was a U.S. Senator from Connecticut during the 1950s. Bush graduated from Yale University in 1948, served in the Navy during the Second World War, and then made Texas his home. He was the founder and president of the Zapata Oil Company, a business firm involved in offshore drilling. Bush was also an active member of the Texas Republican Party, which was a weak organization at the time. He lost a campaign for the U.S. Senate in 1964 but was elected to the U.S. House of Representatives in 1966 for the first of two consecutive terms. After losing a Senate race in 1970, Bush served in a number of executive roles in the Nixon and Ford administrations between 1971 and 1977. Among these were Ambassador to the United Nations, Director of the Central Intelligence Agency, Envoy to the Peoples' Republic of China, and National Chairman of the Republican Party.

Bush sought the Republican presidential nomination in 1980 and achieved an initial success by defeating all of his rivals, including the eventual winner Ronald Reagan, in the Iowa caucuses. Reagan rebounded from this setback and won the New Hampshire primary. Bush continued his battle against Reagan by winning several primaries, but he lost far more than he won and withdrew in May. Reagan offered him the vice presidential nomination. Bush spent the next eight years as the vice president and as a major political surrogate for Reagan. He sought the Republican nomination for President in 1988 and won it after defeating five rivals, of whom Robert Dole was the most formidable. Bush spent much of the general election attacking his Democratic rival Michael Dukakis on a number of issues and defeated him by a margin of 53 to 46 percent. Bush became the first vice president since Martin Van Buren in 1836 to succeed a retiring incumbent as the nation's chief executive.

Bush sought a second term in 1992 but encountered some difficulty because the nation was involved in an economic recession. He lost the election to Bill Clinton. His loss was significant with respect to 2000 because two of his sons, George W. and Jeb, both ran for the governorships of their respective states of Texas and Florida in 1994 and began their own public careers. George W. Bush was able to rely on his father's name and extensive lists of financial contributors when he began his own presidential quest in 1999. His sons might not have run for office in 1994 if Bush had won a second term. Ironically, Bush's public career also helped Al Gore, the man who opposed George W. in the 2000 election. The vice presidency has developed from an insignificant position prior to the Second World War into the most important stepping stone to a nomination of the incumbent party when the incumbent retires. It did so because several of its occupants of the past half century have transformed it into a position of major leadership. Bush was one of the better vice presidents of modern times. His actions helped make the office into the strong position that Gore effectively used to win the nomination of the Democratic Party in 2000.

BUSH, GEORGE W. (1946–)

George W. Bush was the ultimate winner of the disputed election of 2000 and became the nation's forty-third president on January 20, 2001. He is the eldest son of George Bush, who served as president for one term between 1989 and 1993. In becoming president, George W. Bush helped bring about the second instance in American history where a father and son had both served as president. The previous instance was with John Adams (1797–1801) and John Quincy Adams (1825–1829). Bush spent much of his youth in Midland, Texas, where his father was an oil company executive.

He received his undergraduate education at Yale University and acquired a master of business administration from Harvard.

George W. Bush launched his public career in 1978 with a bid for a seat in the U.S. House of Representatives from a district containing Midland as its leading population center. He was defeated that year but quickly became an active member of his father's campaign for the presidency in 1980. Bush worked in each of his father's national campaigns: the 1980 quest for the Republican nomination, the successful efforts as Ronald Reagan's vice presidential running mate in 1980 and 1984, the victorious race for the presidency in 1988, and the defeat for reelection in 1992. These activities enabled Bush to develop extensive contacts with Republican political activists and financial contributors who would prove quite helpful in his own presidential effort in 2000.

Bush was also active in a number of business ventures during these same years, including the establishment of his own oil exploration company. He received significant news attention when he was the major owner of the Texas Rangers major league baseball team between 1989 and 1994. He sold his ownership in 1994 when he ran for the governorship of Texas. He was elected governor that year in a bitter fight with the incumbent Democrat Ann Richards. She had gained national attention in 1988 with her keynote address at the Democratic National Convention when she said that Bush's father, who was the Republican nominee for president that year, had been born with a silver foot in his mouth. Bush was widely perceived as a successful governor and won a second term by an overwhelming margin; 68 percent of the vote. He also ran well among Hispanic voters who are one of the nation's most Democratic oriented groups. These electoral and policy successes convinced many Republicans that Bush would make an excellent candidate for president in 2000.

Bush officially began his presidential campaign in March 1999 with the formation of an exploratory committee. The committee was designed to raise money for the effort, and it succeeded far beyond the expectations of nearly all political observers. By June 30, 1999, the Bush campaign had raised about $30 million, which was more money than the combined totals of the other eleven Republican candidates. The fund raising lead was reflective of Bush's successes as a candidate; he was endorsed by twenty-seven Republican governors and led his rivals in support from voters as measured in public opinion surveys. Six of his rivals abandoned their efforts before the end of 1999, and four of the others were nearly finished as candidates by the time of the first primaries. Unfortunately for Bush, the one remaining rival, Senator John McCain, was still quite strong. McCain surprised Bush and most political observers with a sweeping victory in the nation's first primary, New Hampshire. This led to a major effort by both Bush and McCain in several primaries during February. Bush defeated McCain in South Carolina, Virginia, and Washington while losing in Arizona and Michigan. The final showdown between the two came on March 7 in eleven primaries. Bush won seven of them, and McCain withdrew from the campaign.

Bush was officially nominated by the Republican Party at its national convention in early August, where he chose Richard Cheney as his vice presidential running mate. Bush began the campaign with a modest lead over his Democratic Party rival, Vice President Al Gore, but lost that lead in late August when Gore was officially nominated by his own party. The campaign remained very close throughout the rest of the year. Bush surprised many observers with his performances in the three nationally televised debates that were held during the first three weeks of October. Many observers expected that Bush would fare poorly, but adverse public reactions to Gore, and several postdebate polls, indicated that Bush had done quite well. Bush had a slight lead in the national polls until the eve of the election when Gore tied him.

Bush held a slight lead in the electoral vote and in the state of Florida on the morning after the election but was trailing Gore in the national popular vote. He soon found himself in a defensive action in Florida where he had to fend off efforts by Gore to have manual recounts carried out in some of the state's more Democratic counties. Bush worked through a number of surrogates, including a team of attorneys and political operatives headed by James Baker, and eventually turned both public opinion and the nation's judicial system in his favor. His electoral triumph became obvious with the U.S. Supreme Court ruling in *Bush v. Gore.*

Bush began his presidency with a dilemma; he had won the election through the antiquated device of the electoral college but had not obtained the support of most of his fellow citizens. He had garnered only 47.9 percent of the popular vote, which was in marked contrast to the total of 48.4 percent that Gore had acquired. There was also an important historic parallel; the last time when a father and son had both been presidents, the son, John Quincy Adams, also finished second in the popular vote. Adams was defeated for a second term. How this historic parallel will play out this time is uncertain, but Bush will need a much stronger showing in 2004 to become a two-term president.

BUSH, JOHN ELLIS (JEB) (1953–)

Jeb Bush, as the governor of Florida is often known, is a son of one president and the brother of another. He was born in Midland, Texas, and attained his education at the University of Texas but chose to make Florida his home. In his new state, Bush has been involved in a number of banking ventures and has been politically active in the state Republican Party. His previous political efforts were related to his father's presidential campaigns and to helping other Republicans contest elections.

Bush sought public office for the first time in 1994 when he ran for governor. His candidacy was of particular interest to the national news media and other political observers that year because two sons of former president George Bush were running for governorships in major states. Bush's older brother, George W., was a candidate for the governorship of Texas, which was the nation's third largest state in population. Jeb Bush was running in Florida, the fourth largest state. There have been several political dynasties throughout American history that have attracted the interest of the public, including those of the Adams, Roosevelt, and Kennedy families in particular. The efforts by the "Bush brothers," as some people called them, meant that the Bush family political roles now involved three generations. Prescott Bush, father of George Bush and grandfather of George W. and Jeb Bush, had been a longtime U.S. senator from Connecticut.

These campaigns led some observers to speculate that a second Bush administration might soon be in the nation's future. Many of those same observers, including President Bush, believed that Jeb was the more likely brother to lead that administration. Unfortunately for Jeb, he lost the election for governor of Florida while his brother won in his attempt to become governor of Texas. Jeb Bush devoted the next four years to a second bid for the governorship and succeeded in 1998. By now, his older brother was ready to launch a bid for president.

Jeb Bush played a particularly significant role in the election of 2000. He was the cochair; the other was the Florida Secretary of State Katherine Harris, of the Florida Bush for President Committee. The even division of support for Bush and Gore throughout the nation, coupled with the fact that the three largest states, California, New York, and Texas, were not particularly competitive, forced both campaigns to concentrate on Florida. Jeb Bush's major goal in the campaign was to deliver the twenty-five electoral votes to his brother. The ensuing legal controversies over unequal balloting methods and vote counts encouraged comments that Jeb Bush had tried to fix the election for his brother. None of these charges have ever been proven, but they were problematic for Jeb Bush during his quest for a second term as governor in 2002. They were not strong enough to cost him the election, however; he handily won another term.

CHENEY, RICHARD B., JR. (1941–)

Richard Cheney was the Republican Party nominee for vice president in the election of 2000. Born in Nebraska, Cheney spent much of his childhood in Casper, Wyoming. He received two degrees from the University of Wyoming, a bachelor of arts and master of arts in Political Science. Cheney was the deputy of White House Chief of Staff Donald Rumsfeld during the early months of the administration of Gerald Ford and then served as the White House chief of staff himself after Ford appointed Rumsfeld as secretary of defense in 1975. Cheney left the White House after Ford lost the presidential election of 1976. Cheney launched his own public career shortly afterward, winning election to a seat in the U.S. House of Representatives from Wyoming in 1978. He won reelection to this position by sweeping margins during the next five elections. He resigned from the House in early 1989 to accept appointment by George Bush as secretary of defense. This was a particularly important time; in early 1991 the nation was engaged in the Persian Gulf War where it defeated the military forces of Iraq after about six weeks of air bombardments and four days of armed combat. Cheney left public life after the Republican loss of the presidency in 1992 and soon made his home in Texas, where he was named as the president of an oil supply company, Halliburton. He remained active in public matters, however, serving as an advisor of Governor Bush's presidential bid in 2000. Cheney headed a group designed to recommend a vice presidential candidate to Bush.

Cheney was selected by Governor Bush as the Republican vice presidential nominee during the final days preceding the Republican National Convention, an event that was held in Philadelphia between July 31 and August 3. He received widespread acclaim from both his own partisans and national news reporters for his various legislative and executive experiences, particularly with respect to foreign affairs, and for his ability to work well with all factions of his party. Democrats responded by attacking the conservative votes Cheney had cast as a congressman on several issues such as gun control and funding for Head Start. Head Start is a federal program that provides preschool instruction for economically disadvantaged children.

Cheney spent much of the campaign complementing Bush. Bush used his national convention acceptance speech as an opportunity to emphasize unifying themes, while Cheney used his speech to attack the limitations of the Democratic administration. As is true of all other vice presidential nominees, Cheney traveled the nation and spoke in places separate from Bush and attained far less attention while doing so. His best performance of the campaign came in the nationally televised debate on October 5 between the vice presidential nominees of the two major political parties. Cheney emphasized the major themes of the Republican ticket, and particularly his own strength with respect to foreign affairs. His reception by voters was quite strong. His foreign policy talents have proven quite valuable to the Bush administration. Cheney is helping to expand the nature of the vice presidential office through his actions in diplomacy since the terrorist bombing of 2001.

CLINTON, BILL (1946–)

Bill Clinton was perhaps the most important political issue in the election of 2000. The nation appeared to be nearly evenly divided in their opinions of Clinton; about half of all voters approved of him, while the other half did not. These divisions masked a more disturbing pattern; the vast majority of voters favored the policy accomplishments of the Clinton administration, while an equally overwhelming majority did not respect Clinton as a person because of the various political and sex scandals that had marred his time in office. These divergent trends posed a dilemma that Al Gore could not overcome. Gore tried to present himself to his fellow Democrats as the logical successor of Clinton in executive office, but he also tried to convince voters who were less supportive of Clinton that he was independent and distant from the president that many of them despised.

Clinton was born and raised in Arkansas, received his undergraduate education at Georgetown University, was a Rhodes Scholar, and acquired his law degree from Yale. He returned to Arkansas, married Hillary Rodham, whom he had met in law school, and launched a political career in 1974 with an unsuccessful bid for a seat in congress. Clinton was elected as Attorney General of Arkansas in 1976 at the age of thirty and became governor two years later. He ran a successful campaign for the presidency in 1992 and then won a second term four years later.

The Clinton presidency had some high points, such as the elimination of the chronic budget deficits that had plagued the nation for decades. This accomplishment set the stage for the prosperous economy of the final years of the 1990s. There were also successes in international affairs, such as the resolution of the long-standing crisis in the Balkans. The low points were over the sex scandals involving Paula Jones and Monica Lewinsky and the perjury that Clinton committed before a federal grand jury. This led to the unsuccessful effort by Republican congressmen to impeach Clinton.

Clinton's role in the election campaign of 2000 was unusual in the sense that he was not asked by his own party to spend much time talking about the major accomplishments of his administration. In contrast to this, the retiring incumbent in 1988, Ronald Reagan, spent many of the final days of October speaking on behalf of his vice president, George Bush, in a number of states where the outcome seemed to be in doubt. Reagan attracted huge crowds and extensive media attention. Bush carried the electoral votes of every state in which Reagan appeared.

Clinton ended his eight-year tenure in office with even more controversies, this time over such matters as the granting of pardons to a variety of individuals who had made large financial contributions to his presidential library fund. His historical legacy and the impact of his policies and administration on American political life are still uncertain and are likely to remain so for many years to come.

DALEY, WILLIAM M. (1948–)

William Daley directed the legal and political efforts of the Gore campaign and served as its major spokesman during the Florida vote controversy. Daley hails from Chicago and is the son of that city's legendary mayor from the 1950s and 1960s, Richard J. Daley. He is also the younger brother of the present mayor of Chicago, Richard M. Daley. Daley acquired his undergraduate degree from Loyola University and law degree from John Marshall Law School. He became nationally prominent in 1996, when he served as the major organizer for the Democratic National Convention that was held in Chicago. This site was particularly important because the last time the Democrats met in that city was in 1968, when they were bitterly divided over the conduct of the Vietnam War. Richard J. Daley has often been depicted as a major cause of the disruptions and violence that contributed to the national defeat of the Democratic Party in that year's election. The return of the Democrats to Chicago in 1996 to a convention organized by Daley's son was symbolically important because it indicated how this city's political leaders had once again become significant players in their national party. William Daley joined the Clinton administration in 1997 as the secretary of commerce and later served in a variety of positions in the Gore presidential campaign, including campaign manager. The events of the Florida vote controversy brought him clearly into the public's consciousness.

In leading the Gore efforts in Florida, Daley needed to accomplish two tasks. First, he needed to develop a strategy for challenging the vote counts. Second, he had to use his position as the public face of the Gore campaign to define the controversy in ways that would enhance the Democratic cause. With respect to the first, the Democrats decided to rely on manual recounts in four major counties as their main strategy for winning Florida's twenty-five electoral votes. The reasons were complex, but this course of action seemed to have the greatest likelihood of success. While Gore probably lost far more votes because of the famous butterfly ballot in Palm Beach County than he did with the defective punch card ballots, there did not appear to be any effective way in which the butterfly ballot could be challenged in court. The punch card ballots appeared to contain many errors that could be detected with manual inspections, however. Since the Democratic-oriented counties tended to rely on such ballots, these inspections would probably produce far more new votes for Gore than for Bush. In addition, state law required that candidates had to seek recounts at the county rather than at the state level. With this, the Gore campaign could seek recounts in only places that seemed promising. The Republicans were free to call for recounts in their stronger counties, but their opposition to Gore's efforts prevented them from doing so.

The second part of the Democratic strategy was to demand that all votes be counted. This was an attempt to claim the moral high ground where the party championed the right to vote for everyone, but it may have hurt Gore more than it helped him. Claims of this nature prevented the Gore campaign from challenging Republican practices in two counties where party officials altered some incorrect applications for absentee ballots. It also prevented the Democrats from attempting to disqualify a number of overseas absentee ballots that lacked signatures and postmarks.

The Gore campaign, and William Daley, focused on the one goal of attaining manual recounts with the use of lenient standards in four major counties.

The adverse ruling by the U.S. Supreme Court left them with no alternative strategy when time ran out.

DOLE, ELIZABETH (1936–)

Elizabeth Dole was one of the earliest rivals of George W. Bush for the Republican presidential nomination in 2000, but her bid fell far short of expectations and she ended her quest before the beginning of the actual election year. Born in North Carolina, Dole graduated from Duke University in 1958 and received two advanced degrees from Harvard, a master of arts and a juris doctorate. She held several positions in the Nixon administration including commissioner for the Federal Trade Commission. She also served in two subsequent Republican administrations: as secretary of transportation under Reagan from 1981 to 1985 and as secretary of labor from 1989 to 1991 under Bush. Dole then was the director of the Red Cross from 1991 until 1998, when she resigned to seek the Republican presidential nomination in 2000.

Dole became the first candidate to make a public announcement of candidacy for the presidency, doing so in early January 1999. At first, she seemed to have an excellent chance of winning the nomination. Early opinion polls showed her in second place in Republican preferences behind the early front-runner, George W. Bush. Dole had excellent credentials: high-level political service in three Republican administrations, a captivating speaking style that engaged audiences, and strong connections within the Republican Party. She was helped in the latter partly through her marriage in 1975 to Robert Dole, who was one of the nation's most important leaders of the Republican Party and its presidential nominee in 1996.

Despite these promising beginnings, Dole did not fare well as a candidate. She was unable to raise much money or acquire the endorsements of a significant number of her own partisans. Perhaps even worse, few Republican women seemed particularly interested in joining her effort. Her support actually declined throughout 1999, and it soon became apparent to political observers that her candidacy would be short lived. Much of the national news media had seen her as Bush's major rival for the nomination at the beginning of 1999 and had directed some of their attention to her campaign efforts. They began focusing that same attention on Senator John McCain by mid-summer and soon depicted the campaign as a two-candidate battle, of which Elizabeth Dole was not one.

Dole's campaign effectively ended in mid-August 1999 when she fared poorly in the Iowa Republican Straw Poll. After an investment of considerable money and effort, she finished a weak third behind Bush and Steve Forbes. McCain did not contest the poll but received more new coverage than Dole nonetheless. Dole, with almost no money, backing, or prospects, withdrew from the campaign shortly afterward. Her interest in holding public office is not over, however. She decided to seek the U.S. Senate seat in North Carolina that was being vacated by the retiring Republican Jesse Helms. She was successful and took office in January 2003.

DOLE, ROBERT (1923–)

Robert Dole was the Republican nominee for president in the election of 1996. Although he lost to Bill Clinton that year and decided against any future attempts to seek the nation's highest office, Dole played an important role in the 2000 campaign as a senior statesman within the Republican Party. Dole was born in Russell, Kansas, and continued to call this city his home throughout his public career. In what was to become a defining moment of his life, Dole was severely wounded in combat action in Italy during the Second World War. He was required to spend months in rehabilitation facilities and eventually lost the use of his right arm. After his military service, Dole attended the University of Kansas and Washburn University, where he acquired a bachelor of arts and a law degree. He began his public career in 1950 by winning an election to the Kansas legislature. Dole was then elected as the County Attorney in Russell, Kansas, in 1952 and held that position for eight years. With this experience, Dole began a long and distinguished congressional career. He was elected to a seat in the U.S. House of Representatives in 1960. After eight years in this office, Dole was elected to the U.S. Senate in 1968 and remained as a member of that body until he resigned during the presidential campaign of 1996.

Dole did not confine his political actions exclusively to Congress, however. He served as the national chairman of the Republican Party during the 1972 election and was Gerald Ford's running mate in the presidential election of 1976. Dole used this experience to seek the Republican presidential nomination in 1980 but lost to both Ronald Reagan and George Bush in the New Hampshire primary and soon ended his candidacy. The Republicans won control of the Senate in 1980 and named Dole as the chairman of the Finance Committee. Four years later, Dole was chosen as the majority leader of the Senate. The Democrats won control of the Senate for eight years between 1986 and 1994, thus forcing Dole into the role of minority leader. Dole returned to the majority leader role after 1994.

Dole ran for president a second time in 1988 but lost every primary to George Bush. He ended his candidacy in late March. His final, and most successful, bid for the presidency occurred in 1996. He was the early front-runner and did nothing to lose that distinction. He recorded a narrow victory in Iowa, suffered a close defeat in New Hampshire, but won every other major primary. All of his rivals had left the race by early April. Dole was not as successful in the general election, however. The incumbent Bill Clinton led in every poll and eventually won by a solid but not overwhelming margin of 49 to 41 percent.

Dole played an important role in the Republican Party in 1999 and 2000. While the numerous candidates for the nomination were often attacking one another, Dole aimed his criticisms at the party's eventual target, the Democratic administration. Dole was a unifying figure among his own partisans and helped keep Republicans united in a common cause while they engaged themselves in a hard-fought battle over a presidential nominee. His actions during this time were valuable in helping the Republicans regain the presidency in the election of 2000.

FORBES, STEVE (1947–)

On two occasions, in 1996 and 2000, Steve Forbes was a candidate for the Republican presidential nomination. His two campaigns were unorthodox by modern standards; he paid for his own efforts each time. Fundraising by presidential candidates has been under strict federal regulations since the Watergate scandals of the early 1970s. Candidates are limited in the amounts of money they can spend on their own efforts or accept from contributors. The Federal Election Campaign Act of 1972 limits candidates to spending only $50,000 of their own funds on presidential bids and from accepting contributions larger than $1,000 from individuals and $5,000 from any political committees. While the U.S. Supreme Court set aside some features of this law as violations of free speech, candidates must agree to accept its provisions if they want to receive federal financial assistance in their nomination efforts. Forbes decided to reject the federal funding and instead spend vast amounts of his own personal fortune on his candidacy.

Forbes made his most significant bid in 1996 when he contested both the Iowa precinct caucuses and New Hampshire primary by relying on extensive television advertising. Most of this was done in the form of attacks against the front-runner, Robert Dole. Despite the spending, which some observers have estimated may have been as high as $25 million; Forbes finished in fourth place in both contests and soon withdrew from the campaign. Many Republicans were quite critical of Forbes and placed part of the blame for their defeat at the hands of Bill Clinton on the aggressive attacks he had made against Dole. Despite this criticism, Forbes spent much of the next four years preparing for a second presidential effort, where he would also engage in a free spending effort. He attempted to create imagery to depict he was a champion of conservative values but was unsuccessful. While he managed to attain about 30 percent of the vote in Iowa, his best showing, he was quickly relegated to the status of a minor candidate because of the rise of John McCain as Bush's major rival. Forbes did not have another respectable showing in any state after Iowa and withdrew from the race before the end of February.

Forbes has been the editor of *Forbes Magazine* since 1982. His father founded the business and made the great fortune that made the short-lived political career of Steve Forbes possible. Whether Forbes will have a future in electoral politics is uncertain at this time. He was not solicited by representatives of the Bush campaign for a position in the new Republican administration.

GORE, ALBERT, JR. (1948–)

Al Gore was the Democratic Party's presidential nominee in 2000 and was the losing candidate in one of the most contentious elections in American history. Gore was also the nation's vice president during the election year. He is the son of Albert Gore, Sr., who was a U.S. senator from Tennessee for eighteen years, from 1952 until 1970. While he claims Tennessee as his home, Gore actually spent much of his childhood in Washington, D.C. He attained his undergraduate education at Harvard University, finishing with a bachelor of arts in 1969. He later completed his legal education at Vanderbilt University. After serving in the Army in Vietnam, Gore launched his public career in 1976 by successfully seeking a seat in the U.S. House of Representatives from a district in the greater Nashville area. Gore held that seat for eight years and then ran for a vacant position in the U.S. Senate in 1984. He won that election and then served in the Senate for the next eight years. He was selected by Bill Clinton as the Democratic Party's candidate for vice president in 1992. Once again, he was elected and served for eight years in that office. By the time he sought the presidency in 2000, Gore had acquired twenty-four years of service in elective office distributed evenly among the House, Senate, and vice presidency.

Gore had presidential ambitions even before 2000. He sought the Democratic nomination in 1988, where he tried to develop themes and imagery where he appeared as a moderate Southern candidate in contrast to the more liberal Northern candidates who had been dominating the Democratic Party for many years. He placed his main emphasis on running well in the vast number of primary elections scheduled for the second Tuesday in March, Super Tuesday. He had modest success that day, as he won five of the sixteen primaries. His triumphs occurred in Tennessee, North Carolina, Kentucky, Arkansas, and Oklahoma. His two main rivals were Michael Dukakis and Jesse Jackson, who also won five primaries each that day. Gore did not fare well after this. He finished in third place behind both Dukakis and Jackson in the Wisconsin and New York primaries, which were held at various times in April. With this, he ended his quest for the nomination.

Gore spent much of his eight years as vice president appearing in a surrogate role for Bill Clinton, often speaking to partisan groups about the accomplishments of the Clinton Administration. These activities made him a strong favorite among party leaders and activists for the 2000 nomination when the second and final Clinton term ended. One of Gore's best appearances on behalf of Clinton occurred during the debate on ratification of the North

American Free Trade Agreement (NAFTA) in 1994 when he faced Ross Perot on the television show *Larry King Live*. Gore handily defeated Perot in that encounter. Gore was also a major advisor of Clinton's on a number of important policy questions. One of his major actions as vice president was to lead the administration's efforts toward reinventing government. Here, several thousand federal positions were eliminated, and the delivery of governmental services became more efficient.

Gore began his efforts toward seeking the Democratic nomination in early 1999 but he was often overshadowed by the impeachment trial of Bill Clinton during this time. After some initial troubles in organizing his campaign, Gore moved his headquarters to Nashville and adopted a far more aggressive stance in combating his one nomination rival, Bill Bradley. Gore and Bradley faced one another in late 1999 and in early 2000 in a number of debates. Gore performed quite well and used these appearances to increase his already strong lead over Bradley.

The Democratic campaign was short in duration and never in doubt, with Gore winning every electoral showdown. He defeated Bradley in the January 24 Iowa caucuses by 63 to 35 percent and by 52 to 48 percent in the February 1 New Hampshire primary. The next battles among Democrats took place on March 7, when eleven states held primaries on Super Tuesday. This day in 2000 was much kinder to Gore than the one in 1988. Gore won every primary this time with Bradley ending his candidacy two days later. Gore had clinched the Democratic nomination by mid-March. Later in August, Gore became the fourth vice president since 1960 to be nominated for president in the year in which the incumbent did not seek another term.

Gore had been trailing his Republican rival, George W. Bush, in the polls for many months but eliminated that gap and actually took the lead shortly after the conclusion of the Democratic convention. The polls soon began to show that the nation was about evenly divided in its support for these two candidates, with the final outcome very much in doubt. Gore may have lost his best chances of winning the presidency with several mistakes during the last few weeks of the campaign. One of these occurred when he appeared overly aggressive in the first nationally televised debate with Bush and far too mild during the second. These were not his best debate appearances. A second problem occurred when he failed to link himself to the prosperity and peace that marked the final years of the Clinton administration. Rather than attempting to portray himself as a partner in a successful administration, Gore tried to create imagery in which he claimed to be his "own man." He did this because he wanted to escape any association with the scandals of the Clinton presidency. Finally, Gore failed to campaign adequately in his home state of Tennessee until it was too late. If he had begun his efforts earlier, he might well have won the eleven electoral votes of Tennessee. Victory here would have given Gore 278 electoral votes and would have made the 25 votes from Florida unnecessary.

Gore ended his presidential bid with a mixed legacy. He was one of those rare candidates who won the popular vote only to have lost the election. There is also considerable evidence indicating that if every person who attempted to vote in Florida had been able to cast an accurately counted ballot, Gore would have won that state and the election. In one sense, he is a victim. Some of his critics argue differently, however. They believe he had an excellent opportunity to win the presidency. It is very rare that an incumbent party loses an election during a prosperous time. Gore's critics believe that he should have defeated Bush by a solid and significant margin and that he alone deserves the blame for his defeat.

HARRIS, KATHERINE (1957–)

Katherine Harris was the Florida secretary of state during the 2000 presidential election and was often at the center of most controversies relating to ballot counting and vote certifications. The main theme of the attacks against her was that she had acted in an overly partisan manner when making discretionary decisions and that her main intent had been to help Bush win the election. Her own partisans were as fervent in their defenses of her actions as critics were in their attacks.

Harris is a member of a wealthy Florida agricultural family with long-standing ties to the state's Republican Party. She makes her home in Sarasota, where she has been involved in a number of civic affairs, including membership on the board of trustees of the Ringling Museum. Harris has also served in the Florida Senate. She was elected as the Florida secretary of state in 1998 on a Republican state ticket that was headed by the party's candidate for governor, Jeb Bush. In 2000, Harris was the cochair, with Jeb Bush being the other, of the Florida campaign on behalf of presidential candidate George W. Bush. This campaign had two main purposes: to win the state for Bush during the Republican primaries and to win it again during the general election. The first of these tasks became easy when Bush's only remaining Republican rival, John McCain, ended his campaign on March 9, five days before the primary. The second was far more difficult, however.

Harris did not enter the national consciousness until after the election had ended and she was entrusted with certifying the final election results. Under Florida law, all elections are conducted by the county clerks, whose actions are supervised by the secretary of state. Harris used her position to oppose any manual recounts of ballots that Gore requested. She was overruled by state courts on several occasions but then set the stage for the eventual legal showdown when she said she would refuse all recounts arriving after 5:00 P.M. on November 14. The Florida Supreme Court overturned her ruling, but the U.S. Supreme Court eventually stopped the recounts.

Harris was often held up to serious personal ridicule by mass media and other critics. One of the attacks made against her was over her use of facial make-up. Critics said it was excessive. Editorial cartoonists even depicted her as the animated character Cruella DeVille. Harris cannot seek reelection as secretary of state; prior to the 2000 election the state legislature voted to abolish the office and transfer its duties to other positions. Her actions in 2000, while certainly controversial, have endeared her to many Republicans, however. In early 2001, Harris announced that she would be a candidate for a vacant congressional seat in the Sarasota area in 2002, which she won.

LIEBERMAN, JOSEPH (1942–)

Joseph Lieberman was the Democratic Party's candidate for vice president in 2000. Lieberman is from Connecticut, a state where he was born, was educated, practiced law, and has held a variety of electoral and appointive offices. He acquired his education at Yale, graduating with a bachelor of arts in 1964 and a law degree in 1967. Politics has been a major part of Lieberman's life; he served as the cochairman of Robert Kennedy's presidential bid in 1968 and was elected to the state senate two years later. Lieberman spent ten years in the Senate and served as majority leader for six years. He spent the next eight years as Connecticut's attorney general and was then elected to the U.S. Senate in 1988. By 2000, Lieberman had served in the Senate for twelve years and had to face the voters once again. Connecticut law permitted him to run for two offices simultaneously. While losing the battle for vice president, Lieberman was elected to his third term in the Senate.

Lieberman has established a strong reputation among his Senate colleagues for integrity. Despite the fact that he has been a personal friend and political support of Bill Clinton since the early 1970s—Clinton had worked in one of his campaigns while attending Yale Law School—Lieberman denounced Clinton's behavior during the sex scandal with Monica Lewinsky. In addition, Lieberman has been viewed as being among the less liberal of the Democratic senators. He has often supported foreign policy positions and has taken stands on a number of social issues, such as violence in movies, which are often at odds with those of other members of his party.

Gore selected Lieberman as his running mate partly because of the importance he placed on developing imagery in which he did not seem to be connected to the scandals of the Clinton administration. While this strategy may have worked—few voters blamed Gore for Clinton's misdeeds—it may have been costly because it also prevented Gore from identifying with Clinton's accomplishments.

As is true with vice presidential nominees, Lieberman was constantly overshadowed throughout the general election campaign by the presidential candidate. There were two important developments that attracted attention, however. The first was the important fact that Lieberman was the first person of Jewish faith to be included on the ticket of either party. This led to some discussion about the possible effects of religious bigotry within the news media during the days immediately following his selection, but the fears soon appeared to be exaggerated. It now seems that the religious bigotry that existed in 1960 over John F. Kennedy's Roman Catholic faith is no longer important in American politics. In contrast this time, Lieberman often used religious references in many of his public addresses and tended to generate favorable responses from spokesmen of other religions. The second important development was his excellent performance in the televised debate between the vice presidential candidates. Like the Republican candidate, Richard Cheney, Lieberman emphasized the major themes of his party in a way that led many observers to consider his debate performance as superior to that of his running mate.

Lieberman continues to be a member of the Senate and has now become one of the more important leaders of the Democratic Party. In January 2003, Lieberman announced that he would seek the nomination of the Democratic Party for president in the election of 2004.

McCAIN, JOHN (1936–)

John McCain was the major rival of George W. Bush for the Republican presidential nomination in 2000. McCain was an unusual candidate; unlike most politicians who were born in the post-World War II period, he had a significant career in the armed forces. McCain, whose father and grandfather were both admirals in the Navy, graduated from the U.S. Naval Academy in 1958 and then served for twenty years as a naval officer. Of particular note is the fact that he spent nearly six of those years, from 1967 until 1973, as a prisoner of war in Vietnam. His combat aircraft was shot down while he was on a bombing mission. He was seen in widely published photographs in early 1973 when he returned to the United States at the end of the Vietnam War. McCain was dressed in a white naval uniform, was on crutches, and personally saluted Richard Nixon, who, as president, had welcomed the American forces home in a major public ceremony.

McCain launched a public career in 1982 by winning a seat in the U.S. House of Representatives from Arizona. He was reelected in 1984 and then successfully sought election to a vacant Senate seat in 1986. McCain has been a member of the Senate since that time and was named to a third term in 1998.

McCain's campaign for the Republican nomination in 2000 was as unusual as his background. He concentrated his efforts on one early test state, New Hampshire, and hoped to use a victory in this highly televised primary as a major opportunity for gaining national exposure. The plan worked perhaps even better than McCain had hoped. While his rivals, including Bush, competed in Iowa and used most of their money, McCain spent seventy-seven days campaigning in New Hampshire. His main approach was to hold a "town meeting" where he would speak to whoever attended and then answer their questions in a somewhat conversational manner. Two themes highlighted McCain's appeal; his personal heroism and his advocacy of campaign finance reform. With respect to the former, McCain stressed his war record and used it to develop the theme that he would be a fighter in the political world rather than an agent of special interests. He also blamed many of the ills of American government on the reliance that most elected officials have on corporate financial contributions. McCain sought a ban on the use of soft money, contributions given to political parties that are not subject to federal campaign finance laws. Many of the most prominent leaders of the Republican Party were opposed to his candidacy because of this stand.

McCain won the New Hampshire primary over Bush by an overwhelming margin of 49 to 31 percent. While this total seems impressive, there was one problem. Independents and Democrats were allowed to participate in the New Hampshire Republican primary and many did so. Exit polls indicated that these voters had been the foundation of McCain's support. Bush actually won the support of a majority of the Republicans who voted in New Hampshire.

McCain opposed Bush in sixteen additional primaries over the next five weeks, but this same problem continued to harm him. He always carried the votes of Independents and Democrats but lost the support of his own partisans. Since most states restricted primary voting exclusively to party members, McCain lost ten of them, including the major states of California, New York, and Ohio and withdrew from the race on March 9. Despite this loss, he continued to pursue campaign finance reform in the Senate and succeeded in the early months of 2002 in the wake of the Enron scandal. Congress passed and President Bush signed the bill for which McCain had worked so hard for for so many years.

NADER, RALPH (1934–)

Ralph Nader was either the major cause of Al Gore's defeat in the election of 2000 or he was a reflection of far deeper problems that exist in the political appeal of the Democratic Party. The answer to this question depends on the observer's ideological perspective. Nader was the nominee of the Green Party and garnered 2.7 percent of the popular vote. According to numerous public opinion polls, approximately half of Nader's supporters would have voted for Gore if Nader had not been a candidate, while about 20 percent would have cast their ballots for Bush. The rest told pollsters they would not have voted for president if Nader had not been a candidate. Responses such as these are significant because Nader acquired about 100,000 votes in Florida. If half of those people had indeed voted for Gore, the vice president would have carried Florida by a solid margin, regardless of butterfly ballots, inadequate voter registration data, or hanging chads. Many of Gore's supporters blame Nader for drawing off these votes. They also blame Nader for causing

Gore to devote considerable campaign time during the final weeks of October and early November to an effort aimed at reducing the Green Party's appeal in Wisconsin, Minnesota, Iowa, Oregon, New Mexico, and Washington. Gore carried each of these states by close margins. The critics say Gore would have won the election if he could have devoted that same time to Florida and Tennessee.

Others disagree. The nation has seen a number of presidential efforts over the past decades by candidates who have used minor political parties as their vehicles for attaining access to the ballot. Candidates such as George Wallace, John Anderson, and Ross Perot were unlike Nader, however. They created their own parties for the single purpose of running for president; the Greens asked Nader to be their standard bearer. The Greens are a relatively new party from the political left and are often opposed to the ideological directions of both Democrats and Republicans. They see candidates like Gore and Bush as advocates for the interests of industry and consider them as threats to the continuation of American democracy. If this analysis of the views of Green Party members and followers is accurate, the Democratic Party will likely face major problems in future elections from a group of voters it has considered as loyal.

Nader is a long-time consumer advocate who first gained national attention with his attacks on the quality of the cars produced by General Motors. He was born in Connecticut and acquired his undergraduate education at Princeton. Afterward, he finished with distinction in the Harvard University law school. He told voters that his major goal in 2000 was to attain 5 percent of the vote. This would make the Greens a major party under federal law and entitle them to several million dollars in governmental funding in the presidential election of 2004. Under the law, the Democrats and Republicans each received $67.5 million and the Reform Party $12.4 million for the 2000 election because of their showings in 1996. Nader did not succeed in his endeavor, however, so the Greens will have to try once again if they want major party status.

While the Green Party may not have qualified, there is a strong chance that it will have a candidate in 2004. The major question now is whether that candidate will be Ralph Nader.

REHNQUIST, WILLIAM (1924–)

William Rehnquist was the chief justice of the United States Supreme Court during the Florida vote controversy. He was also one of the more significant justices in the five-person Court majority that ended the manual recounts and decided the election in *Bush v. Gore*. Rehnquist was appointed to the Supreme Court as an associate justice in 1972 by Richard Nixon and was advanced to the position of chief justice in 1986 by Ronald Reagan. Since his initial appointment, Rehnquist has been the primary leader of the Court's conservative faction. In those cases when the Court has made rulings consistent with conservative views, Rehnquist has often written the majority opinion. In other instances, when the Court has decided a case in a more liberal direction, Rehnquist has frequently written strong dissenting opinions. Some of his dissents have served as the intellectual foundation of conservative majorities of future years.

Rehnquist acquired his undergraduate and law school education at Stanford University, completing the legal part in 1952. He was a member of several major law firms in Arizona before 1969 when Nixon appointed him to the post of deputy attorney general. This experience within the Nixon administration led Rehnquist to excuse himself from taking part in the landmark ruling in 1974 where Nixon had to turn over the Watergate tapes to the special prosecutor. Many Americans have seen Rehnquist perform some of the most important roles required of the chief justice, including administering the oath of office to a new president. Rehnquist gave the oath to Presidents Ford (1974), Carter (1977), Reagan (1981), Bush (1989), Clinton (1993), and Bush (2001). In addition, Rehnquist also fulfilled another role required by the Constitution; he presided over the impeachment trial of a president, Clinton in this instance, in 1999.

During his tenure, Rehnquist has often led the Court in a direction that seems inconsistent with his ruling in *Bush v. Gore*. He has interpreted the Constitution's Tenth Amendment, a provision that says in part that "all powers not delegated to the national government nor prohibited are reserved to the states" in ways that have limited the ability of the national government to overrule the actions of state governments. Some of his rulings have prevented the national government from forcing state governments to comply with federal employment laws that apply to private enterprises. Others have upheld the ability of state legislatures and executives to make broad interpretations of their powers. This history is often used by critics of the *Bush v. Gore* decision to question the motives of the conservative majority. These critics charge that an application of Rehnquist's past practices would have seen the Supreme Court defend the ability of a state court to define the meaning of state law without the intervention of the national government. Rehnquist is nearly eighty years old, and many political observers expect him to retire soon.

STEVENS, JOHN PAUL (1920–)

John Paul Stevens was an associate justice of the United States Supreme Court at the time of the *Bush v. Gore* ruling. After Chief Justice Rehnquist, who was appointed to the Court in 1971, Stevens is the next most senior justice with respect to time served on the Court. He was appointed to his current position by Gerald Ford in 1975. Since that time, Stevens has been looked upon by a fairly large number of observers as the primary spokesman and leader and of the Court's liberal minority. He was the most prominent member of this four-person group during the controversial election ruling. Stevens was particularly critical of both the reasoning behind the *Bush v. Gore* ruling and of the earlier decision by the Court even to become involved in this controversy. He concluded his dissenting opinion by saying that the greatest losers in the ruling would be the legitimacy of the judges in federal and state courts who work to interpret and apply laws.

Stevens is a native of Illinois and lived in the state for most of his life prior to his appointment to the Court. He was born in Chicago and attained his education at two of the most important universities in that city. He graduated from the University of Chicago in 1941 and completed his legal education at Northwestern University in 1947. His early career involved membership in major Chicago area law firms, one term in the U.S. House of Representatives, and service in the lower federal courts. Stevens was a federal district court justice in Illinois for several years and was a member of the U.S. Court of Appeals for the Seventh Circuit immediately prior to his appointment to the Supreme Court. His one term in congress, from 1951 to 1953, gave Stevens an opportunity to become acquainted with Ford, who was a congressman from Michigan at the time.

While a member of the Supreme Court, Stevens has been a major player in a large number of landmark rulings. His positions have reflected the Court's modern tendency of interpreting laws in ways that defended the constitutional rights of unpopular minorities. Stevens has been quite critical of Court efforts to expand the powers of police to seize evidence without the use of valid search warrants and has opposed the efforts of governments to limit free speech and press in their efforts to legislate moral behavior. He has also interpreted the equal protection clause of the Fourteenth Amendment in ways that have expanded the right to vote of African-Americans and other racial minorities. He advanced the argument in *Bush v. Gore* that the Court's interpretation of equal protection was inconsistent with past rulings. Stevens is more than eighty years old now and is expected by many political observers to retire from the court in the near future.

PRIMARY DOCUMENTS OF THE ELECTION

A. Supreme Court Decision of *Bush v. Gore*

The Florida vote controversy eventually resulted in more than thirty court decisions. The most important of these, by far, was the one entitled *Bush v. Gore* that was decided by the U.S. Supreme Court on December 12, 2000. The court ordered an immediate end to the manual recounts of disputed ballots in Florida and effectively decided the election in favor of George W. Bush. It voted, by a margin of 5 to 4, that the Florida recounts, as being conducted, violated the equal protection clause of the Fourteenth Amendment of the federal constitution. That clause reads, "Nor shall any state... deny to any person within its jurisdiction equal protection of the laws." The full text of the decision is printed below. There was one concurring opinion, written by Chief Justice Rehnquist, and four dissenting opinions, written by justices Stevens, Breyer, Ginsburg, and Souter. The Stevens dissent is reprinted here.

SUPREME COURT OF THE UNITED STATES
No.00–949
531 U.S. 98, 121 S.CT. 525, 148 L.Ed. 2d 388 (2000)
GEORGE W. BUSH, ET AL., PETITIONERS v.
ALBERT GORE, JR., ET AL.
531 U.S. 98, 121 S.Ct. 525, 148 L.Ed.2d 388 (2000)
ON WRIT OF CERTIORARI TO
THE FLORIDA SUPREME COURT
December 12, 2000

PER CURIAM

On December 8, 2000, the Supreme Court of Florida ordered that the Circuit Court of Leon County tabulate by hand 9,000 ballots in Miami-Dade County. It also ordered the inclusion in the certified vote totals of 215 votes identified in Palm Beach County and 168 votes identified in Miami-Dade County for Vice President Albert Gore, Jr., and Senator Joseph Lieberman, Democratic Candidates for President and Vice President. The Supreme Court noted that petitioner, Governor George W. Bush asserted that the net gain for Vice President Gore in Palm Beach County was 176 votes, and directed the Circuit Court to resolve that dispute on remand. The court further held that relief would require manual recounts in all Florida counties where so-called "undervotes" had not been subject to manual tabulation. The court ordered all manual recounts to begin at once. Governor Bush and Richard Cheney, Republican Candidates for the Presidency and Vice Presidency, filed an emergency application for a stay of this mandate. On December 9, we granted the application, treated the application as a petition for a writ of certiorari, and granted certiorari.

The proceedings leading to the present controversy are discussed in some detail in our opinion in *Bush v. Palm Beach County Canvassing Bd.*, (per curiam) (Bush I). On November 8, 2000, the day following the Presidential election, the Florida Division of Elections reported that petitioner, Governor Bush, had received 2,909,135 votes, and respondent Vice President Gore, had received 2,907,351 votes, a margin of 1,784 for Governor Bush. Because Governor Bush's margin of victory was less than "one-half of a percent... of the votes cast," an automatic machine recount was conducted under Sec. 102.141(4) of the election code, the results of which showed Governor Bush still winning the race but by a diminished margin. Vice President Gore then sought manual recounts in Volusia, Palm Beach, Broward, and Miami-Dade Counties, pursuant to Florida's election protest provisions. Fla. Stat. Sec. 102.166 (2000). A dispute arose concerning the deadline for local county canvassing boards to submit their returns to the Secretary of State (Secretary). The Secretary declined to waive the November 14 deadline imposed by statute. Sec. 102.111, 102.112. The Florida Supreme Court, however, set the deadline at November 26. We granted certiorari and vacated the Florida Supreme Court's decision, finding considerable uncertainty as to the grounds on which it was based. Bush I. On December 11, the Florida Supreme Court issued a decision on remand reinstating that date.

On November 26, the Florida Elections Canvassing Commission certified the results of the election and declared Governor Bush the winner of Florida's 25 electoral votes. On November 27, Vice President Gore, pursuant to Florida's contest provisions, filed a complaint in Leon County Circuit Court contesting the certification. Fla. Stat. Sec. 102.168 (2000). He sought relief pursuant to Sec. 102.168(3)(c.), which provides that "receipt of a number of illegal votes or rejection a number of legal votes sufficient to change or place in doubt the result of the election" shall be grounds for a contest. The Circuit Court denied relief, stating that Vice President Gore failed to meet his burden of proof. He appealed to the First District Court of Appeal, which certified the matter to the Florida Supreme Court.

Accepting jurisdiction, the Florida Supreme Court affirmed in part and reversed in part. *Gore v. Harris.* The court held that the Circuit Court had been correct to reject Vice President Gore's challenge to the results certified in Nassau County and his challenge to the Palm Beach county canvassing board's determination that 3,300 ballots cast in that county were not, in the statutory phrase, "legal votes."

The Supreme Court held that Vice President Gore had satisfied his burden of proof under Sec. 102.168(3)(c.) with respect to his challenge to Miami-Dade County's failure to tabulate, by manual count, 9,000 ballots on which the machines had failed to detect a vote for President ("undervotes"). Noting the closeness of the election, the Court explained that "on this record, there can be no question that there are legal votes within the 9,000 uncounted votes sufficient to place the results of this election in doubt." A "legal vote," as determined by the Supreme Court, is "one in which there is a 'clear indication of the intent of the voter.'" The court therefore ordered a hand recount of the 9,000 ballots in Miami-Dade County. Observing that the contest provisions vest broad discretion in the circuit judge to "provide any relief appropriate under such circumstances," Fla. Stat. Sec. 102.168(8) (2000), the Supreme court further held that the Circuit court could order "the Supervisor of elections and the Canvassing Boards, as well as the necessary public officials, in all counties that have not conducted a manual recount or tabulation of the undervotes... to do so forthwith, said tabulation to take place in the individual counties where the ballots are located."

The Supreme Court also determined that both Palm Beach County and Miami-Dade County, in their earlier manual recounts, had identified a net gain of 215 and 168 legal votes for Vice President Gore. Rejecting the Circuit Court's conclusion that Palm Beach County lacked the authority to include the 215 net votes submitted past the November 26 deadline, the Supreme Court explained that the deadline was not intended to exclude votes identified after that date through ongoing manual recounts. As to Miami-Dade County, the Court concluded that although the 168 votes identified were the result of a partial recount, they were "legal votes that could change the outcome of the election." The Supreme Court therefore directed the Circuit court to include those totals in the certified results, subject to resolution of the actual vote total from the Miami-Dade partial recount.

The petition presents the following questions: whether the Florida Supreme court established new standards for resolving Presidential election contests, thereby violating Art. II, Sec. 1 cl. 2, of the United States Constitution and failing to comply with 3 U.S.C. Sec. 5, and whether the use of standardless manual recounts violates the Equal Protection and Due Process Clauses. With respect to the equal protection question, we find a violation of the Equal Protection Clause.

II

A.

The closeness of this election and the multitude of legal challenges, which have followed in its wake, have brought into sharp focus a common, if heretofore unnoticed, phenomenon. Nationwide statistics reveal that an estimated 2% of ballots cast do not register a vote for President for whatever reason, including deliberately choosing no candidate at all or some voter error, such as voting for two candidates or insufficiently marking a ballot. Se Ho, *More Than 2M Ballots Uncounted, AP Online* (Nov. 28, 2000); Kelley, *Balloting Problems Not Rare But Only In A Very Close Election Do Mistakes And Mismarking Make a Difference, Omaha World-Herald* (Nov. 15, 2000). In certifying election results, the votes eligible for inclusion in the certification are the votes meeting the properly established legal requirements.

This case has shown that punch card balloting machines can produce an unfortunate number of ballots which are not punched in a clean, complete way by the voter. After the current counting, it is likely legislative bodies nationwide will examine ways to improve the mechanisms and machinery for voting.

B.

The individual citizen has no federal constitutional right to vote for elections for the President of the United States unless and until the state legislature chooses a statewide election as the means to implement its power to appoint members of the Electoral College. U.S. Const., Art. II, Sec 1. This is the source for the statement in *McPherson v. Blacker, 146 U.S. 1, 35 (1892),* that the State legislature's power to select the manner for appointing electors is plenary; it may, if it so chooses, select the electors itself, which indeed was the manner used by State legislatures in several States for many years after the Framing of our Constitution. Id., at 28–33. History has now favored the voter, and in each of the several States the citizens themselves vote for Presidential electors. When the state legislature vests the right to vote for President, in its people, the right to vote as the legislature has prescribed is fundamental; and one source of its fundamental nature lies in the same equal weight accorded to each vote and the equal dignity owed to each voter. The State, of course, after granting the franchise in the special context of Article II, can take back the power to appoint electors. See id., at 35 ("there is no doubt of the right of the legislature to resume the power at any time, for it can neither be taken away nor abdicated") (quoting S. Rep. No. 395, 43d Cong., 1st Sess.).

The right to vote is protected in more than the initial allocation of the franchise. Equal protection applies as well to the manner of its exercise. Having once granted the right to vote on equal terms, the State may not, by later arbitrary and disparate treatment, value one person's vote over that of another. See, e.g., *Harper v. Virginia Bd. Of Elections, 383 U.S. 663, 665 (1966)* ("Once the franchise is granted to the electorate, lines may not be drawn which are inconsistent with the Equal Protection Clause of the Fourteenth Amendment"). It must be remembered that "the right of suffrage can be denied by a debasement or dilution of the weight of a citizen's vote just as effectively as by wholly prohibiting the free exercise of the franchise." *Reynolds v. Sims, 377 U.S. 533, 555 (1964).*

There is no difference between the two sides of the present controversy on these basic propositions. Respondents say that the very purpose of vindicating the right to vote justifies the recount procedures now at issue. The question before us, however, is whether the recount procedures the Florida Supreme Court has adopted are consistent with its obligation to avoid arbitrary and disparate treatment of the members of its electorate.

Much of the controversy seems to revolve around ballot cards designed to be perforated by a stylus but which, either through error or deliberate omission, have not been perforated with sufficient precision for a machine to count them. In some cases a piece of the card—a chad—is hanging, say by two corners. In other cases there is no separation at all, just an indentation.

The Florida Supreme Court has ordered that the intent of the voter be discerned from such ballots. For purposes of resolving the equal protection challenge, it is not necessary to decide whether the Florida Supreme Court had the authority under the legislative scheme for resolving election disputes to define what a legal vote is and to mandate a manual recount implementing that definition. The recount mechanisms implement in response to the decisions of the Florida Supreme Court do not satisfy the minimum requirement for non-arbitrary treatment of voters necessary to secure the fundamental right. Florida's basis command for the count of legally cast votes is to consider the "intent of the voter." *Gore v. Harris.* This is unobjectionable as an abstract proposition and a starting principle. The problem inheres in the absence of specific standards to ensure its equal application. The formulation of uniform rules to determine intent based on these recurring circumstances is practicable and, we conclude, necessary.

The law does not refrain from searching for the intent of the actor in a multitude of circumstances; and in some cases the general command to ascertain intent is not susceptible to much further refinement. In this instance, however, the question is not whether to believe a witness but how to interpret the marks or holes or scratches on an inanimate object, a piece of cardboard or paper which, it is said, might not have registered as a vote during the machine count. The factfinder confronts a thing, not a person. The search for intent can be confined by specific rules designed to ensure uniform treatment.

The want of those rules here has led to unequal evaluation of ballots in various respects. See *Gore v. Harris,* (Wells, J., dissenting) ("Should a county canvassing board count or not count a 'dimpled chad' where the voter is able to successfully dislodge the chad in every other contest on that ballot? Here, the county canvassing boards disagree"). As seems to have been acknowledged at oral argument, the standards for accepting or rejecting contested ballots might vary not only from county to county but indeed within a single county from one recount team to another.

The record provides some examples. A monitor in Miami-Dade County testified at trial that he observed that three members of the county canvassing board applied different standards in defining a legal vote. 3 Tr. 497, 499

(Dec. 3, 2000). And testimony at trial also revealed that at least one county changed its evaluative standards during the counting process. Palm Beach County, for example, began the process with a 1990 guideline which precluded counting completely attached chads, switched to a rule that considered a vote to be legal if any light could be seen through a chad, changed back to the 1990 rule, and then abandoned any pretense of a per se rule, only to have a court order that the county consider dimpled chads legal. This is not a process with sufficient guarantees of equal treatment.

An early case in our one person, one vote jurisprudence arose when a State accorded arbitrary and disparate treatment to voters in its different counties. *Gray v. Sanders, 372 U.S. 368 (1963)*. The Court found a constitutional violation. We relied on these principles in the context of the Presidential selection process in *Moore v. Ogilvie, 394, W. S. 814 (1969)*, where we invalidated a county-based procedure that diluted the influence of citizens in larger counties in the nominating process. There we observed that "the idea that one group can be granted greater voting strength than another is hostile to the one man, one vote basis of our representative government." Id., at 819.

The State Supreme court ratified this uneven treatment. It mandated that the recount totals from two counties, Miami-Dade and Palm Beach, be included in the certified total. The court also appeared to holds sub silentio that the recount totals from Broward County, which were not completed until after the original November 14 certification by the Secretary of State, were to be considered part of the new certified vote totals even though the county certification was not contested by Vice President Gore. Yet each of the counties used varying standards to determine what was a legal vote. Broward County used a more forgiving standard than Palm Beach County, and uncovered almost three times as many new votes, a result markedly disproportionate to the difference in population between the counties.

In addition, the recounts in these three counties were not limited to so-called undervotes but extended to all of the ballots. The distinction has real consequences. A manual recount of all ballots identifies not only those ballots which show no vote but also those which contain more than one, the so-called overvotes. Neither category will be counted by the machine. This is not a trivial concern. At oral argument, respondents estimated there are as many as 110,000 overvotes statewide. As a result, the citizen whose ballot was not read by a machine because he failed to vote for a candidate in a way readable by a machine may still have his vote counted in a manual recount; on the other hand, the citizen who marks two candidates in a way discernable by the machine will not have the same opportunity to have his vote count, even if a manual examination of the ballot would reveal the requisite indicia of intent. Furthermore, the citizen who marks two candidates, only one of which is discernable by the machine, will have his vote counted even though it should have been read as an invalid ballot. The State Supreme court's inclusion of vote counts based on these variant standards exemplifies concerns with the remedial processes that were under way.

That brings the analysis to yet a further equal protection problem. The votes certified by the court included a partial total from one county, Miami-Dade. The Florida Supreme Court's decision thus gives no assurance that the recounts included in a final certification must be complete. Indeed, it is respondent's submission that it would be consistent with the rules of the recount procedures to include whatever partial counts are done by the time of final certification, and we interpret the Florida Supreme court's decision to permit this. See *Gore v. Harris* (noting "practical difficulties" may control outcome of election, but certifying partial Miami-Dade total nonetheless). This accommodation no doubt results from the truncated contest period established by the Florida Supreme court in *Bush I,* at respondents' own urging. The press of time does not diminish the constitutional concern. A desire for speed is not a general excuse for ignoring equal protection guarantees.

In addition to these difficulties the actual process by which the votes were to be counted under the Florida Supreme Court's decision raises further concerns. That order did not specify who would recount the ballots. The county canvassing boards were forced to pull together ad hoc teams comprised of judges from various Circuits who had no previous training in handling and interpreting ballots. Furthermore, while others were permitted to observe, they were prohibited from objecting during the recount.

The recount process, in its features here described, is inconsistent with the minimum procedures necessary to protect the fundamental right of each voter in the special instance of a statewide recount under the authority of a single state judicial officer. Our consideration is limited to the present circumstances, for the problem of equal protection in election processes generally presents many complexities.

The question before the Court is not whether local entities, in the exercise of their expertise, may develop different systems for implementing elections. Instead, we are presented with a situation where a state court with the power to assure uniformity has ordered a statewide recount with minimal procedural safeguards. When a court orders a statewide remedy, there must be at least some assurance that the rudimentary requirements of equal treatment and fundamental fairness are satisfied.

Given the Court's assessment that the recount process underway was probably being conducted in an unconstitutional manner, the court stayed the order directing the recount so it could hear this case and render an expedited decision. The contest provision, as it was mandated by the State Supreme Court, is not well calculated to sustain the confidence that all citizens must have in the outcome of elections. The State has not shown that its procedures include the necessary safeguards. The problem, for instance, of the estimated 110,000 overvotes has not been addressed, although Chief Justice Wells called attention to the concern in his dissenting opinion. See *Gore v. Harris.*

Upon due consideration of the difficulties identified to this point, it is obvious that the recount cannot be conducted in compliance with the requirements of equal protection and due process without substantial additional work. It would require not only the adoption (after opportunity for argument) of adequate statewide standards for determining what is a legal vote, and practicable procedures to implement them, but also orderly judicial review of any disputed matters that might arise. In addition, the Secretary of State has advised that the recount of only a portion of the ballots requires that the vote tabulation equipment be used to screen out undervotes, a function for which the machines were not designed. If a recount of overvotes were also required, perhaps even a second screening would be necessary. Use of the equipment for this purpose, and any new software developed for it, would have to be evaluated for accuracy be the Secretary of State, as required by Fla. Stat. Sec. 101.015 (2000).

The Supreme Court of Florida has said that the legislature intended the State's electors to "participate fully in the federal electoral process," as provided in 3 U.S.C. Sec. 5., see also *Palm Beach Canvassing Bd. V. Harris, 2000 WL 1725434, *13 (Fla. 2000)*. That statute, in turn, requires that any controversy or contest that is designed to lead to a conclusive selection of electors be completed by December 12. That date is upon us, and there is no recount procedure in place under the State Supreme Court's order that comports with minimal constitutional standards. Because it is evident that any count seeking to meet the December 12 date will be unconstitutional for the reasons we have discussed, we reverse the judgment of the Supreme Court of Florida ordering a recount to proceed.

Seven Justices of the Court agree that there are constitutional problems with the recount ordered by the Florida Supreme Court that demand a remedy. See post, at 6 (SOUTER, J., dissenting); post, at 2 15 (BREYER, J., dissenting). The only disagreement is as to the remedy. Because the Florida Supreme court has said that the Florida Legislature intended to obtain the safe-harbor benefits of 3 U.S.C. Sec. 5, JUSTICE BREYER's proposed remedy—remanding to the Florida Supreme Court for its ordering of a constitutionally proper contest until December 18—contemplates action in violation of the Florida election code, and hence could not be part of an "appropriate" order authorized by Fla. Stat. Sec. 102.168 (8) (2000).

None are more conscious of the vital limits on judicial authority than are the members of this Court, and none stand more in admiration of the Constitution's design to leave the selection of the President to the people, through their legislatures, and to the political sphere. When contending parties invoke the process of the courts, however, it becomes our unsought responsibility to resolve the federal and constitutional issues the judicial system has been forced to confront.

The judgment of the Supreme Court of Florida is reversed, and the case is remanded for further proceedings not inconsistent with this opinion.

Pursuant to this Court's Rule 45.2, the Clerk is directed to issue the mandate in this case forthwith.

It is so ordered.

JUSTICE STEVENS, with whom JUSTICE GINSBURG
and JUSTICE BREYER join, dissenting.

The Constitution assigns to the States the primary responsibility for determining the manner of selecting the Presidential electors. See Art. II, sec 1, cl. 2. When questions arise about the meaning of state laws, including election laws, it is our settled practice to accept the opinions of the higher courts of the States as providing the final answers. On rare occasions, however, either federal statutes or the Federal Constitution may require federal judicial intervention I state elections. This is not such an occasion.

The federal questions that ultimately emerged in this case are not substantial. Article II provides that, "each State shall appoint, in such Manner as the Legislature thereof may direct, a Number of Electors." It does not create state legislatures out of whole cloth, but rather takes them as they come—as creatures born of, and constrained by, their state constitutions. Lest there be any doubt, we stated over 100 years ago in *McPherson v. Blacker*, 146 U.S. 1,25 (1892), that "what is forbidden or required to be done by a State" in the Article II context "is forbidden or required of the legislative power under state constitutions as they exist." In the same vein, we also observed that "the State's legislative power is the supreme authority except as limited by the constitution of the State." The legislative power in Florida is subject to the judicial review pursuant to Article V of the Florida Constitution, and nothing in Article II of the Federal Constitution frees the state legislature from the constraints in the state constitution that created it. Moreover, the Florida Legislature's own decision to employ a unitary code for all elections indicates that it intended the Florida Supreme Court to play the same role in Presidential elections that it has historically played in resolving electoral disputes. The Florida Supreme Court's exercise of appellate jurisdiction therefore was wholly consistent with, and indeed contemplated by, the grant of authority in Article II.

It hardly needs stating that Congress, pursuant to 3 U.S.C. sec. 5, did not impose any affirmative duties upon the States that their governmental branches could "violate." Rather, sec. 5 provides a safe harbor for States to select electors in contested elections "by judicial or other methods" established by laws prior to the election day. Section 5, like Article II, assumes the involvement of the state judiciary in interpreting state election laws and resolving election disputes under those laws. Neither sec. 5 nor Article II grants federal judges any special authority to substitute their views for those of the state judiciary on matters of state law.

Not are petitioners correct in asserting that the failure of the Florida Supreme Court to specify in detail the precise manner in which the "intent of the voter," Fla. Stat. sec 101.5614(5) (Supp. 2001), is to be determined rises to the level of a constitutional violation. We found such a violation when individual votes within the same State were weighted unequally, see, *e.g.*

Reynolds v. Sims, 377 U.S. 533,568 (1964), but we have never before called into question the substantive standard by which a State determines that a vote has been legally cast. And there is no reason to think that the guidance provided to the fact finders, specifically the various canvassing boards, by the "intent of the voter" standard is any less sufficient—or will lead to results any less uniform—than, for example, the "beyond a reasonable doubt" standard employed everyday by ordinary citizens in courtrooms across this country.

Admittedly, the use of differing substandards for determining voter intent in different counties employing similar voting systems may raise serious concerns. Those concerns are alleviated—if not eliminated—by the fact that a single impartial magistrate will ultimately adjudicate all objections arising from the recount process. Of course, as a general matter, "the interpretation of constitutional principles must not be too literal. We must remember that the machinery of government would not work if it were not allowed a little play in its joints." ... If it were otherwise, Florida's decision to leave to each county the determination of what balloting system to employ-despite enormous differences in accuracy-might run afoul of equal protection. So, too, might the similar decisions of the vast majority of state legislatures to delegate to local authorities certain decisions with respect to voting systems and ballot design.

Even assuming that aspects of the remedial scheme might ultimately be found to violate the Equal Protection Clause, I could not subscribe to the majority's disposition of the case. As the majority explicitly holds, once a state legislature determines to select electors through a popular vote, the right to have one's vote counted is of constitutional stature. As the majority further acknowledges, Florida law holds that all ballots that reveal the intent of the voter constitute valid votes. Recognizing these principles, the majority nonetheless orders the termination of the contest proceeding before all such votes have been tabulated. Under their own reasoning, the appropriate course of action would be to remand to allow more specific procedures for implementing the legislature's uniform general standard to be established.

In the interest of finality, however, the majority effectively orders the disenfranchisement of an unknown number of voters whose ballots reveal their intent—and are therefore legal votes under state law—but were for some reason rejected by ballot-counting machines. It does so on the basis of the deadlines set forth in Title 3 of the United States code. But, as I have already noted, those provisions merely provide rules of decision for Congress to follow when selecting among conflicting slates of electors. They do not prohibit a State from counting what the majority concedes to be legal votes until a bona fide winner is determined. Indeed, in 1960, Hawaii appointed two slates of electors and Congress chose to count the one appointed on January 4, 1961, well after the Title 3 Deadlines ... thus, nothing prevents the majority, even if it properly found an equal protection violation, from ordering relief appropriate to remedy that violation without depriving

Florida voters of their right to have their votes counted. As the majority notes, "a desire for speed is not a general excuse for ignoring equal protection guarantees."

Finally, neither in this case, nor in its earlier opinion in *Palm Beach County Canvassing Bd. v. Harris,* did the Florida Supreme Court make any substantive change in Florida electoral law. Its decisions were rooted in long-established precedent and were consistent with the relevant statutory provisions, taken as a whole. It did what courts do—it decided the case before it in light of the legislature's intent to leave no legally cast vote uncounted. In so doing, it relied on the sufficiency of the general "intent of the voter" standard articulated by the state legislature, coupled with a procedure for ultimate review by an impartial judge, to resolve the concern about disparate evaluations of contested ballots. If we assume—as I do—that the members of that court and the judges who would have carried out its mandate are impartial, its decision does not even raise a colorable federal question.

What must underlie petitioners' entire federal assault on the Florida election procedures is an unstated lack of confidence in the impartiality and capacity of the state judges who would make the critical decisions if the vote count were to proceed. Otherwise, their position is wholly without merit. The endorsement of that position by the majority of this court can only lend credence to the most cynical appraisal of the work of judges throughout the land. It is confidence in the men ad women who administer the judicial system that is the true backbone of the rule of law. Time will one day heal the wound to that confidence that will be inflicted by today's decision. One thing, however, is certain. *Although we may never know with complete certainty the identity of the winner of this year's Presidential election, the identity of the loser is perfectly clear. It is the Nation's confidence in the judge as an impartial guardian of the rule of law.* (Italics added)

I respectfully dissent.

B. *Gore v. Harris* in Circuit Court

Katherine Harris, the Secretary of State for Florida and the state's chief election official, certified the vote as recorded on November 26, 2000 as the final vote in the presidential election. It showed Governor Bush winning the state by a margin of 537 votes out of more than six million that had been cast. In making her ruling, Harris decided that several hundred votes that had been found through the manual recounts to have been cast for Vice President Gore should not be included in this total because they had arrived at her office after the 5:00 P.M. deadline that had been established by the Florida Supreme Court. Gore sued Harris in state district court in order to have additional recounts conducted and votes included in the total. The court ruled against Gore.

In the Circuit Court of the Second Judicial Circuit in and for
Leon County, Florida
Case No. CV-00–2808

Albert Gore, Jr., Nominee of the Democratic Party of the United States for President of the United States, and Joseph I. Lieberman, Nominee of the Democratic Party of the United States for Vice President of the United States, Plaintiffs.

v.

Katherine Harris, as Secretary of State, State of Florida, ET AL., Defendants

Final Judgment

This action was tried before the court. The finding and conclusions in the ruling of the court from the bench is open court this day shall become a part hereof. Accordingly, it is ORDERED AND ADJUDGED THAT Plaintiffs Albert Gore, Jr., and Joseph I. Lieberman shall take nothing by the action and the defendants may go hence without day.

DONE AND ORDERED in Chambers, this 4th day December 2000.

N. Sanders Sauls
Circuit Judge

At this time, the court finds and concludes as follows: The complaint filed herein states in its first paragraph that this is an action to contest the state certification in the presidential election of 2000, asserting that the State Elections Canvassing Commission's certification on November 26, 2000, is erroneous as the vote totals wrongly include illegal votes and do not include legal votes that were improperly rejected.

Plaintiffs further contest the State of Florida's certification of the election for George W. Bush and Richard Cheney as being elected.

Plaintiffs further challenge and contest the election certifications of the canvassing boards of Dade, Palm Beach and Nassau counties.

As to the Dade Canvassing Board, plaintiffs seek to compel the Dade Board to include in its certification, and the State elections Canvassing Commission to include in the state certification, a six-vote change in favor of plaintiffs, resulting from the Board's initial test partial manual recount of 1 percent of the countywide vote total conducted with respect to three precincts designated by the plaintiffs' designees; also additional votes manually hand counted in a further partial recount total resulting from the board's discretionary decision to stop completion of a full manual recount of all the votes in all of the precincts of Dade because of insufficiency of time to complete the same. These represent the result of the count of an additional 136 precincts of the 635 precincts in Dade County. And also the results of any court-ordered manual review and recount of some 9,000 to 10,000 voter cards or ballots, which at the plaintiffs' request have been separated or were separated as alleged undervotes by the Dade Canvassing Board or the Dade supervisor of elections as a result of all the countywide ballots being processed through the counting machines a third time and being nonreadable by the machine.

As to the Palm Beach Canvassing Board, plaintiffs seek to compel the Palm Beach Board to include in its certification, and the state Elections Canvassing

Commission to include in the state certification, additional votes representing the results of an attempted partial certification of results completed before the November 26, 2000, deadline mandated by the Florida Supreme Court, as well as the additional reminder of the results of the manual recount, which was completed after the deadline and the attempted certification thereof on December 1; and in addition, the results of any court-ordered manual review and recount of some 3,300 ballots, which were objected to during the Palm Beach Board's manual recount, which plaintiffs alleged should have been counted as valid votes because that board used an improper standard.

As to Nassau, the Nassau County Canvassing Board, the plaintiffs seek to compel the Nassau Board to amend its certification, and the State Elections Canvassing Commission to amend the state certification, to reflect and include the results of the board's machine recount rather than the results of the board's original machine count, thereby resulting in a favorable net gain to plaintiffs of 51 votes.

It is the established law of Florida, as reflected in *State v. Smith* [(7 Fla. 134, 144 So. 333 (1932)], that where changes or charges of irregularity of procedure or inaccuracy of returns in balloting and counting processes have been alleged, the court must find as a fact that a legal basis for ordering any recount exists before ordering such recount.

Further, it is well established, as reflected in the opinion of Judge Jonas in *Smith v. Tynes* [412 S. 2d 925 (Fla. 1st DCA 1982)], that in order to contest election results under Section 102.168 of the Florida statutes, the plaintiff must show that but for the irregularity or inaccuracy claimed, the result of the election would have been different, and he or she would have been the winner. It is not enough to show a reasonable possibility that election results could have been altered by such irregularities or inaccuracies. Rather, a reasonable probability that the results of the election would have been changed must be shown.

In this case, there is no credible statistical evidence and no other competent substantial evidence to establish by preponderance a reasonable probability that the results of the statewide election in the State of Florida would be different from the result which has been certified by the State Canvassing Commission.

The court further finds and concludes the evidence does not establish any illegality, dishonesty, gross negligence, improper influence, coercion or fraud in the balloting and counting processes.

Secondly, there is no authority under Florida law for certification of an incomplete manual recount of a portion of or less than all ballots from any county by the State Elections Canvassing Commission, nor authority to include any returns submitted past the deadline established by the Florida Supreme Court in this election.

Thirdly, although the record shows voter error and/or less than total accuracy in regard to the punch-card voting devices utilized in Dade and Palm

Beach Counties, which these counties have been aware of for many years, these balloting and counting problems cannot support or effect any recounting necessity with respect to Dade County, absent the establishment of a reasonable probability that the statewide election result would be different, which has not been established in this case.

The court further finds the Dade Canvassing Board did not abuse its discretion in any of its decisions in its review and recounting processes.

Fourthly, with respect to the approximate 3,300 Palm Beach County ballots of which plaintiffs seek review, the Palm Beach Board properly exercised its discretion in its counting process and has judged those ballots which plaintiffs wish this court to again judge de novo.

All cases upon which plaintiffs rely were rendered upon mandamus prior to the modern statutory election system and remedial scheme enacted by the Legislature of the State of Florida in Section 102 of the Florida statutes, or Chapter 102 of the Florida Statutes. The local boards have been given broad discretion, which no court may overrule absent a clear abuse of discretion. The Palm Beach County Board did not abuse its discretion in its review and recounting process. Further, it acted in full compliance with the order of the Circuit Court in and for Palm Beach County. Having done so, plaintiffs are stopped from further challenge of its process and standards. It should be noted, however, that such process and standards were changed from the prior 1990 standards, perhaps contrary to 3 U.S.C. Sec. 5.

Furthermore, with respect to the standards utilized by the Board in its review and counting processes, the court finds that the standard utilized was in full compliance with the law, and review under another standard would not be authorized, thus creating a two-tier situation within one county as well as with respect to other counties.

The court notes that the attorney general of the State of Florida enunciated his opinion of the law with respect to this in a letter dated November 14, 2000 to the Hon. Charles E. Burton, chair of the Palm Beach County Canvassing Board, which in part is as follows:

> A two-tier system would have the effect of treating voters differently depending upon what county they voted in. A voter in a county where a manual count was conducted would benefit from having a better chance of having his or her vote actually counted than a voter in a county where a hand count was halted. As the state's chief legal officer, I feel a duty to warn that if the final certified total for balloting in the State of Florida includes figures generated from this two-tier system of differing behavior by official canvassing boards, the state will incur a legal jeopardy under both the United States and State Constitutions. This legal jeopardy could potentially lead Florida to having all of its votes, in effect, disqualified, and this state being barred from the Electoral College's selection of a president.

The court finds further that the Nassau County Canvassing Board did not abuse its discretion in its certification of Nassau County's voting results. Such actions were not void or illegal and it was done within the proper exercise of its discretion upon adequate and reasonable public notice.

Further, this court would further conclude and find that the properly stated cause of action under section 102.168 of the Florida Statutes to contest a statewide federal election, the plaintiff would necessarily have to place an issue and seek as a remedy with the attendant burden of proof a review and recount of all ballots in all the counties in this state with respect to the particular alleged irregularity or inaccuracy in the balloting or counting processes alleged to have occurred.

As recently stated by Judge Klein, with the concurrence of Chief Judge Warner in the Fourth District Court of Appeal case of *Fladell v. Palm Beach Canvassing Board* [No. 4D00–4145 (November 27, 2000)(Klein, J. dissenting)], section 102.168 provides in subsection 1 that the certification of election may be contested for presidential elections., Section 103.011 provides that "the Department of State shall certify, as elected the presidential electors of the candidates for president and vice president who receive the highest number of votes."

There is in this type of election one statewide election and one certification. Palm Beach County did not elect any person as a presidential elector, but rather the election was a winner-take-all proposition dependent on the statewide vote.

Finally, for the purpose of expedition due to the exigencies surrounding these proceedings, this court will deny those portions of the pending motions to dismiss of the various parties herein not affected by or ruled upon in these findings and conclusions with those portions consisting solely of matters of law being reviewable upon such denial.

In conclusion, the court finds that the plaintiffs have failed to carry the requisite burden of proof and judgment shall be and hereby is entered that plaintiffs shall take nothing by this action and the defendants may go hence without day.

All ballots in the custody of the clerk of this court shall remain pending review.

C. *Gore v. Harris* before the Florida Supreme Court

Vice President Gore appealed the unfavorable ruling he had received from the trial court of Judge Sauls in the case of *Gore v. Harris* to the Florida Supreme Court. The higher court issued its ruling, printed below, on December 8 and overturned the lower court ruling. The Florida Supreme Court, in a vote of 4 to 3, ordered that manual recounts be conducted in every Florida county and then added several hundred votes that had already been counted to Gore's total. One day later, the U.S. Supreme Court issued an injunction stopping the recounts pending its decision on an appeal of the Florida court ruling. The U.S. Supreme Court overturned the Florida court ruling on December 12.

Supreme Court of Florida
No. SC00–243
Albert Gore, Jr., and Joseph I. Lieberman, Appellants,
v.
Katherine Harris, as Secretary, ETC., ET AL., Appellees
December 8, 2000

PER CURIAM.

We have for review a final judgment of a Leon County trial court certified by the First District Court of Appeal as being of great public importance and requiring immediate resolution by this Court. We have jurisdiction... the final judgment under review denies all relief requested by appellants Albert Gore, Jr. and Joseph I. Lieberman, the Democratic candidates for President and Vice President of the United States, in their complaint contesting the certification of the state results in the November 7, 2000, presidential election. Although we find that the appellants are entitled to reversal in part of the trial court's order and are entitled to a manual count of the Miami-Dade county undervote, we agree with the appellees that the ultimate relief would require a counting of the legal votes contained within the undervotes in all counties where the undervote has not been subjected to a manual tabulation. Accordingly, we reverse and remand for proceedings consistent with this opinion.

I. BACKGROUND

On November 26, 2000, the Florida Election Canvassing Commission... certifies the results of the election and declared Governor George W. Bush and Richard Cheney, the Republican candidates for President and Vice President, the winner of Florida's electoral votes. The November 26, 2000, certified results shows a 537-vote margin in favor of Bush. On November 27, pursuant to the legislatively enacted "contest" provisions, Gore filed a complaint in Leon County Circuit Court, contesting the certification on the grounds that the results certified by the Canvassing Commission included "a number of illegal votes" and failed to include "a number of legal votes sufficient to change or place in doubt the result of the election."

Pursuant to the legislative scheme providing for an "immediate hearing" in a contest action, the trial court held a two-day evidentiary hearing on December 2 and 3, 2000, and on December 4, 2000, made an oral statement in open court denying all relief and entered a final judgment adopting the oral statement. The trial court did not reference any of the testimony adduced in the two-day evidentiary hearing, other than to summarily state that the plaintiffs failed to meet their burden of proof. Gore appealed to the First District Court of Appeal, which certified the judgment to this Court.

The appellants' election contest is based on five instances where the official results certified involved either the rejection of a number of legal votes or the receipt of a number of illegal votes. These five instances, as summarized by appellants' brief, are as follows:

The rejection of 215 net votes for Gore identified in a manual count by the Palm Beach Canvassing Board as reflecting the clear intent of the voters;

The rejection of 168 net votes for Gore, identified in the partial recount by the Miami-Dade County Canvassing Board.

The receipt and certification after Thanksgiving of the election night returns from Nassau County, instead of the statutorily mandated machine recount tabulation, in violation of section 102.14, Florida Statutes, resulting in an additional 51 net votes for Bush.

The reject of an additional 3,300 votes in Palm Beach County, most of which Democrat observers identified as votes for Gore but which were not included in the Canvassing Board's certified results; and

The refusal to review approximately 9,000 Miami-Dade ballots, which the counting machine registered as non-votes and which have never been manually reviewed.

For the reasons stated in this opinion, we find that the trial court erred as a matter of law in not including (1) the 215 net votes for Gore identified by the Palm Beach County Canvassing Board and (2) in not including the 168 net votes for Gore identified in a partial recount by the Miami-Dade County Canvassing Board. However, we find no error in the trial court's findings, which are mixed questions of law and fact, concerning (3) the Nassau County Canvassing Board and the (4) additional 3300 votes in Palm Beach County that the Canvassing Board did not find to be legal votes. Lastly, we find the trial court erred as a matter of law in (5) refusing to examine the approximately 9000 additional Miami-Dade ballots placed in evidence, which have never been examined manually.

II. APPLICABLE LAW

Article II, section I, clause 2 of the United States Constitution, grants the authority to select presidential electors "in such Manner as the Legislature thereof may direct." The Legislature of this State has place the decision for election of President of the United States, as well as every other elected office, in the citizens of this State through a statutory scheme. We consider these statutes cognizant of the federal grant of authority derived from the United States Constitution and derived from 3 U.S.C. sec 5 (1994) entitled "Determination of controversy as to appointment of electors." That section provides:

> If any State shall have provided, by laws, enacted prior to the day fixed for the appointment of the electors, for its final determination of any controversy or contest concerning the appointment of all or any of the electors of such State, by judicial or other methods or procedures, and such determination shall have been made at least six days before the time fixed for the meeting of the electors, such determination made pursuant to such law so existing on said day, and made at least six days prior to said time of meeting of the electors, shall be conclusive, and shall govern in the counting of the electoral

votes as provided in the constitution, and as hereinafter regulated, so far as the ascertainment of the electors appointed by such state is concerned.

This case today is controlled by the language set forth by the Legislature in section 102.168 Florida Statutes (2000). Indeed, an important part of the statutory election scheme is the State's provision for a contest process, section 102.168, which laws were enacted prior to the 2000 election. Although courts are, and should be, reluctant to interject themselves in essentially political controversies, the Legislature has directed in section 102.168 that an election contest shall be resolved in a judicial forum ... This court has recognized that the purpose of the election contest statute is "to afford a simple and speedy means of contesting election to stated offices." *Farmer v. Carson* 110 Fla. 245, 251, 148 So. 557, 559 (1933)....

Section 102.168(2) sets forth the procedures that must be followed in a contest proceeding, providing that the contestant file a complaint in the circuit court within ten days after certification of the election returns or five days after certification following a protest pursuant to section 102.166 (1), Florida Statutes (2000), whichever occurs later. Section 102.168(3) outlines the grounds for contesting an election and includes: "receipt of a number of illegal votes or rejection of a number of legal votes sufficient to change or place in doubt the result of the election." Finally, section 102.168(8) authorizes the circuit court judge to "fashion such orders as he or she deems necessary to ensure that each allegation in the complaint is investigated, examined, or checked, to prevent or correct any alleged wrong, and to provide any relief appropriate under the circumstances."

III. ORDER ON REVIEW

Vice President Gore claims that the trial court erred in the following three ways: (1) The trial court held that an election contest proceeding was essentially an appellate proceeding where the County Canvassing Board's decision must be reviewed with an "abuse of discretion," rather than "de novo," standard of review; (2) The court held that in a contest proceeding in a statewide election a court must review all the ballots cast throughout the state, not just the contested ballots; and (3) The court failed to apply the legal standard for relief expressly set forth in section 102.168(3).

A. The Trial Court's Standard of Review

The Florida election Code sets forth a two-pronged system for challenging vote returns and election procedures. The "protest" and "contest" provisions are distinct proceedings. A protest proceeding is filed with the County Canvassing Board and addresses the validity of the vote returns. The relief that may be granted includes a manual recount. The Canvassing Board is a neutral ministerial body...A contest proceeding, on the other hand, is filed in circuit court and addresses the validity of the election itself. Relief that may be granted is varied and can be extensive. No appellate relationship exits between a "protest" and a "contest"; a protest is not a prerequisite for a contest ... Moreover, the trial court in the contest action does not sit as an appellate court over the decisions of the Canvassing Board. Accordingly, while the Board's action concerning the elections process may constitute evidence in a contest proceeding, the Board's decisions are not to be accorded the highly deferential "abuse of discretion" standard of review during a contest proceeding.

In the present case, the trial court erroneously applied an appellate abuse of discretion standard to the Boards' decisions...In applying the abuse of discretion standard of review to the Boards' actions, the trial court relinquished an improper degree of its own authority to the Boards. This was error.

B. Must All the Ballots Be Counted Statewide?

Appellees contend that even if a count of the undervotes in Miami-Dade were appropriate, section 102.168, Florida Statutes (2000), requires a count of all votes in Miami-Dade County and the entire state as opposed to a selected number of votes challenged. However, the plain language of section 102.168 refutes Appellees' argument.

Section 102.168(2) sets forth the procedures that must be followed in a contest proceeding, providing that the contestant file a complaint in the circuit court within ten days after certification of the election returns or five days after certification following a protest pursuant to section 102.166(1), whichever occurs later. Section 102.168(3)(c) outlines the grounds for contesting an election, and includes: "Receipt of a number of illegal votes or rejection of a number of legal votes sufficient to change or place in doubt the result of the election." ... Finally, section 102.168(8) authorizes the circuit court judge to "fashion such orders as he ... deems necessary to ensure that each allegation in the complaint is investigated, examined, or checked, to prevent or correct any alleged wrong, and to provide any relief appropriate under the circumstances."

As explained above, section 102.168(3)(c) explicitly contemplates contests based upon a "rejection of a number of legal votes sufficient to change the outcome of an election." Logic dictates that to bring a challenge based upon the rejection of a specific number of legal votes, under section 102.168(3)(c), the contestant must establish the "number of legal votes" which the county canvassing board failed to count. This number, therefore, under the plain language of the statute, is limited to the votes identified and challenged under section 102.168(3)(c), rather than the entire county. Moreover, counting uncontested votes in a contest would be irrelevant to a determination of whether certain uncounted votes constitute legal votes that have been rejected.

On the other hand, a consideration of "legal votes" contained in the category of "undervotes" identified statewide may be properly considered as evidence in the contest proceedings and, more importantly, in fashioning any relief.

We do agree, however, that it is absolutely essential in this proceeding and to any final decision, that a manual recount be conducted for all legal votes in this State, not only in Miami-Dade County, but in all Florida counties where there was an undervote, and hence a concern that not every citizen's vote was counted. This election should be determined by a careful examination of the votes of Florida's citizens and not by strategies extraneous to the voting process. This essential principle, that the outcome of elections be determined by the will of the voters, forms the foundation of the election code enacted by the Florida Legislature and has been consistently applied by this Court in resolving election disputes.

We are dealing with the essence of the structure of our democratic society; with the interrelationship, within that framework, between the United States Constitution and the statutory scheme established pursuant to that authority by the Florida Legislature. Pursuant to the authority extended by the United States Constitution,... the Legislature has expressly vested in the citizens of the State of Florida the right to select the electors for President and Vice President of the United States:... In so doing, the Legislature has placed the election of presidential electors squarely in the hands of Florida's voters under the general election laws of Florida. Hence, the Legislature has expressly recognized the will of the people of Florida as the guiding principle for the selection of all elected officials in the State of Florida, whether they be county commissioners or presidential electors.

When an election contest is filed under section 102.168, Florida Statutes (2000), the contest statute charges trial courts to:

> Fashion such orders as he or she deems necessary to ensure that each allegation in the complaint is investigated, examined, or checked, to prevent or correct any alleged wrong, and to provide any relief appropriate under such circumstances.

Through this statute, the Legislature has granted trial courts broad authority to resolve election disputes and fashion appropriate relief. In turn, this Court, consistent with legislative policy, has pointed to the "will of the voters" as the primary guiding principle to be utilized by trial courts in resolving election contests ...

The demonstrated problem of not counting legal votes inures to any county utilizing a counting system which results in undervotes and "no registered vote" ballots. In a countywide election, one would not simply examine such categories of ballots from a single precinct to insure the reliability and integrity of the countywide vote. Similarity, in this statewide election, review should not be limited to less than all counties whose tabulation has resulted in such categories of ballots. Relief would not be [appropriate] "under the circumstances" if it failed to address the "otherwise valid exercise of the right of a citizen to vote" of all those citizens of this State who, being similarly situated, have had their legal votes rejected. This is particularly important in a Presidential election, which implicates both State and uniquely important national interests. The contestant here satisfied the threshold requirement by demonstrating that, upon consideration of the thousands of undervote or "no registered vote" ballots presented, the number of legal votes therein were sufficient to at least place in doubt the result of the election. However, a final decision as to the result of the statewide election should only be determined upon consideration of the legal votes contained within the undervote or "no registered vote" ballots of all Florida counties, as well as the legal votes already tabulated.

C. The Plaintiff's Burden of Proof

It is immediately apparent... that the trial court failed to apply the statutory standard and instead applied an improper standard in determining the contestant's burden under the contest statute. The trial court... overlooks and fails to recognize the specific and material changes to the statute which the Legislature made in 1999 that control these proceedings. While the earlier version, like the current version, provided that a contestant shall file a complaint setting forth "the grounds on which the contestant intends to establish his or her right to such office or set aside the result of the election," the prior version did not specifically enumerate the "grounds for contesting an election under this section." Those grounds, as contained in the 1999 statute, now explicitly include, in subsection 9 (c), the "receipt of a number of illegal votes or rejection of a number of legal votes sufficient to change or place in doubt the result of the election." Assuming that reasonableness is an implied component of such a doubt standard, the determination of whether the plaintiff has met his or her burden of proof to establish that the result of an election is in doubt is far different standard that the "reasonable probability" standard, which was applicable to contests under the old version of the statute, and erroneously applied and articulated as a "preponderance of a reasonable probability" standard by the trial court here. A person authorized to contest an election is required to demonstrate that there have been legal votes cast in the election that have not been counted (here characterized as "undervotes" or "no vote registered" ballots) and that available data shows that a number of legal votes would be recovered from the entire pool of the subject ballots which, if cast for the unsuccessful candidate, would change or place in doubt the result of the election. Here, there has been an undisputed showing of the existence of some 9,000 "undervotes" in an election contest decided by a margin measured in the hundreds. Thus a threshold contest showing that the result of an election has been placed in doubt, warranting a manual count of all undervotes or "no vote registered" ballots has been made.

IV. LEGAL VOTES

Having first identified the proper standard of review, we turn now to the allegations of the complaint filed in this election contest. To test the sufficiency of those allegations and the proof, it is essential to understand what, under Florida law, may constitute a "legal vote," and what constitutes rejection of such vote.

Section 101.5614(5), Florida Statutes (2000), provides that "no vote shall be declared invalid or void if there is a clear indication of the intent of the voter as determined by the canvassing board." Section 101.5614(6) provides, conversely, that any vote in which the board cannot discern the intent of the voter must be discarded. Lastly, section 102.166(7)(b) provides that, "if a counting team is unable to determine a voter's intent in casting a ballot, the ballot shall be presented to the county canvassing board for it to determine the voter's intent." This legislative emphasis on discerning the voter's intent is mirrored in the case law of this State, and in that of other states.

This Court has repeatedly held, in accordance with the statutory law of this State, that so long as the voter's intent may be discerned from the ballot, the vote constitutes a "legal vote" that should be counted...As the State has moved toward electronic voting, nothing in this evolution has diminished the long-standing case law and statutory law that the intent of the voter is of paramount concern and should always be given effect if the intent can be determined....

Accordingly, we conclude that a legal vote is one in which there is a "clear indication of the intent of the voter"...We next address whether the term "rejection" used in section 102.168(3)(c) includes instances where the County Canvassing Board has not counted legal votes. Looking at the statutory scheme as a whole, it appears that the term "rejected" does encompass votes that may exist but have not been counted. As explained above, in 1999, the Legislature substantially revised the contest provision of the Election Code...One of the revisions to the contest provision included the codification of the grounds for contesting an election...The House Bill noted that one of the grounds for contesting an election at common law was the "Receipt of a number of illegal votes or rejection of a number of legal votes sufficient to change or place in doubt the result of the election." As noted above, the contest statute ultimately contained this ground for contesting the results of an election.

To further determine the meaning of the term "rejection," as used by the Legislature, we may also look to Florida case law. In State ex rel. *Clark v. Klingensmith,* 121 Fla. 297, 163 So. 704 (1935)...this Court concluded that "the rejection of votes from legal voters, not brought about by fraud, and not of such magnitude as to demonstrate that a free expression of the popular will has been suppressed," is insufficient to void an election, "at least unless it be shown that the votes rejected would have changed the result"... Therefore, the Court appears to have equated a "rejection" of legal votes with the failure to count legal votes, while at the same time recognizing that a sufficient number of such votes must have been rejected to merit relief. This notion of "rejected" is also in accordance with the common understanding of rejection of votes as used in other election cases. In discussing the facts in *Roudebush v. Hartke,* 405 U.S. 15, (1972), the United States Supreme Court explained:

> If a recount is conducted in any county, the voting machine tallies are checked and the sealed bags containing the paper ballots are opened. The recount commission may make new and independent determinations as to which ballots shall be counted. In other words, it may reject ballots initially counted and count ballots initially rejected....

This also comports with cases from other jurisdictions that suggest that a legal vote will be deemed to have been "rejected" where a voting machine fails to count a ballot, which has been executed in substantial compliance with applicable voting requirements and reflects, the clear intent of the voter to express a definite choice.

Here, then, it is apparent that there have been sufficient allegations made which, if analyzed pursuant to the proper standard, compel the conclusion that legal votes sufficient to place in doubt the election results have been rejected in this case.

V. THIS CASE

We must review the instances in which appellants claim that they established that legal votes were rejected or illegal voters were included in the certifications.

The refusal to review approximately 9,000 additional Miami-Dade Ballots, which the counting machine registered as non-vote and which have never been manually reviewed.

On November 9, 2000, the Miami-Dade County Democratic Party made a timely request under section 102.166 for a manual recount. After first deciding against a full manual recount, the Miami-Dade County Canvassing Board voted to begin a manual recount of all ballots cast in Miami-Dade County for the Presidential election, and the manual recount began on November 19, 2000. On November 21, 2000, this Court issued its decision in *Palm Beach Canvassing Board v. Harris,* stating that amended certifications must be filed by 5 P.M. on Sunday, November 26, 2000. The Miami-Dade Canvassing Board thereafter suspended the manual recount and voted to use the election returns previously compiled. Earlier that day, the panel had decided to limit its recount to the 10,750 "undervotes," that is, ballots on which no vote was registered by counting machines. The Board's stated reason for the suspension of the manual recount was that it would be impossible to complete the recount before the deadline set forth by this Court. At the time that the Board suspended the recount, approximately 9,000 of the

10,750 undervotes had not yet been reviewed. In the two days that the Board had counted ballots, the Board identified 436 additional legal votes (from 20 percent of the precincts, representing 15 percent of the votes cast) which the machines failed to register, resulting in a net vote of 168 votes for Gore. Nonetheless, in addition to suspending further recounting, the Board also determined that it would not include the additional 436 votes that had been tabulated in its partially completed recount.

Specifically as to Miami-Dade County, the trial court found:

> Although the record shows voter error, and/or less than total accuracy in regard the punchcard voting devices utilized in Miami-Dade and Palm Beach Counties, which these counties have been aware of for many years, these balloting and counting problems cannot support or effect any recounting necessity with respect to Miami-Dade County, absent the establishment of a reasonable probability that the statewide election result would be different, which has not been established in this case.

The Court further finds that the Dade Canvassing Board did not abuse its discretion in any of its decisions in its review in recounting processes. This statement is incorrect as a matter of law. In fact, as the Third District determined in *Miami-Dade County Democratic Party v. Miami-Dade County Canvassing Board*, 25 Fla. L. Weekly D2723 (Fla. 3d DCA Nov. 22, 2000), the results of the sample manual recount and the actual commencement of the full manual recount triggered the Canvassing Board's "mandatory obligation to recount all of the ballots in the county." In addition, the circuit court was bound at the time it ruled to follow this appellate decision. This Court has determined the decisions of the district courts of appeal represent the law of this State unless and until they are overruled by this Court, and therefore, in the absence of inter-district conflict, district court decisions bind all Florida trial courts.

However, regardless of this error, we again note the focus of the trial court's inquiry in an election contest authorized by the Legislature pursuant to the express statutory provisions of section 102.168 is not appellate review to determine whether the Board properly or improperly failed to complete the manual recount. Rather, as expressly set out in section 102.168, the court's responsibility is to determine whether "legal votes" were rejected sufficient to change or place in doubt the results of the election. Without ever examining or investigating the ballots that the machine failed to register as a vote, the trial court in this case concluded that there was no probability of a different result. First, as we stated the trial court erred as a matter of law in utilizing the wrong standard. Second, and more importantly, by failing to examine the specifically identified group of uncounted ballots that is claimed to contain the rejected legal votes, the trial court has refused evidence that they have relied on to establish their ultimate entitlement to relief. The trial court has presented the plaintiffs with the ultimate Catch-22, acceptance of the only evidence that will resolve the issue but a refusal to examine such evidence. We also note that whether or not the Board could have completed the manual recount by November 26, 2000, or whether the Board should have fulfilled its responsibility and completed the full manual recount, the fact remains that the manual recount was not completed through no fault of the Appellant.

3300 Votes in Palm Beach County

Appellants also contend that the trial court erred in finding that they failed to satisfy their burden of proof with respect to the 3300 votes that the Palm Beach County Canvassing Board reviewed and concluded did not constitute "legal votes" pursuant to section 102.168(3)(c). However, unlike the approximately 9000 ballots in Miami-Dade that the County Canvassing Board did not manually recount, the Palm Beach County Canvassing Board did complete a manual recount of these 3300 votes and concluded that, because the intent of the voter in these 3300 ballots was not discernible, these ballots did not constitute "legal votes"...We find no error in the trial court's determination that appellants did not establish a preliminary basis for relief as to the 3300 Palm Beach county votes because the appellants have failed to make a threshold showing that "legal votes" were rejected. Although the protest and contest proceedings are separate statutory provisions, when a manual count of ballots has been conducted by the Canvassing Board pursuant to section 102.166, the circuit court is a contest proceeding does not have the obligation de novo to simply repeat an otherwise-proper manual count of the ballots. As state above, although the trial court does not review a Canvassing Board's actions under an abuse of discretion standard, the Canvassing Board's actions may constitute evidence that a ballot does or does not qualify as a legal vote. Because the appellants have failed to introduce any evidence to refute the Canvassing Board's determination that the 3300 ballots did not constitute "legal votes," we affirm the trial court's holding as to this issue. This reflects the proper interaction of section 102.166 governing protests and manual recounts and section 102.168 governing election contests.

Whether the vote totals must be revised to include the legal votes actually identified in the Palm Beach County and Miami-Dade County manual recounts?

Appellants claim that the certified vote totals must be amended to include legal votes identified as being for one of the presidential candidates by the County Canvassing Boards of Palm Beach County and Miami-Dade during their manual recounts. After working for a period of many days, the Palm Beach County Canvassing Board conducted and completed a full manual recount in which the Board identified a net gain of 215 votes for Gore. As discussed above, the Miami-Dade Canvassing Board commenced a manual recount but did not complete the recount. During the partial recount it identified additional legal votes, of which 302 were for Gore and 134 were for Bush, resulting in a net gain of 168 votes for Gore.

The circuit court concluded as to Palm Beach County that there was not any authority to include any returns submitted past the deadline established by the Florida Supreme Court in this election." This conclusion was erroneous as a matter of law. The deadline of November 26, 2000, at 5 P.M. was established in order to allow maximum time for contests pursuant to section 102.168. The deadline was never intended to prohibit legal votes identified after that date through ongoing manual recounts to be excluded from the statewide official results in the Election Canvassing Commission's certification of the results of a recount of less than all of a county's ballots. In the same decision we held that all returns must be considered unless their filing would effectively prevent an election contest from being conducted or endanger the counting of Florida's electors in the presidential election. As to Miami-Dade County, in light of our holding that the circuit court should have counted the undervote, we agree with appellants that the partial recount results should also be included in the total legal votes for this election. Because the county canvassing boards identified legal votes and these votes could change the outcome of the election, we hold that the trial court erred in rejecting the legal votes identified in the Miami-Dade County and Palm Beach County manual recounts. These votes must be included in the certified vote totals. We find that appellants did not establish that the Nassau County Canvassing Board acted improperly.

CONCLUSION

Through no fault of appellants, a lawfully commenced manual recount in Dade County was never completed and recounts that were completed were not counted. Without examining or investigating the ballots that were not counted by the machines, the trial court concluded there was no reasonable probability of a different result. However, the proper standard required by section 102.168 was whether the results of the election were placed in doubt. On this record there can be no question that there are legal votes within the 9000 uncounted votes sufficient to place the results of this election in doubt. We know this not only by evidence of statistical analysis but also by the actual experience of recounts conducted. The votes for each candidate that have been counted are separated by no more than approximately 500 votes and may be separated by as little as approximately 100 votes. Thousands of uncounted votes could obviously make a difference. Although in all elections the Legislature and the courts have recognized that the voter's intent is paramount, in close elections the necessity for counting all legal votes becomes critical. However, the need for accuracy must be weighed against the need for finality. The need for prompt resolution and finality is especially critical in presidential elections where there is an outside deadline established by federal law. Notwithstanding, consistent with the legislative mandate and our precedent, although the time constraints are limited, we must do everything required by law to ensure that legal votes that have not been counted are included in the final results. As recognized by the Florida House of Representatives Committee on Election Reform 1997 Interim Project on election Contests and Recounts:

All election contests and recounts can be traced to either an actual failure in the election system or a perception that the system has failed. Public confidence in the election process is essential to our democracy. If the voter cannot be assured of an accurate vote count, or an election unspoiled by fraud, they will not have faith in other parts of the political process. Nonetheless, it is inevitable that legitimate doubts of the validity and accuracy of election outcomes will arise. It is crucial, therefore, to have clearly defined legal mechanisms for contesting or recounting election results.

Only by examining the contested ballots, which are evidence in the election contest, can a meaningful and final determination in this election contest be made. As stated above, one of the provisions of the contest statute, section 102.168(8), provides that the circuit court judge may "fashion such orders as he... deems necessary to ensure that each allegation in the complaint is investigated, examined or checked, to prevent any alleged wrong, and to provide any relief appropriate under such circumstances."

In addition to the relief requested by appellants to count the Miami-Dade undervote, claims have been made by the various Appellees and intervenors that because this is a statewide election, statewide remedies would be called for. As we discussed in this opinion, we agree. While we recognize that time is desperately short, we cannot in good faith ignore both the appellant's right to relief as to their claims concerning the uncounted votes in Miami-Dade County nor can we ignore the correctness of the assertions that any analysis and ultimate remedy should be made on a statewide basis.

We note that contest statutes vest broad discretion in the circuit court to "provide any relief appropriate under the circumstances." Section 102.168(5). Moreover, because venue of an election contest that covers more than one county lies in Leon County,... the circuit court has jurisdiction, as part of the relief it orders, to order the Supervisor of Elections and the Canvassing Boards, as well as the necessary public officials, in all counties that have not conducted a manual recount or tabulation of the undervotes in this election to do so forthwith, said tabulation to take place in the individual counties where the ballots are located.

Accordingly, for the reasons stated in this opinion, we reverse the final judgment of the trial court dated December 4, 2000, and remand this cause for the circuit court to immediately tabulate by hand the approximate 9000 Miami-Dade ballots, which the counting machine registered as non-votes, but which have never been manually reviewed, and for other relief that may thereafter appear appropriate. The circuit court is directed to enter such orders as are necessary to add any legal votes to the total statewide certifications and to enter any orders necessary to ensure the inclusion of the additional legal votes for Gore in Palm Beach County, and the 168 additional legal votes from Miami-Dade County.

Because time is of the essence, the circuit court shall commence the tabulation of the Miami-Dade ballots immediately. The circuit court is authorized, in accordance with the provisions of section 102.168(8), to be assisted by the Leon County Supervisor of elections or its sworn designees. Moreover, since time is also of the essence in any statewide relief that the circuit court must consider, any further statewide relief should also be ordered forthwith and simultaneously with the manual tabulation of the Miami-Dade undervotes.

In tabulating the ballots and in making a determination of what is a "legal" vote, the standards to be employed is that established by the Legislature in our election Code which is that the vote shall be counted as a "legal" vote if there is "clear indication of the intent of the voter. Section 101.5614(5), Florida Statutes (2000).

D. Constitutional Provisions Relating to Presidential Elections

There are several provisions in the U.S. Constitution relating to presidential elections. Article II creates the presidency, lists its powers, the qualifications persons must have for holding the office, and prescribes the means by which presidents shall be elected. The most significant part of the election procedure is the existence of the Electoral College. The following language from Article II was contained in the original draft of the constitution but was repealed in 1804 with the ratification of the Twelfth Amendment. The Twelfth Amendment is also printed here. Two other constitutional amendments, numbers 14, which contains the equal protection clause used by the U.S. Supreme Court in the case of *Bush v. Gore,* and 23, which altered the composition of the Electoral College to provide the District of Columbia with three votes, are included here.

ARTICLE II.

Section 1. The executive Power shall be vested in a President of the United States of America. He shall hold his Office during the Term of four Years, and, together with the Vice President, chosen for the same Term, be elected as follows.

Each state shall appoint, in such Manner as the Legislature thereof may direct, a Number of Electors, equal to the whole Number of Senators and Representatives to which the State may be entitled in the Congress; but no Senator or Representative, or Person holding an Office of Trust or Profit under the United States, shall be appointed an Elector.

[The Electors shall meet in their respective States, and vote by Ballot for two Persons, of whom one at least shall not be an Inhabitant of the same State with themselves. And they shall make a List of all the Persons voted for, and the Number of Votes for each; which List they shall sign and certify, and transmit sealed to the Seat of Government of the United States, directed to the President of The Senate. The President of the Senate shall, in the Presence of the Senate and House of Representatives, open all the Certificates, and the Votes shall then be counted. The Person having the greatest Number of Votes shall be the President, if such Number be a Majority of the whole Number of Electors appointed; and if there be more than one who have such Majority, and have an equal Number of Votes, then the House of Representatives shall immediately chuse by Ballot one of them for President; and if no Person have a majority, then from the five highest on the List the Said House shall in like Manner chuse the President. But in chusing the President, the Votes shall be taken by States, the Representation from each State having one Vote; a quorum for this purpose shall consist of a Member or Members from two thirds of the States, and a Majority of all the States shall be necessary to a Choice. In every Case, after the Choice of the President, the Person having the greatest Number of Votes of the Electors shall be the Vice President. But if there should remain two or more who have equal Votes, the Senate shall chuse from them by Ballot the Vice President].*

The Congress may determine the Time of chusing the Electors, and the Day on which they shall give their Votes; which Day shall be the same throughout the United States.

* The paragraph in brackets was superseded by the Twelfth Amendment.

AMENDMENT XII (1804)

The Electors shall meet in their respective states and vote by ballot for President and Vice-President, one of whom, at least, shall not be an inhabitant of the same state with themselves; they shall name in their ballots the person voted for as President, and in distinct ballots, the person voted for as Vice-President, and they shall make distinct lists of all persons voted for as President, and of all persons voted for as Vice-President, and of the number of votes for each, which lists they shall sign and certify, and transmit sealed to the seat of the government of the United States, direct to the President of the Senate;—The President of the Senate shall, in the presence of the Senate and House of Representatives, open all the certificates and the votes shall then be counted;—The person having the greatest number of votes for President, shall be the President, it such number be a majority of the whole number of electors appointed; and if no person have such majority, then from the persons having the highest numbers not exceeding three on the list of those voted for as President, the House of Representatives shall choose immediately, by ballot, the President. But in choosing the President, the votes shall be taken by states, the representation from each state having one vote; a quorum for this purpose shall consist of a member or members from two-thirds of the states, and a majority of all the states shall be necessary to a choice. [And if the House of Representatives shall not choose a President whenever the right of choice shall devolve upon them before the fourth day of March next following, then the Vice-President shall act as President, as in the case of the death or other constitutional disability of the President.]** The person having the greatest number of votes as Vice-President, shall be the Vice-President, if such number be a majority of the whole number of electors appointed, and if no person have a majority, then from the two highest numbers on the list, the Senate shall choose the Vice-President; a quorum for the purpose shall consist of two-thirds of the whole number of senators, and a majority of the whole number shall be necessary to a choice. But no person constitutionally ineligible to the office of President shall be eligible to that of Vice-President of the United States.

** The sentence in brackets was superseded by the Twentieth Amendment which changed the fourth of March to the twentieth of January.

AMENDMENT XIV (1868)

Section 1. all persons born or naturalized in the United States and subject to the jurisdiction thereof, are citizens of the United States and of the State wherein they reside. No state shall make or enforce any law which shall abridge the privileges or immunities of citizens of the United States, or shall any State deprive any person of life, liberty, or property, without due process of law; nor deny to any person within its jurisdiction the equal protection of the laws.

AMENDMENT XXIII (1961)

Section 1. The District constituting the seat of Government of the United States shall appoint in such manner as the Congress may direct;

A number of electors of President and Vice President equal to the whole number of Senators and Representatives in Congress to which the District would be entitled if it were a State, but in no event more than the least populous State; they shall be considered, for the purposes of the election of President and Vice President, to be electors appointed by a State; and they shall meet in the District and perform such duties as provided by the twelfth article of amendment.

E. Selected Provisions of Federal Law Relating to Presidential Elections

While the constitution places the responsibility for conducting elections, even those for president, with the states, Congress does have the right to determine such matters as the time, place, and manner of elections and to decide on the resolution of disputed choices of state electors. Several provisions of the United States Code were relevant to the Florida vote controversy. Those provisions are printed below.

UNITED STATES CODE

TITLE 3—THE PRESIDENT

Chapter 1: Presidential Elections and Vacancies.

Section 1. Time of appointing electors.

The electors of President and Vice President shall be appointed, in each state, on the Tuesday next after the first Monday in November, in every fourth year succeeding every election of a President and Vice President.

Section 2. Failure to make choice on prescribed day.

Whenever any State has held an election for the purpose of choosing electors, and has failed to make a choice on the day prescribed by law, the electors may be appointed on a subsequent day in such a manner as the legislature of such State may direct.

Section 3. Number of electors.

The number of electors shall be equal to the number of Senators and Representatives to which the several States are by law entitled at the time when the President and Vice President to be chosen come into office; except, that where no appointment of Representatives has been made after any enumeration, at the time of choosing electors, the number of electors shall be according to the then existing appointment of Senators and Representatives.

Section 5. Determination of controversy as to appointment of electors.

If any State shall have provided, by laws enacted prior to the day fixed for the appointment of electors, for its final determination of any controversy or contest concerning the appointment of all or any of the electors of such State, by judicial or other methods or procedures, and such determination shall have been made at least six days before the time fixed for the meeting of the electors, such determination made pursuant to such law so existing on said day, and made at least six days prior to said time of meeting of the electors, shall be conclusive, and shall govern in the counting of the electoral votes as provided in the Constitution, and as hereinafter regulated, so far as the ascertainment of the electors appointed by such State is concerned.

Section 6. Credentials of electors; transmission to Archivist of the United States and to Congress; public inspection.

It shall be the duty of the executive of each State, as soon as practicable after the conclusion of the appointment of the electors in such State by the final ascertainment, under and in pursuance of the laws of such State providing for such ascertainment, to communicate by registered mail under the seal of the State to the Archivist of the United States a certificate of such ascertainment of the electors appointed, setting forth the names of such electors and the canvass or other ascertainment under the laws of such State of the number of votes given or cast for each person for whose appointment any and all votes have been given or cast; and it shall also thereupon be the duty of the executive of each State to deliver the electors of such State, on or before the day on which they are required by section 7 of this title to meet, six duplicate-originals of the same certificate under the seal of the State; and if there shall have been any final determination in a State in the manner provided for by law of a controversy or contest concerning the appointment of all or any of the electors of such State, it shall be the duty of the executive of such State, as soon as practicable after such determination, to communicate under the seal of the State to the Archivist of the United States a certificate of such determination in form and manner as the same shall have been made; and the certificate or certificates so received by the Archivist of the United States shall be preserved by him for one year and shall be part of the public records of his office and shall be open to public inspection; and the Archivist of the United States at the first meeting of Congress thereafter shall transmit to the two Houses of Congress copies in full of each and every such certificate as received at the National Archives and Records Administration.

Section 7. Meeting and vote of electors.

The electors of President and Vice President of each State shall meet and give their votes on the first Monday after the second Wednesday in December next following their appointment at such place in each State as the legislature of such State shall direct.

Section 15. Counting electoral votes in Congress.

Congress shall be in session on the sixth day of January succeeding every meeting of the electors. The Senate and House of Representatives shall meet in the Hall of the House of Representatives at the hour of 1 o'clock in the afternoon on that day, and the President of the Senate shall be their presiding officer. Two tellers shall be previously appointed on the part of the Senate and two on the part of the House of Representatives, to whom shall be handed, as they are opened by the President of the Senate, all the certificates and papers purporting to be certificates of the electoral votes, which certificates and papers shall be opened, presented, and acted upon in the alphabetical order of the States, beginning with the letter A; and said tellers, having then read the same in the presence and hearing of the two Houses, shall make a list of the votes as they shall appear from the said certificates; and the votes having been ascertained and counted according to the rules in this subchapter provided, the result of the same shall be delivered to the President of the Senate, who shall thereupon announce the state of the vote, which announcement shall be deemed a sufficient declaration of the persons, if any, elected President and Vice President of the United States, and, together with a list of the votes, be entered on the Journals of the two Houses. Upon such reading of any certificate or paper, the President of the Senate shall call for objections, if any. Every objection shall be made in writing, and shall state clearly and concisely, and without argument, the ground thereof, and shall be signed by at least one Senator and one Member of the House of Representatives before the same shall be received. When all objections so made to any vote or paper from a

State shall have been received and read, the Senate shall thereupon withdraw, and such objections shall be submitted to the Senate for its decision; and the Speaker of the House of Representatives shall, in like manner, submit such objections to the House of Representatives for its decision; and no electoral vote or votes from any State which shall have been regularly given by electors whose appointment has been lawfully certified to according to section 6 of this title from which but one return has been received shall be rejected, but the two Houses concurrently may reject the vote or votes when they agree that such vote or votes have not been so regularly given by electors whose appointment has been so certified. If more than one return or paper purporting to be a return from a State shall have been received by the President of the Senate, those votes, and those only, shall be counted which shall have been regularly given by electors who are shown by the determination mentioned in section 5 of this title to have been appointed, if the determination in said section provided for shall have been made, or by such successors or substitutes, in case of a vacancy in the board of electors so ascertained, as have been appointed to fill such vacancy in the mode provided by the laws of the State; but in case there shall arise the question which of two or more of such State authorities determining what electors have been appointed, as mentioned in section 5 of this title, is the lawful tribunal of such state, the votes regularly given of those electors, and those only, of such state shall be counted whose title as electors the two Houses, acting separately, shall concurrently decide is supported by the decision of such State so authorized by its law; and in such case of more than one return or paper purporting to be a return from a State, if there shall have been no such determination of the question in the State aforesaid, then those votes, and those only, shall be counted which the two Houses shall concurrently decide were cast by lawful electors appointed in accordance with the laws of the State, unless the two Houses, acting separately, shall concurrently decide such votes not to be the lawful votes of the legally appointed electors of such State. But if the two Houses shall disagree in respect of the counting of such votes, then, and in that case, the votes of the electors whose appointment shall have been certified by the executive of the State, under the seal thereof, shall be counted. When the two Houses have voted, they shall immediately again meet, and the presiding officer shall then announce the decision of the questions submitted. No votes or papers from any other State shall be acted upon until the objections previously made to the votes or papers from any State shall have been finally disposed of.

F. Provisions of Florida Election Law Cited in the U.S. Supreme Court Case of *Bush v. Gore*

All American elections, even ones for choosing members of the Electoral College, are conducted by the states. This section lists the various components of the Florida election laws that were relevant in the vote controversy and in the rulings made by the various courts.

SECTION 101.015 STANDARDS FOR VOTING SYSTEMS.

(Sections 1–3 only)

(1) The Department of State shall adopt rules which establish minimum standards for hardware and software for electronic and electromechanical voting systems. Such rules shall contain standards for:

(a) Functional requirements;

(b) Performance levels;

(c) Physical and design characteristics;

(d) Documentation requirements; and

(e) Evaluation criteria.

(2) Each odd-numbered year the Department of State shall review the rules governing standards and certification of voting systems to determine the adequacy and effectiveness of such rules in assuring that elections are fair and impartial.

(3) The Department of State shall adopt rules to achieve and maintain the maximum degree of correctness, impartiality, and efficiency of the procedures of voting, including write-in voting, and of counting, tabulating, and recording votes by voting systems used in this state.

SECTION 101.151 SPECIFICATIONS FOR GENERAL ELECTION BALLOT.

(Section 4 only)

(4) the names of the candidates of the party which received the highest number of votes for Governor in the last election in which a Governor was elected shall be placed first under the heading for each office, together with an appropriate abbreviation of party name; the names of the candidates of the party which received the second highest vote for Governor shall be second under the heading for each office, together with an appropriate abbreviation of the party name.

SECTION 101.5614 CANVASS OF RETURNS.

(Section 5 only)

(5) If any ballot card of the type for which the offices and measures are not printed directly on the card is damaged or defective so that it cannot properly be counted by the automatic tabulating equipment, a true duplicate copy shall be made of the damaged ballot card in the presence of witnesses and substituted for the damaged ballot. Likewise, a duplicate ballot card shall be made of a defective ballot which shall not include the invalid votes. All duplicate ballot cards shall be clearly labeled "duplicate," bear a serial number which shall be recorded on the damaged or defective ballot card, and be counted in lieu of the damaged or defective ballot. If any ballot card of the type for which offices and measures are printed directly on the card is damaged or defective so that it cannot properly be counted by the automatic tabulating equipment, a true duplicate copy may be made of the damaged ballot card in the presence

of witnesses in the manner set forth above, or the valid votes on the damaged ballot card may be manually counted at the counting center by the canvassing board, whichever procedure is best suited to the system used. If any paper ballot is damaged or defective so that it cannot be counted properly by the automatic tabulating equipment, the ballot shall be counted manually at the counting center by the canvassing board. The totals for all such ballots or ballot cards counted manually shall be added to the totals for the several precincts or election districts. No vote shall be declared invalid or void if there is a clear indication of the intent of the vote as determined by the canvassing board. After duplicating a ballot, the defective ballot shall be placed in an envelope provided for that purpose and the duplicate ballot shall be tallied with the other ballots for that precinct.

SECTION 102.111 ELECTIONS CANVASSING COMMISSION.

(1) Immediately after certification of any election by the county canvassing board, the results shall be forwarded to the Department of State concerning the election of any federal or state officer. The Governor, the Secretary of State, and the Director of the Division of Elections shall be the Elections Canvassing Commission. The Elections Canvassing Commission shall, as soon as the official results are compiled from all counties, certify the returns of the election and determine and declare who has been elected for each office. In the event that any member of the Elections Canvassing Commission is unavailable to certify the returns of any election, such member shall be replaced by a substitute member of the Cabinet as determined by the Director of the Division of Elections. If the county returns are not received by the Department of State by 5 P.M. of the seventh day following an election, all missing counties shall be ignored, and the results shown by the returns on file shall be certified.

SECTION 102.112. DEADLINE FOR SUBMISSION OF COUNTY RETURNS TO THE DEPARTMENT OF STATE; PENALTIES.

(1) The county canvassing board or a majority thereof shall file the county returns for the election of a federal or state officer with the Department of State immediately after certification of the election results. Returns must be filed by 5 P.M. on the 7th day following the first primary and general election and by 3 P.M. on the 3rd day following the second primary. If the returns are not received by the department by the time specified, such returns may be ignored and the results on file at that time may be certified by the department.

SECTION 102.141 COUNTY CANVASSING BOARD; DUTIES.

Section 102.141(4) If the returns for any office reflect that a candidate was defeated or eliminated by one-half of a percent or less of the votes cast for such office, that a candidate for retention to a judicial office was retained or not retained by one-half of a percent or less of the votes cast on the question of retention, or that a measure appearing on the ballot was approved or rejected by one-half of a percent or less of the votes cast on such measure, the board responsible for certifying the results of the vote on such race or measure shall order a recount of the votes cast with respect to such office or measure. A recount need not be ordered with respect to the returns for any office, however if the candidate or candidates defeated or eliminated from contention for such office by one-half of a percent or less of the votes cast for such office request in writing that a recount not be made. Each canvassing board responsible for conducting a recount shall examine the counters on the machines or the tabulation of the ballots cast in each precinct in which the office or issue appeared on the ballot and determine whether the returns correctly reflect the votes cast. If there is a discrepancy between the returns and the counters of the machines or the tabulation of the ballots cast, the counters of such machines or the tabulation of the ballots cast shall be presumed correct and such votes shall be canvassed accordingly.

SECTION 102.166 PROTEST OF ELECTION RETURNS; PROCEDURE.

(1) Any candidate for nomination or election, or any elector qualified to vote in the election related to such candidacy, shall have the right to protest the returns of the election as being erroneous by filing with the appropriate canvassing board a sworn, written protest.

(2) Such protest shall be filed with the canvassing board prior to the time the canvassing board certifies the results for the office being protested or within 5 days after midnight of the date the election is held, whichever occurs later.

(3) Before canvassing the returns of the election, the canvassing board shall:

(a) When paper ballots are used, examine the tabulation of the paper ballots cast.

(b) When voting machines are used, examine the counters on the machines of nonprinter machines or the printer-pac or printer machines. If there is a discrepancy between the returns and the counters of the machines or the printer-pac, the counters of such machines or the printer-pac shall be presumed correct.

(c) When electronic or electromechanical equipment is used, the canvassing board shall examine precinct records and election returns. If there is a discrepancy which could affect the outcome of an election, the canvassing board may recount the ballots on the automatic tabulating equipment.

(4) (a) Any candidate whose name appeared on the ballot, any political committee that supports or opposes an issue which appeared on the ballot, or any political party whose candidates' names appeared on the ballot may file a written request with the county canvassing board for a manual recount. The written request shall contain a statement of the reason the manual recount is being requested.

(b) Such request must be filed with the canvassing board prior to the time the canvassing board certifies the results for the office being protested or within 72 hours after midnight of the date the election was held, whichever occurs later.

(c) The county canvassing board may authorize a manual recount. If a manual recount is authorized, the county canvassing board shall make a reasonable effort to notify each candidate whose race is being recounted of the time and place of such recount.

(d) The manual recount must include at least three precincts and at least 1 percent of the total votes cast for such candidate or issue. In the event there are less than three precincts involved in the election, all precincts shall be counted. The person who requested the recount shall choose three precincts to be recounted, and, if other precincts are recounted, the county canvassing board shall select the additional precincts.

(5) If the manual recount indicates an error in the vote tabulation which could affect the outcome of the election, the county canvassing board shall:

(a) Correct the error and recount the remaining precincts with the vote tabulation system;

(b) Request the Department of State to verify the tabulation software; or

(c) Manually recount all ballots.

(6) Any manual recount shall be open to the public.

(7) Procedures for a manual recount are as follows:

(a) The county canvassing board shall appoint as many counting teams of at least two electors as is necessary to manually recount the ballots. A counting team must have, when possible, members of at least two political parties. A candidate involved in the race shall not be a member of the counting team.

(b) If a counting team is unable to determine a voter's intent in casting a ballot, the ballot shall be presented to the county canvassing board for it to determine the voter's intent.

(8) If the county canvassing board determines the need to verify the tabulation software, the county canvassing board shall request in writing that the Department of State verify the software.

(9) When the Department of State verifies such software, the department shall:

(a) Compare the software used to tabulate the votes with the software filed with the Department of State pursuant with s. 101.5607; and

(b) Check the election parameters.

(10) The Department of State shall respond to the county canvassing board within 3 working days.

SECTION 102.168 CONTEST OF ELECTION.

(1) Except as provided in s. 102.171, the certification of election or nomination of any person to office, or of the result on any question submitted by referendum, may

be contested in the circuit court by any unsuccessful candidate for such office or nomination thereto or by any elector qualified to vote in the election related to such candidacy, or by any taxpayer respectively.

(2) Such contestant shall file a complaint, together with the fees prescribed in chapter 28, with the clerk of the circuit court within 10 days after midnight of the date the last county canvassing board empowered to canvass the returns certifies the results of the election being contested or within 5 days after midnight of the date the last county canvassing board empowered to canvass the returns certifies the results of that particular election (following a protest pursuant to s. 102.166 91), whichever occurs later.

(3) The complaint shall set forth the grounds on which the contestant intends to establish his or her right to such office or set aside the result of the election on a submitted referendum. The grounds for contesting an election under this section are:

(a) Misconduct, fraud, or corruption on the part of any election official or any member of the canvassing board sufficient to change or place in doubt the result of the election.

(b) Ineligibility of the successful candidate for the nomination or office in dispute.

(c) Receipt of a number of illegal votes or rejection of a number of legal votes sufficient to change or place in doubt the result of the election.

(d) Proof that any elector, election official, or canvassing board member was given or offered a bribe or reward in money, property, or any other thing of value for the purpose of procuring the successful candidate's nomination or election or determining the result on any question submitted to referendum.

(e) Any other cause or allegation which, if sustained, would show that a person other than the successful candidate was the person duly nominated or elected to the office in question or that the outcome of the election on a question submitted by referendum was contrary to the result declared by the canvassing board or election board.

(4) The canvassing board or election board shall be the proper party defendant, and the successful candidate shall be an indispensable party to any action brought to contest the election or nomination of a candidate.

(5) A statement of the grounds of contest may not be rejected, nor the proceedings dismissed, by the court for any want of form if the grounds of contest provided in the statement are sufficient to clearly inform the defendant of the particular proceeding or cause for which the nomination or election is contested.

(6) A copy of the complaint shall be served upon the defendant and any other person named therein in the same manner as in other civil cases under the laws of this state. Within 10 days after the complaint has been served, the defendant must file an answer admitting or denying the allegations on which the contestant relies or stating that the defendant has no knowledge or information concerning the allegations, which shall be deemed a denial of the allegations, and must state any other defenses, in law or fact, on which the defendant relies. If an answer is not filed within the time prescribed, the defendant may not be granted a hearing in court to assert any claim or objection that is required by this subsection to be stated in an answer.

(7) Any candidate, qualified elector, or taxpayer presenting such a contest to a circuit judge is entitled to an immediate hearing. However, the court in its discretion may limit the time to be consumed in taking testimony, with a view therein to the circumstances of the matter and to the proximity of any succeeding primary or other election.

(8) The circuit judge to whom the contest is presented may fashion such orders as he or she deems necessary to ensure that each allegation in the complaint is investigated, examined, or checked, to prevent or correct any alleged wrong, and to provide any relief appropriate under such circumstances.

G. National and Florida Election Results

Below are two tables indicating the votes attained by the two major candidates, George W. Bush and Al Gore, in the presidential election of 2000. The first table contains the national vote and is illustrated in a state-by-state format while the second table displays the Florida vote in a county-by-county format. Both tables show the total popular vote and the percentages attained by Bush and Gore in the respective state or county. The first table also contains the electoral votes won by each candidate.

Table G-1.
Presidential Vote by State—2000 Election

State	Popular Vote Total	Percentage of Popular Vote—Bush	Percentage of Popular Vote—Gore	Electoral Vote—Bush	Electoral Vote—Gore
Alabama	1,666,272	56.5	41.6	9	
Alaska	285,560	58.6	27.7	3	
Arizona	1,532,016	51.0	44.7	8	
Arkansas	921,781	51.3	45.9	6	
California	10,965,856	41.7	53.4		54
Colorado	1,741,368	50.8	42.4	8	
Connecticut	1,459,525	38.4	55.9		8
Delaware	327,622	41.9	55.0		3
District of Columbia	201,894	9.0	85.2		2*
Florida	5,963,110	48.8	48.8	25	
Georgia	2,596,645	54.7	43.0	13	
Hawaii	367,951	37.5	55.8		4
Idaho	501,621	67.2	27.6	4	
Illinois	4,742,123	42.6	54.6		22
Indiana	2,199,302	56.6	41.0	12	
Iowa	1,315,563	48.2	48.5		7

(Continued)

Table G-1 *(continued)*

State	Popular Vote Total	Percentage of Popular Vote—Bush	Percentage of Popular Vote—Gore	Electoral Vote—Bush	Electoral Vote—Gore
Kansas	1,072,218	58.0	37.2	6	
Kentucky	1,544,187	56.5	41.4	8	
Louisiana	1,765,656	52.6	44.9	9	
Maine	651,817	44.0	49.1		4
Maryland	2,020,480	40.3	56.5		10
Massachusetts	2,702,984	32.5	59.8		12
Michigan	4,232,711	46.1	51.3		18
Minnesota	2,438,685	45.5	47.9		10
Mississippi	994,184	57.6	40.7	7	
Missouri	2,359,892	50.4	47.1	11	
Montana	410,997	58.4	33.4	3	
Nebraska	697,019	62.2	33.3	5	
Nevada	608,970	49.5	46.0	4	
New Hampshire	569,081	48.1	46.8	4	
New Jersey	3,187,226	40.3	56.1		15
New Mexico	598,605	47.8	47.9		5
New York	6,821,999	35.2	60.2		33
North Carolina	2,911,262	56.0	43.2	14	
North Dakota	288,256	60.7	33.1	3	
Ohio	4,701,998	50.0	46.4	21	
Oklahoma	1,234,229	60.3	38.4	8	
Oregon	1,533,968	46.5	47.0		7
Pennsylvania	4,913,119	46.4	50.6		23
Rhode Island	409,047	31.9	61.0		4
South Carolina	1,382,717	56.8	40.9	8	
South Dakota	316,269	60.3	37.6	3	
Tennessee	2,076,181	51.1	47.3	11	
Texas	6,407,637	59.3	38.0	32	
Utah	770,754	66.8	26.3	5	
Vermont	294,308	40.7	50.6		3
Virginia	2,739,447	52.5	44.4	13	
Washington	2,487,433	44.6	50.2		11
West Virginia	648,124	51.9	45.6	5	
Wisconsin	2,598,607	47.6	47.8		11
Wyoming	218,351	67.8	27.7	3	
United States	**105,396,627**	**47.9**	**48.4**	**271**	**266***

*One elector from the District of Columbia abstained from casting a ballot for Gore to protest the District's lack of representation in Congress.

Source: Scammon, Richard M., Alice V. McGillivrey, and Rhodes Cook. *America Votes 24: A Handbook of Contemporary American Election Statistics 2000.* Washington, D.C.: Congressional Quarterly Press, 2001.

Table G-2.
Presidential Vote by Florida Counties— 2000 Election

County	Popular Vote Total	Percentage of Popular Vote—Bush	Percentage of Popular Vote—Gore
Alachua	85,729	39.8	55.2
Baker	8,154	68.8	29.3
Bay	58,805	65.7	32.1
Bradford	8,673	62.4	35.5
Brevard	218,395	52.7	44.6
Broward	575,143	30.9	67.4
Calhoun	5,174	55.5	41.7
Charlotte	66,896	53.0	44.3
Citrus	57,204	52.0	44.6
Clay	57,353	72.8	25.5
Collier	92,163	65.6	32.5
Columbia	18,508	59.2	38.1
Dade	625,449	46.3	52.6
Desoto	7,811	54.5	42.5
Dixie	4,666	57.8	39.1
Duval	264,636	57.5	40.8
Escambia	116,648	62.6	35.1
Flagler	27,111	46.5	51.3
Franklin	4,644	52.8	44.1
Gadsden	14,727	32.4	66.1
Gilchrist	5,395	61.2	35.4
Glades	3,365	54.7	42.9
Gulf	6,144	57.8	39.0
Hamilton	3,964	54.1	43.4
Hardee	6,233	60.4	37.5
Hendry	8,139	58.3	39.8
Hernando	65,219	47.0	50.1
Highlands	35,149	57.5	40.3
Hillsborough	360,395	50.2	47.1
Holmes	7,395	67.8	29.4
Indian River	49,622	57.7	39.8
Jackson	16,300	56.1	42.1
Jefferson	5,643	43.9	53.9
Lafayette	2,505	66.7	31.5
Lake	88,611	56.4	41.3
Lee	184,377	57.6	39.9
Leon	103,124	37.9	59.6
Levy	12,724	53.9	42.4
Liberty	2,410	54.6	42.2
Madison	6,162	49.3	48.9
Manatee	110,221	52.6	44.6
Marion	102,956	53.6	43.4

(Continued)

Table G-2 *(continued)*

County	Popular Vote Total	Percentage of Popular Vote—Bush	Percentage of Popular Vote—Gore
Martin	62,013	54.8	42.9
Monroe	33,887	47.4	48.6
Nassau	23,780	69.0	29.2
Okalossa	70,680	73.7	24.0
Okeechobee	9,853	51.3	46.6
Orange	280,125	48.0	50.1
Osceola	55,658	47.1	50.6
Palm Beach	433,186	35.3	62.3
Pasco	142,731	48.0	48.7
Pinellas	398,472	46.4	50.3
Polk	168,607	53.6	44.6
Putnam	26,222	51.3	46.2
St. Johns	60,746	65.1	32.1
St. Lucia	77,989	44.5	53.3
Santa Rosa	50,319	72.1	25.4
Sarasota	160,942	51.6	45.3
Seminole	137,634	55.0	43.0
Sumter	22,261	54.5	43.3
Suwannee	12,457	64.3	32.7
Taylor	6,808	59.6	38.9
Union	3,826	61.0	36.8
Volusia	183,653	44.8	53.0
Wakulla	8,587	52.5	44.7
Walton	18,318	66.5	30.8
Washington	8,025	62.2	33.6
Federal Absentees	2,490	63.3	33.6
State Total	**5,963,110**	**48.8**	**48.8**

Source: Scammon, Richard M., Alice V. McGillivrey, and Rhodes Cook. *America Votes 24: A Handbook of Contemporary American Election Statistics 2000.* Washington, D.C.: Congressional Quarterly Press, 2001.

ANNOTATED BIBLIOGRAPHY

Abbott, David W., and James P. Levine. *Wrong Winner: The Coming Debacle in the Electoral College*. Westport, Conn.: Praeger, 1991.

This is a critical evaluation of the electoral college that points out its major weaknesses and calls for its elimination. The authors discuss how the electoral college sometimes allows popular vote losers to win, and they describe the variety of biases that seems to be built into the electoral college. In addition, they show how the distributions of electoral votes can distort the meaning of an election by creating appearances that winners of close elections by popular vote outcomes frequently look like sweeping winners through the electoral college.

Barone, Michael, Richard E. Cohen, and Grant Ujifusa. *The Almanac of American Politics 2002*. Washington, D.C.: The National Journal, 2001.

This almanac contains information about recent American voting patterns. It begins with a brief overview of the outcomes of the 2000 presidential and congressional elections and follows with biographies of the leading elected officials throughout the nation: president, vice president, governors and members of congress. It also provides state-by-state and congressional district-by–congressional district analysis of cultural and political patterns including descriptions of the states and districts and the results of recent elections.

Best, Judith A. *The Choice of the People? Debating the Electoral College*. Lanham, Md.: Rowman and Littlefield, 1996.

This book offers a defense of the electoral college and argues that it is a valuable institution in American constitutional theory. The author divides it into two parts: the first focuses on a discussion and defense of the electoral college, and the second includes the complete "Report of the Senate Judiciary Committee on Direct Popular Election of the President and Vice President" from 1977 and the testimony of several persons before the committee. The author, who testified before the committee, is critical of the report that called for the abolition of the electoral college.

Bugliosi, Vincent. *The Betrayal of America: How the Supreme Court Undermined the Constitution and Chose Our President.* New York: Thunder's Mouth Press/Nation Books, 2001.

This is a critical indictment of the U.S. Supreme Court for its ruling in the *Bush v. Gore* case. Much of the book contains an extended editorial that first appeared in the February 5, 2001, issue of *The Nation,* a magazine that espouses a left-radical political perspective on contemporary issues. The author raises questions about the reasoning of the Supreme Court and the motivations of the five conservative judges who comprised the majority. He is particularly critical of what he sees as a novel use of the equal protection argument. There are forewords by well-known authors Molly Ivins and Jerry Spence.

Ceaser, James W., and Andrew E. Busch. *The Perfect Tie: The True Story of the 2000 Presidential Election.* Lanham, Md.: Rowman and Littlefield, 2001.

This book describes and evaluates the leading events of Election 2000 and explains why it ended so closely. There are chapters relating to the beginnings of the campaign in 1999 and of candidates attempting to raise money and endorsements; the long battles for the party nominations; Vice President Gore's problems as a candidate and of how he frequently tried to create a new public image; distributions of the popular and electoral votes by both geographic regions and demographic groups; and the court struggles over the final vote count in Florida.

Cook, Rhodes. *Race for the Presidency: Winning the 2000 Nomination.* Washington, D.C.: Congressional Quarterly Press, 2000.

This book is a guide for understanding the rules that were in operation during the nomination campaigns of 2000. It begins with an overview of how the current nomination system works and looks at the enhanced role primary elections now play in deciding final outcomes. It follows with chapters about the procedures and dates employed in each state by both major political parties for selecting the delegates who will attend the national nominating conventions. The order of presentation of the states is by the sequence in which they selected their convention delegates; the initial states of Iowa and New Hampshire were considered first.

Crotty, William, ed. *America's Choice 2000.* Boulder, Colo.: Westview Press, 2001.

This book provides a review and social scientific analysis of the outcomes and meanings of several important features of Election 2000. It begins with an overview of the leading events of the campaign and its final outcome and then follows with a variety of essays by individual authors who focus on such matters as the role of the courts in deciding the winner, the different levels of political participation attributed to specific types of voters, the events and meaning of the nomination campaign, the events and outcome of the general election campaign, an overview of congressional elections, the patterns of state and local elections, and a perspective on the meaning of all the events of Election 2000.

Dershowitz, Alan M. *Supreme Injustice: How the High Court Hijacked Election 2000.* New York: Oxford University Press, 2001.

This book offers a critical evaluation of the decision of the U.S. Supreme Court in the case of *Bush v. Gore* and concludes that the decision has little merit. The author, a prominent law professor, argues that the decision was inconsistent with recent court principles related to equal protection of the law, was designed by conservative Republican judges who mainly wanted to elect Bush as President, and likely would never have taken place if the roles of the two candidates had been reversed, that is, with Gore leading in the Florida vote and Bush demanding a number of recounts in Republican-dominated counties.

Dionne, E.J., Jr., and William Kristol. *Bush v. Gore: The Court Cases and the Commentary.* Washington, D.C.: The Brookings Institution, 2001.

This book contains complete texts of the leading legal decisions related to the Florida vote counting controversy in the 2000 election. Included here are the decisions of a variety of Florida trial courts, the state's Supreme Court, and the U.S. Supreme Court. The book also provides the text of several advisory opinions issued by the Florida Attorney General to election officials involved in the controversy. Of particular interest is the variety of concurring and dissenting opinions written by several justices on the U.S. Supreme Court in the *Bush v. Gore* case. There are also copies of major editorials from such leading newspapers as the *New York Times, Wall Street Journal,* and *Washington Post.*

Dover, E.D. *Missed Opportunity: Gore, Incumbency, and Television in Election 2000.* Westport, Conn.: Praeger, 2002.

This book looks at the relationship between surrogate incumbency and media reporting in the 2000 election and of how the two major candidates, Bush and Gore, adapted to their individual roles of incumbent and challenger. The book begins with a discussion of the importance of the vice presidency in contemporary elections when the president retires. There are also descriptions and evaluations of how television news media illustrated and depicted the leading events of the nomination and general election phases of the campaign and the performances of Bush and Gore to their viewing audiences.

Gillman, Howard. *The Votes That Counted: How the Court Decided the 2000 Presidential Election.* Chicago: The University of Chicago Press, 2001.

This book provides a detailed explanation of the events and court decisions related to the Florida vote controversy. It includes a chronology of the major events, a description of how these events unfolded, reviews of the political strategies of the major participants, explanations of the numerous judicial cases and the rulings that came from them, and a critical evaluation of the U.S. Supreme Court for becoming involved in what the author believes should have been a matter for state courts and Congress. The Appendix contains relevant provisions of federal, state, and constitutional law and a summary of the legal issues and rulings of leading cases.

Glennon, Michael J. *When No Majority Rules: The Electoral College and Presidential Succession*. Washington, D.C.: Congressional Quarterly Press, 1992.

This book discusses the creation and operation of the electoral college with particular emphasis given to the roles of Congress and the courts. There is a review of the important historical factors that led to the creation of the electoral college and of other historical factors that eventually forced the college to develop in a manner quite different from the one intended by the authors of the federal constitution. There is also a discussion of the legitimacy of the electoral college in the eyes of voters and an appendix with relevant provisions of federal law and U.S. Supreme Court decisions related to the electoral college.

Goldstein, Michael L. *Guide to the 2000 Presidential Election*. Washington, D.C.: Congressional Quarterly Press, 2000.

This book was published early in 2000 and was intended to provide an overview of the variety of events that would occur during the election campaign. There are chapters about the changing political context in which the 2000 election will occur and about the various demands that are now placed on candidates, including changed rules for selecting delegates to national nominating conventions and the need for raising extensive amounts of money to contest primary elections. There are also chapters about the nomination and general election phases of the campaign and a series of short biographies of the likely candidates.

Greene, Abner. *Understanding the 2000 Election: A Guide to the Legal Battles That Decided the Presidency.* New York: New York University Press, 2001.

This book explains the political and legal meanings of the numerous issues that became part of the Florida vote controversy. There are chapters focusing on the hand counting of disputed ballots; on the various provisions of the federal constitution and law that were relevant in the Supreme Court's ruling; on what the author describes as wild-card legal matters such as the butterfly ballot in Palm Beach County; on problems with voting by absentee ballots; and on the role of a state legislature in resolving a disputed election.

Greenfield, Jeff. "*Oh Waiter! One Order of Crow!*" New York: G.P. Putnam's Sons, 2001.

This provides an overview and commentary about several features of Election 2000, including the remarkable failure of the television networks to correctly project the winner of the vote in Florida. There is a discussion of the social and political context of the election year, a review of some of the leading events of the nomination and general election campaigns and of the candidates themselves, and a summary of the main themes that comprised the vote recount controversy. The author relies on some of his own personal experiences to provide insight into political events.

Hardaway, Robert. *The Electoral College and the Constitution: The Case for Preserving Federalism*. Westport, Conn.: Praeger, 1994.

The author advances a highly favorable view of the background and operations of the electoral college while showing how the existence of the college is an integral part of the constitutional doctrine of American federalism. He discusses political events related to the creation of the electoral college, explains the variety of laws that govern its present operation, reviews the college's unexpected historical development, evaluates current problems, and reviews some of the leading proposals for reform.

Issacharoff, Samuel, Pamela S. Karlan, and Richard H. Pildes. *When Elections Go Bad: The Law of Democracy and the Presidential Election of 2000*. Rev. Ed. New York: New York Foundation Press, 2001.

This book explains the variety of laws and court decisions that were relevant in the Florida vote controversy. Included here are reviews of the federal interest, from both constitutional and legal perspectives, in election procedures; the role of the state in conducting elections and the nature of state election law; previous decisions by the U.S. Supreme Court relating to votes and voting rights; and questions about possible methods that might prevent disputed elections.

Jacobson, Gray C. *The 2000 Elections and Beyond*. Washington, D.C.: Congressional Quarterly Press, 2001.

This book provides a short summary of the most important features of the 2000 elections. It begins by showing how voters were evenly divided in their preferences between the two major political parties with respect to both the presidency and congress. It follows by reviewing the leading events of the various campaigns, by looking at the divisions of opinion as reflected in Election Day exit polls, and concludes with a review of some of the leading problems that electoral system will need to confront in coming years.

Jamieson, Kathleen Hall, and Paul Waldman. *Electing the President 2000: The Insiders' View*. Philadelphia: University of Pennsylvania Press, 2001.

This book contains the remarks made by the individual participants in a ten-hour seminar on the 2000 election that was held on February 10, 2001, at the Annenberg School of Communication at the University of Pennsylvania. The participants were Matthew Dowd, Fred Steeper, Mark McKinnon, Lionel Sosa, Alex Castellanos, and Karl Rove, who held various positions in the Bush campaign; Carter Eskew, Bob Shrum, Stanley Greenberg, and Bill Knapp, who held comparable roles in the Gore effort; and Kathleen Frankovic of *CBS News*.

Jarvis, Robert M., Phyllis Coleman, and Johnny C. Burris. *Bush v. Gore: The Fight for Florida's Vote*. New York: Kluwer Law International, 2001.

The authors, all three of whom are law professors at Nova Southeastern University in Fort Lauderdale, Florida, provide complete transcripts of the major court rulings in the Florida vote controversy. The cases, which number thirty-four in total, range from the actions of trial courts concerned with such matters as the use of a butterfly ballot in Palm Beach County, to battles over the standards that should be employed in counting ballots with attached chads, to the reviews of various decisions by the Florida and U.S. Supreme Courts.

Jones, Randall J., Jr. *Who Will Be in the White House? Predicting Presidential Elections*. New York: Longman, 2002.

This book reviews the methods that are frequently employed to explain the outcomes of presidential elections. Consideration is given to bellwether states, that is, places that always vote for the winner; presidential approval ratings and how the popularity of an incumbent affects the final result; exit polls that ask actual voters to describe their choices and the reasons they made them; multivariate techniques that attempt to show how certain statistical factors account for the outcome; the dynamics of the nomination processes, which help some candidates and hurt others; and the performance of the national economy.

Kaplan, David A. *The Accidental President*. New York: HarperCollins, 2001.

This book provides a description of the actions of the individuals who were involved in the Florida vote controversy and its related court cases. The primary emphasis is on three sets of participants: members of the Gore and Bush campaign and legal staffs, Florida election officials including the office of the secretary of state, and both Florida and federal judges. Included are reviews of the personal backgrounds of the major players, descriptions of what they said in various circumstances, and explanations of their intentions in responding to events in the manners they did.

Kellner, Douglas. *Grand Theft 2000: Media Spectacle and a Stolen Election*. Lanham, Md.: Rowman and Littlefield Publishers, 2001.

This book provides a review and critical commentary on the conclusion of the 2000 election. It begins with a description of the mistakes that national media made in forecasting the outcome of the Florida vote. It continues with a review of the events relating to vote recounts, court challenges, and the efforts of the Bush and Gore campaigns to influence the content of media reporting to gain public support for their vote contesting efforts. The book concludes with commentary about some of the major media failings in reporting about the content of election 2000.

Kura, Alexandra. *Electoral College and Presidential Elections.* Huntington, N.Y.: Nova Science Publishers, 2001.

This book provides a thorough description of the operations of American elections and the variety of uses that have been made of the electoral college. There are chapters about election processes, including the rules and legal institutions that exist for resolving party nominations; descriptions of the workings of partisan campaigns, reviews of voting procedures and patterns, and a discussion of the role of the electoral college in deciding close elections.

Kuroda, Tadahisa. *The Origins of the Twelfth Amendment: The Electoral College in the Early Republic, 1787–1804.* Westport, Conn.: Greenwood Press, 1994.

This book discusses the beginnings and early uses of the electoral college. It begins by describing the events related to the creation of the electoral college at the constitutional convention in 1787. It then follows by showing how the college operated in the first four presidential elections, a pattern that is quite different from the manner in which the college works in today's political order. After showing how the college failed to achieve the goals of the constitutional authors who created it, the book then describes the congressional debates and ratification battles that led to the eventual adoption of the Twelfth Amendment in 1804 that altered the electoral college into the institution that exists today.

Lewis, Charles. *The Buying of the President 2000: The Authoritative Guide to the Big-Money Interests behind This Year's Presidential Candidates.* New York: Avon Books, 2000.

This book, published during the 2000 presidential election, looks at the sources of campaign funding for the major political parties and leading candidates. It has individual chapters about the Democratic, Republican, and Reform parties and such leading candidates as Bill Bradley, Al Gore, Gary Bauer, George W. Bush, Elizabeth Dole, Steve Forbes, Orrin Hatch, Alan Keyes, John McCain, Dan Quayle, and Patrick Buchanan. Included are charts of the top fifty contributors to the two major parties and the top ten contributors to each of the above named candidates.

Longley, Lawrence D., and Neal R. Peirce. *The Electoral College Primer 2000.* New Haven, Conn.: Yale University Press, 1999.

This book looks at the historical and political reasons that governed the creation of the electoral college and explores how a variety of unanticipated factors have altered the college's purposes. It also examines important features of several disputed and close elections and closes with an appendix that contains the results of those elections and relevant excerpts from the Constitution and the United States Code relating to the electoral college.

Mayer, William G, ed. *In Pursuit of the White House 2000: How We Choose Our Presidential Nominees.* New York: Chatham House Publishers, 2000.

This book describes and evaluates the current processes by which the major political parties choose their presidential nominees. Topics considered include the rules for selecting delegates for the national nominating conventions; the front-loading of presidential primaries; the unusual influences of the first primary of the year, New Hampshire; the importance of televised debates; the voting behavior of the American electorate that participates in nomination campaigns; and current patterns of vice presidential selection. The book is comprised of chapters written by leading political scientists.

Merzer, Martin, and the Staff of the Miami Herald. *The Miami Herald Report: Democracy Held Hostage.* New York: St. Martin's Press, 2001.

This book describes the leading features of the Florida vote controversy and then focuses attention on its unique contribution, the results of a post-controversy count, sponsored by the *Miami Herald,* of the 64,000 disputed ballots that were not considered in the various recounts. While the official recounts ended with the December 12 decision of the U.S. Supreme Court, this newspaper sought to find out what would have happened if all ballots had been counted by a variety of different standards. The authors concluded that Bush would still have won if three of the four available methods had been used. The race would have been too close to call with the fourth method.

Nelson, Michael, ed. *The Elections of 2000.* Washington, D.C.: Congressional Quarterly Press, 2001.

This book contains several chapters written by various political scientists about specific features of the elections of 2000. The chapters include such matters as the nomination campaigns within each party for the presidency, an overview of the voting patterns of the general election by both geography and demographic groups, the outcome of various ballot initiatives in several states, and the national division of the vote in elections for Congress. There are also chapters providing context and perspective on the outcome and meaning of the elections.

New York Times: *36 Days: The Complete Chronicle of the 2000 Presidential Election Crisis.* New York: Time Books, Henry Holt and Company, 2001.

This book contains reprints of news stories and editorials that appeared in the *New York Times* newspaper relating to the Florida vote controversy. The material is arranged in thirty-six specific chapters that correspond to each day of the thirty-six-day controversy. They begin on November 8, the day immediately following the election, when the problems first became known, and end on December 13, the day after the U.S. Supreme Court halted the recounts and Gore conceded the election.

Polsby, Nelson W., and Aaron Wildavsky. *Presidential Elections: Strategies and Structures of American Politics.* 10th ed. New York: Chatham House Publishers, 2000.

This most recent edition of a classic political science textbook looks at the environment, sequences, and issues involved in presidential selection. It describes and evaluates the roles of voters, political parties, interest groups, rules for selecting national convention delegates, the importance of primary elections, the laws and practices of fund raising, the roles of the conventions, and general election campaigns. It was published before the 2000 campaign began and draws on examples from every election since 1972.

Pomper, Gerald M., ed. *The Election of 2000.* New York: Chatham House Publishers, 2001.

This book looks at various features of the 2000 election relating to the nomination and selection of the president and members of Congress. It directs attention to such topics as the role of money in modern campaigns, the influences of mass media on campaign styles and voter perceptions, the voting behavior of an ambivalent electorate, and the electoral effects that may have derived from the policies and personal behavior of Bill Clinton. The individual chapters on specialized topics are written by major political scientists.

Posner, Richard A. *Breaking the Deadlock: The 2000 Election, the Constitution, and the Courts.* Princeton, N.J.: Princeton University Press, 2001.

This book, written by a prominent conservative theorist and federal judge, provides commentary on a variety of issues related to the Florida vote controversy. Among the topics considered are a review of the history and meaning of the right to vote; a number of statistical models relating to the validity of the charges relating to such factors as race, overvotes, undervotes, type of voting machine used, and literacy; a description of the leading events and issues at stake in the court cases; a critique of the participants in the battle; and a discussion of proposals for reform of voting procedures.

Rakove, Jack N., ed. *The Unfinished Election of 2000.* New York: Basic Books, 2001.

This book provides a series of articles about various questions arising from the 2000 election. It is divided into two parts that focus on the politics of presidential elections and the role of the court and the constitution in elections. The first part offers chapters about voting behavior over the span of several elections, reaching as far back in time as 1896, and the 2000 election itself. The second part focuses on the role of the courts in resolving election disputes, at the meaning of equal protection of the law, and the role of the electoral college in an electronic age when geographic boundaries seem increasingly irrelevant.

Sabato, Larry, J. *Overtime: The Election 2000 Thriller.* New York: Longman, 2002.

This book provides several short essays about various aspects of the 2000 election. Included are descriptions of the nomination campaigns within both parties, the general election battles between Gore and Bush, the role of mass media as a source of information and influence on the conduct of events, distributions of the national popular and electoral vote, the leading events of the Florida controversy from the perspectives of both Bush and Gore, and an overview of the legal issues involved in the court cases that followed.

Sammon, Bill. *At Any Cost: How Al Gore Tried to Steal the Election.* Washington, D.C.: Regnery Publishing, 2001.

This book looks at the behavior and motivations of the Gore campaign team and legal staff in their efforts at demanding manual recounts of questionable votes in Florida. There is emphasis on the flow of events throughout the controversy and of how the various participants adapted to and were sometimes responsible for creating them. The book is quite critical of Gore and his Democratic Party operatives. It attempts to place much of the blame for the controversy and related court decisions on their unwillingness to concede to what the author considers the obvious, that they had lost the election.

Scammon, Richard M., Alice V. McGillivrey, and Rhodes Cook. *America Votes 24: A Handbook of Contemporary American Election Statistics 2000.* Washington, D.C.: Congressional Quarterly Press, 2001.

This is the most recent volume in a series of books that compile the results of major American elections. It contains a state-by-state and county-by-county breakdown of votes in the presidential election of 2000, a review of the outcomes of the 2000 primary elections, and the results of state elections for members of congress and for governors. There are also state-by-state results of presidential, congressional, and state elections over the past several decades.

Simon, Roger. *Divided We Stand: How Al Gore Beat George Bush and Lost the Presidency.* New York: Crown Publishers, 2001.

The author, a major political reporter, describes several important features of the 2000 election from the perspective of the personal characteristics of the leading candidates. He focuses much of his attention on the topic of the book, Al Gore, but also looks at George W. Bush, John McCain, Bill Bradley, and Bill Clinton. There is some discussion of the nomination battles, the events of the national conventions, the general election campaign and the debates, and the Florida vote controversy. Of particular interest is the commentary on the state of the personal relationship between Gore and Clinton and how it might have influenced the campaign.

Stevens, Stuart. *The Big Enchilada: Campaign Adventures with the Cockeyed Optimists from Texas Who Won the Biggest Prize in Politics.* New York: The Free Press, 2001.

This book is an insider's account of activities within the Bush campaign for President. The author, a member of the Bush staff, provides descriptions and commentaries about how the Bush effort developed and operated through the many phases of the two-year-long campaign. The author begins with how Bush decided on seeking the presidency and then follows by looking at the leading events of the campaign. He focuses on fundraising efforts, the primary elections, national conventions, the fall campaign, the debates, and the final drive to the election.

Tapper, Jack. *Down and Dirty: The Plot to Steal the Presidency.* New York: Little, Brown, and Company, 2001.

This book, written by a political reporter, providers an insider's description of the events and personalities related to the Florida vote controversy. The author looks at the personal backgrounds of the leading participants, describes events from the vantage points of the main players, shows how the variety of arguments advanced by both sides were self-serving, and criticizes the U.S. Supreme Court for creating an unusual interpretation of Equal Protection of the Law to elect Bush as president.

Toobin, Jeffrey. *Too Close To Call: The Thirty-Six-Day Battle to Decide the 2000 Election.* New York: Random House, 2001.

This book provides an extensive description of the personalities, issues, politics, strategies, and court rulings that dominated the Florida vote controversy. It begins by introducing the participants and by describing how each viewed the controversy from their own particular vantage point. The author, a national network reporter who specializes in legal issues, then explains how the numerous participants responded to the fast-breaking and frequently unpredictable events and constantly changing day-to-day developments. There is a particular emphasis on the legal issues and of how they often played out in the many court cases that eventually dominated the vote controversy.

Vanderbilt Television News Archive. *Evening News Abstracts.* Nashville, Tenn.: Vanderbilt University Publications, 2002.

This archive contains tapes of the daily news broadcasts of the four major television networks of the American Broadcasting Company (ABC), the Cable News Network (CNN), the Columbia Broadcasting System (CBS), and the National Broadcasting Company (NBC). Summaries of the broadcasts are available at the Web site of www.tvnews.com, while tapes of individual broadcasts can be purchased from the archive. The archive contains all network broadcasts related to the election of 2000, the controversy over the Florida vote, and the U.S. Supreme Court decision of *Bush v. Gore*.

Washington Post. *Deadlock: The Inside Story of America's Closest Election.* New York: Public Affairs Press, 2001.

The political staff of the *Washington Post* newspaper wrote this book about the events of the Florida vote controversy. They relied upon hundreds of interviews with the leading participants, including members of the Bush and Gore legal and campaign staffs and a variety of Florida election officials. The authors look at the tensions that existed within the Bush and Gore teams while those teams were trying to understand and respond to fast-breaking events. The book also attempts to answer questions about what might have happened if the candidates had responded differently. There is a thorough narrative of events and discussion of relevant legal issues.

Wayne, Stephen J. *The Road to the White House: The Politics of Presidential Elections.* Boston: Bedford/St. Martin's Press, 2000.

Written prior to the conclusion of the 2000 election, this book explains the processes by which the nation chooses a president. There are chapters about such matters as campaign finance, including the legal limits that exist for contributions and the limited federal role in financing nomination and general election campaigns; about the processes presently employed for selecting the delegates who attend the national nominating conventions; about the influences and themes of mass media in reporting and in defining the context of a campaign; and of a variety of methods used by political scientists to predict the outcomes of national elections.

Zelnick, Robert. *Winning Florida: How the Bush Team Fought the Battle.* Stanford, Calif.: Hoover Institute Press, 2001.

This book is an insider's view of how the Bush legal team responded to the issues and court cases that rose from the Florida vote controversy. The author begins his review by outlining the different legal and political interests that motivated the Bush and Gore teams. He follows with a narrative of how the Bush team became aware of each new problem, interpreted it, and then crafted and presented a legal and political response. The issues range from the butterfly ballot in Palm Beach County to the decision of the Florida Supreme Court favoring the Gore position on vote recounts. The book contains some of the arguments that both sides used in various court cases.

INDEX

About the Author

E.D. Dover is Professor of Political Science, Public Policy, and Administration at Western Oregon University. He is the author of *Presidential Elections in the Television Age* (Praeger, 1994), *The Presidential Election of 1996* (Praeger, 1998), and *Missed Opportunity* (Praeger, 2002).